More Than a Prophet

EMIR FETHI CANER

ERGUN MEHMET CANER

More Than a Prophet

An Insider's Response to Muslim Beliefs About Jesus & Christianity

Kregel
Publications

More Than a Prophet: An Insider's Response to Muslim Beliefs About Jesus & Christianity

Published by Kregel Publications, a division of Kregel, Inc., P.O. Box 2607, Grand Rapids, MI 49501.

English translation quotations from the Qur'an are from Abdullah Yusuf 'Ali, *The Meaning of the Holy Qur'an* (Brentwood, Md.: Amana, 1992).

Unless otherwise indicated, Scripture quotations are from the *New King James Version.* © 1979, 1980, 1982, Thomas Nelson, Inc., Publishers.

Scripture quotations marked NIV are from the *Holy Bible, New International Version®.* © 1973, 1978, 1984 by International Bible Society. Used by permission of Zondervan Publishing House. All rights reserved.

Library of Congress Cataloging-in-Publication Data
Caner, Emir Fethi
More than a prophet: an insider's response to Muslim beliefs about Jesus and Christianity / by Emir Fethi Caner and Ergun Mehmet Caner.
    p. cm.
Includes bibliographicl references.
    1. Islam—Controversial literature. 2. Jesus Christ—Islamic interpretations. 3. Islam—Relations—Christianity. 4. Christianity and other religions—Islam
I. Caner, Ergun Mehmet. II. Title.
BP169.C34   2003
261.2'7—dc21   2003009060

ISBN 0-8254-2401-1

Printed in the United States of America

3 4 5 6 / 08 07 06

For our sons,
John Mark Caner and
Braxton Paige Caner.
May we be fathers worthy of your respect,
effusive in our love, and
constant in our encouragement.

*I want to know Christ and the power of his resurrection
and the fellowship of sharing in his sufferings,
becoming like him in his death.*
—Philippians 3:10 NIV

We covenant to pray for our Muslim friends,
That they find the Jesus Christ who is . . .

More than a Messenger . . .
He is Messiah.

More than a Servant . . .
He is Savior.

More than the Word of God . . .
He is God.

More than Virgin Born . . .
He was Crucified, Buried, and Resurrected.

More than Assumed at death . . .
He conquered death and Ascended on High.

More than a Prophet . . .
He is Prophet, Priest, and King.

TABLE OF CONTENTS

3. Questions Concerning the Nature of the Qur'an and the Bible

4. Questions Concerning the Old Testament

5. Questions Concerning the New Testament

6. Questions Concerning the Atonement and Salvation

7. Questions Concerning Eschatology (End Times)

8. Questions Concerning Ethics and Politics

Acknowledgments

The authors are indebted to a number of individuals who have profoundly influenced our work in apologetics and comparative religions:

Jim, Dennis, Paul, and the entire Kregel team, for their forbearance and patience with our teaching, speaking, and family schedules, as well as Janyre Tromp, for her constant encouragement and diligent labor as our manager and director.

Phyllis Jackson, for her eagle eye and patient editing of the manuscript.

Dr. Jim Sibley and Diana Owen, for their expertise in Hebrew and Jewish theology.

Dr. Harvey Solganick, professor at LeTourneau University, for his formidable work in the philosophical arena. His work specifically on the questions of the nature of God and Allah is profound.

The entire team at answering-islam.org. Your work is nothing short of indispensable.

Our pastors, Dr. Mac Brunson and Rev. Dan Main, for preaching the incomparable Christ through the inerrant Word.

The presidents of the institutions where we teach, Drs. Paige Patterson and C. Richard Wells.

The Ledbetters, for their everlasting gift of Barnabas.

Steve Davidson, quite simply a twenty-year, every-juncture friend.

Our students at Southeastern Seminary and the Criswell College, for engaging us to dig deeper in our studies and communication.

And as always, our wives, who have earned crowns in glory for putting up with us.

INTRODUCTION

AN APOLOGETIC HANDBOOK

IT'S TUESDAY. THIS MUST BE ATLANTA.

In the year since publication of our first book, *Unveiling Islam*,[1] we have spoken more than four hundred times—at conferences, churches, conventions, state denominational meetings, national press conferences. Our voices were heard over tiny radio stations in the middle of wheat fields and on national television. We have addressed audiences of nine thousand and congregations of thirty-one. Often we have slept on airplanes, in airports, and on strange hotel beds. We faced questions, queries, demands, hostilities, anger, and broken hearts.

The effort has been worthwhile. For the first time in a generation in our culture, Christians are thinking seriously about reaching the one billion Muslims. Granted, we did not enjoy some of the attention we have received in our corner of this new discourse. At one California church, more than one hundred Muslims appeared to shout us down. Muslims began to pass out Islamic tracts during the offering at a church in Virginia. We are called evil, divisive hatemongers. The reason is that, along with 50 million other evangelical Christians, we believe in the central tenet of Christianity: *Jesus Christ—God who became human to share our lives and take away the punishment for our sins—is the only hope that we might be made acceptable in the sight of a perfect God. Only Jesus is worthy of receiving our complete trust and ultimate loyalty.* We testify that He died for the world, so that anyone on the planet can be forgiven and can have an eternal relationship with God. One must simply understand the true awfulness of our self-centered rebellion and surrender our failed efforts to new management. Jesus died and then rose from death to buy worthless enemies and give them eternal value.

After quotations (and misquotations) of our book fueled an already contentious debate in the summer of 2002, *Unveiling Islam* became a Christian best-seller in the religious books market. Since then, we have devoted much of our lives to answering the kinds of questions found on the following pages. We have answered questions from every major Christian broadcaster and virtually every major news outlet. We have answered questions over a myriad local television stations. Skeptical Muslims, angry Muslims, and interested Muslims all have posed questions. Liberal Christians who desire to meld Islam with Christianity ask questions. Biased reporters ask because they want an inflammatory quote, and sincere journalists ask because they are grappling with the enormity of the subject.

Along the way, we began to see patterns to these questions, whether from the secular media or Muslim *ulema* (scholars). *More Than a Prophet* was born as we studied these patterns of objection and argument. The ubiquitous question among the Christians begins with the explanation: *"I have a Muslim friend. . . . How do I answer my Islamic friend, who says . . . ?"* We wrote *Unveiling Islam* to explain Islam to Christians. Now both Muslims and Christians need a book designed to explain Christianity to Muslims. Most of the questions and objections considered here have been raised by Muslim scholars as reasons why they refuse to believe in Jesus Christ as the Son of God and Savior of humanity. Here lies the foundation of Islamic arguments against Christ and the stark points of contrast between the two religions.

We prefer to engage in constructive dialogue instead of debate over these issues. In fact, we no longer engage in the "debate" format interactions. Hundreds of university debates, interpersonal face-offs, and split-screen television interviews have shown why debate falls short of dialogue. The confrontational Jerry Springer style of shouting, booing, and hissing cuts off meaningful interchange of ideas. Guests interrupt each other in television interviews until the scene rivals what must have happened at the Tower of Babel. Retorts become attacks on the messenger, rather than discussions of the issues. Dialogue is no longer possible in the mass sense, since participants seldom listen to what their opponents are actually saying. This problem is lamented by sincere Christians and Muslims alike. Even the carefully planned intellectual encounter of August 1988 between Christian scholar Anis A. Shorrosh and Islamic scholar Ahmed Deedat in the Royal Albert Hall in the U.K. degenerated into a fracas, although the rules were framed to avoid such anarchy.

In the interest of fairness and candor, let us disclose a few details of our background.

First, we are proud to be Turkish in ancestry. To many Middle Eastern Muslims, though, this means we were "half-breed secular Muslims." In the nineteenth century, the Ottoman Empire, under the leadership of Mustafa Kemal Atatürk (1881-1938), abolished the caliphate and established a secular government without mullah rule. So many believe that Turkish Islam is not the real thing, so we are disqualified to discuss the subject as former members of the Islamic faith. Certainly we were both raised to be faithful Muslims within the Turkish culture, yet our religious upbringing and understandings were those of devout Sunni Muslims anywhere. We are more influenced in our Turkish culture by our homeland's horrible treatment of the Kurds during the twentieth century than by the fall of the Ottoman Empire after World War I. We do not come from an Arabic-speaking heritage, but then only a minority of the world's Muslims do come from homes in which Arabic was the primary language.

Second, we both converted from Islam to Christianity before we reached adulthood. Some Muslims contend that we left the faith while we were too young to fully comprehend Islam. Whatever deficiencies we may have had in our understanding have been compensated by over twenty years of study in Islam as we have tried to understand the Muslim mind.

Third, we are citizens of the United States and we cherish the religious liberty we enjoy. The concept of *religious liberty* as it is practiced in the United States and Canada is a foreign concept to many Muslims, so let us be explicit. *Religious liberty* means that the authors would defend to the death the right of anyone to worship as they wish. We defend a Muslim's right to build a mosque and worship Allah. Likewise, we insist on the right of Christians to stand on the street corner and tell those same Muslims about Jesus. This is our foundational freedom of conscience. Islam has no such concept. *Sharia* law establishes religious toleration but not the freedom to build new churches, share the gospel without fear, or leave Islam for faith in Christ without harsh consequence. Christians do not ask for power or favoritism but only for unfettered rights in other countries like those espoused in the U.S. Constitution.

If that request seems unrealistic in the world scene of today, the intention of this book may also seem naive. We offer a handbook that can impart useful information both to Muslims and to Christians.

For the Christian, we hope to examine and defend our faith with sensitivity to the kinds of issues that are on the minds of curious and sincere seekers of truth in the Islamic community. Without apology we suggest that Christians use these points to more effectively offer new life in Jesus Christ. Such one-on-one engagement between Christians and other religions has been going on for two millennia. It is a handbook and training manual for the pastor or church leader who lives and works in an Islamic culture as well as for the Christian who is burdened for Muslim neighbors in a pluralistic society. It is Christian education curriculum that all Christians need to master to understand world issues, whether they ever meet Muslims in the public forum.

For the curious Muslim, we have organized the questions, footnoted the sources and cited the speakers to answer your questions to the best of our ability. We hope that Muslim readers will use this book to answer questions or objections they may have regarding Christianity. To that end, we have provided answers to many of the questions we have heard repeatedly from Muslims at different times in various settings. In every case, we have sought to answer these questions thoughtfully and respectfully, and we hope our readers will consider our views in the same manner.

To make the book useful for Muslims and Christians alike, we have organized the nearly 150 questions under twelve headings. The discussions include citations and footnotes to be authoritative, but we have tried to keep the answers simple and conversational in tone. We want to approach these issues in the same manner that friends might talk about them. Another organizing scheme might have been used, but we have opted for simplicity, and others may use the information as they will.

This book is not a comprehensive guide to Islam. There is no such thing. It is the labor of two evangelical Christian professors of church history and Christian theology who are former Muslims and wish to bridge the gap between Christian and Islamic worlds. Others have called us "experts" in the subject. No one—not even a Muslim ulema—is an expert in all the complexities of Islam. Many sects and theological distinctions mark that religion, and no one group speaks for the whole. We continue to grow in our knowledge of this historic religion.

Josh McDowell answered the prevailing ignorance about the person of Jesus Christ in the 1970s with a simple little apologetic that he titled *More Than a Carpenter*.[2] Our variation on McDowell's title, *More Than a Prophet*, hints at a similarity of aim. We too want to simplify core distinctions between Christianity and Islam. While Muslims respect Jesus as a prophet in the line leading toward the final prophet Muhammed, the Bible points to Jesus as the redeeming Son of God and second person of the Godhead. Since no one comes to the Father except through believing in Jesus Christ as Lord and God, this is no small difference.

A radical dichotomy exists between evangelical Christianity and Islamic faith. Some say that we stand for one spiritual view of reality because we are bigoted. We accept the charge that we believe in an absolute truth, but we strongly deny that this is evidence of bigotry. Rather, we have been motivated to write by an overwhelming burden of love. Our culture finds offense in a statement that there is one truth, and all conflicting beliefs are false. Who are we to believe that ours is the only way to heaven? In fact, we are not the ones who have chosen Christ to be the only way. The Bible, which we are convinced is utterly without falsehood, proclaims Jesus to be a perfectly holy God's only response to the unholiness separating humanity from Him. If the Bible is absolutely true, as orthodox Christianity purports, then the point is nonnegotiable. One Lamb of God, who was more than a mere prophet, took upon Himself the guilt of sinners. He offered His own righteousness in return, so that His most bitter enemies might be liberated and live, be they Saddam Hussein, Usamah Bin Ladin, or that Jewish radical Saul of Tarsus, who became more frequently known to us as the Christian evangelist Paul. If any of the earth's billions of people turn to Christ in repentance and faith, then they shall be forgiven and liberated as well.

The Cross and Christ is not about the defeat or death of the infidel but their new life. We are not called to vanquish with guns or bombs. We are called to touch with the precious truth.

The central issue of *More Than a Prophet* is Jesus Christ.

Notes

1. Ergun Mehmet Caner and Emir Fethi Caner, *Unveiling Islam* (Grand Rapids: Kregel, 2002).
2. Josh McDowell, *More Than a Carpenter* (Carol Stream, Ill.: Tyndale House, 1977).

1

QUESTIONS CONCERNING THE
NAME AND NATURE OF GOD

ISLAM BEGAN AS A REACTION TO THE Christian God, either as understood or as misconceived. Disagreements over the name and nature
of God are central to the conflict between Islam and Christianity.
The pluralist argues that Islam and Christianity are both monotheistic religions that claim spiritual descendancy from Abraham, so
the same God is worshiped by either. Such an easygoing ecumenism
is a distortion. We simply do not share the most essential understandings of God and to claim otherwise shows disrespect. It fails
to take seriously what a religion claims about ultimate truth.[1]

Thirteen questions illuminate some possible openings and clear
away cultural errors and misunderstandings that have arisen concerning our respective faiths.

Isn't Allah the same God that
Christianity and Judaism distorted?

In Islamic literature, the concept of *Allah* is that of the one true
God. All other gods are idols. Christianity and Judaism, in their
original form, were correct in teaching the tawhid (unique and
absolute oneness) of Allah, but these teachings were later distorted.
In Abdullah Yusuf 'Ali's commentary on the Qur'an, he writes:

There is really only one true Religion, the Message of Allah, submission to the Will of Allah: this is called Islam. It was the religion preached by Moses and Jesus; it was the religion of Abraham, Noah, and all the prophets, by whatever name it may be called. If people corrupt that pure light, and call their religions by different names, we must bear with them, and we may allow the names for convenience. But Truth must prevail over all.[2]

Muhammed fervently believed that Jews and Christians were at one time "People of the Book." However, they now are infidels, no better than other pagans. In fact, they are worse, as they have denied the very truth they were called by Allah to proclaim.

In Surah al-Taubah (9:29–33) the severity of their sin is outlined:

Fight those who believe not in Allah nor the Last Day, nor hold that forbidden which has been forbidden by Allah and His Messenger, nor acknowledge the Religion of Truth, from among the People of the Book, until they pay the Jizyah (poll tax) with willing submission and feel themselves subdued.

The Jews call ʿUzayr (Ezra) a son of God, and the Christians call Christ the Son of God. That is a saying from their mouth; (In this) they but imitate what the unbelievers of old used to say. Allah's curse be on them: how they are deluded away from the Truth!

They take their priests and their anchorites to be their lords in derogation of Allah, and (they take as their Lord) Christ, the son of Mary; Yet they were commanded to worship but One God: There is no god but He. Praise and glory to Him: (Far is He) from having the partners they associate (with Him).

Fain would they extinguish Allah's Light with their mouths, but Allah will not allow but that His Light should be perfected, even though the unbelievers may detest (it).

It is He who hath sent His Messenger with guidance

and the Religion of Truth, to proclaim it over all religion, even though the pagans may detest (it).

Clearly Muhammed based his teaching at least partly on a mis-understanding of what the Bible taught. He believed that Jews and Christians had both deified humanity and made idols out of their prophets Ezra and Jesus, respectively. Actually, orthodox Old Testament believers would have been in agreement with Muslims that the Old Testament term *sons of God* referred to spiritual relationship, not literal physical generation. ʿAli shows the errant understanding as he complains about the theology of Job 38:7: "'When the morning stars sang together, and all the sons of God shouted for joy.' . . . If used figuratively these and like words refer to the love of Allah. Unfortunately 'son' used in a physical sense, or 'beloved' in an exclusive sense as if Allah loved only the Jews, makes a mockery of religion."[3]

Apparently Muhammed knew of some sect that called Ezra a "son of God" and thought that all Jews ascribed some sort of divinity to the post-Babylonian exile Jewish priest Ezra. ʿAli cites Baidhawi as a source of this belief.

Misunderstanding what the Old Testament writers meant by the concept of sonship, the early Muslim understanding was that Jews took the "primitive ignorance and superstition" of deifying their leaders from their idol-worshiping neighbors.[4] Christians had further "deluded the Truth" by adapting the ancient Jewish heresy to deify Jesus Christ. This is the highest *shirk* (sin).

Use of the term *anchorites* in 9:31 is an apparent reference to the intercessory position Muhammed believed the priests of his day took between God and people. He saw these priests and monks as claiming to stand in the place of Allah in a quite literal sense, again a sin of the highest order.

Muhammed is thus sent as the final prophet to correct their errors, as we can deduce from 9:33. This messenger (Muhammed) would proclaim the "Religion of Truth" over all the religions, leading either to their extermination or subjugation. This proclamation is of the highest importance, as one can readily see by 9:29.

To "fight those who believe not in Allah nor in the Last Day" has been variously interpreted as literal, intellectual, or spiritual, but within the context of the verse, the submission of the unbelievers is unquestionably demanded. If they remain under Islamic rule, they must pay a tax (Jizyah).

In any interpretation of the Qur'anic text, Christianity and Judaism have left the truth taught by their founders and have followed idolatrous practices to their eternal peril. The belief that Christians and Jews substantially changed the message of God is further expounded in surah 5:18: "Both the Jews and the Christians say, 'We are sons of Allah, and His beloved.' Say: 'Why then doth He punish you for your sins?' Nay, ye are but men—of the men He hath created: He forgiveth whom He pleaseth, and He punisheth whom He pleaseth."

Didn't Allah originate as a pagan moon god?

One contemporary Christian view is that Muhammed borrowed his concept of Allah from a pagan "moon god" identified with the Ka'aba.[5] Thus, the crescent found in Islamic architecture is symbolic of the moon. This argument identifies Islam as a syncretistic pagan phenomenon.

In his books *Islamic Invasion* and *The Moon-god: Allah in the Archeology of the Middle East*, Robert A. Moray submits the thesis that Muhammed actually took both the word Allah and the nature of Allah from a pre-Islamic Arabian mythology.[6] His thesis has three parts:

1. Before the rise of Islam in the seventh century, the term *Allah* was used to refer to any of 360 gods worshiped in the Ka'aba.
2. This one god may have been a "high god," greater than the other deities, but it was never viewed as the absolute one true God.
3. *Allah* can be traced back to the Babylonian term *Il* and the Bedouin term *al-Il'ah*.

Morey believes that he has found strong evidence in thousands of books and articles for an adaptation view of the word *Allah*. However, there are problems with this view:

First, Muhammed believed in Allah's absolute separation from creation, not identification with it. Further, the Qur'an clearly stipulates in surah 41:37: "Among His Signs are the Night and the Day and the Sun and Moon. Prostrate (adore) not to the Sun and the Moon but prostrate to Allah, Who created them, if it is Him you wish to serve."

Second, whatever might have contributed to Muhammed's theology, the historical criticism of Islamic doctrine has little to do with the beliefs of the modern Muslim. For fifteen hundred years, Muslims have held to the *tawhid* nature of Allah. It is more profitable to evaluate what the Qur'an now says and Muslims now confess. Christians can find ample points to dispute without bringing in some moon god that neither Muhammed nor Muslims have accepted.

Third, Morey makes the common mistake of relying on Christian sources for his citations. Muslims correctly assert that Christian scholarship is hardly an unbiased observer in proving anything about Islam. His hundreds of citations from Christian academic works seem unfair, at best, to Muslims.

Certainly this provocative thesis demands further investigation from ancient sources that can be uncovered. Meanwhile such statements are open to dispute. Even if they were unassailable, the conclusions are irrelevant to the evaluation of Islam as it now exists. The Christian would be well advised to study and discuss the nature and attributes of Allah as found in the Qur'an.

Is the God of Muhammed the Father of Jesus?

Related to the question of the origins of Islam is a raging controversy that we have been called to address repeatedly.[7] The basic question frequently is stated: "Christians claim to know the one true God. Muslims claim to know the one true God. Are you not talking about the same God? Are you not both historically monotheistic religions?"

We like the manner in which Timothy George framed the issue

in the February 2002 issue of *Christianity Today:* "Is the God of Muhammad the Father of Jesus?"[8] Dr. George suggests that Christianity and Islam share a number of suppositions. Both are monotheistic, historical, textual, and moral systems, and speak of the one God in terms of holiness and justice. He answers the question:

> Is the Father of Jesus the God of Muhammad? The answer is surely Yes and No. Yes, in the sense that the Father of Jesus is the only God there is. He is the Creator and Sovereign Lord of Muhammad, Buddha, Confucius, of every person who has ever lived. He is the one before whom all shall one day bow (Phil. 2:5–11). Christians and Muslims can together affirm many important truths about this great God—his oneness, eternity, power, majesty. As the Qur'an puts it, he is "the Living, the Everlasting, the All-High, the All-Glorious" (2:256). But the answer is also No, for Muslim theology rejects the divinity of Christ and the personhood of the Holy Spirit—both essential components of the Christian understanding of God. No devout Muslim can call the God of Muhammad "Father," for this, to their mind, would compromise divine transcendence. But no faithful Christian can refuse to confess, with joy and confidence, "I believe in God the Father . . . Almighty!" Apart from the Incarnation and the Trinity, it is possible to know that God is, but not who God is.[9]

The article goes on to explain how Islam and Christianity differ in the fundamental descriptions and attributes of God, and how such a distortion can have eternally deleterious effects. However, others have taken the position that, since Muslims worship a monotheistic, just, righteous God of creation, then that God—under whatever name—is the same God. Some missiologists, even purported evangelical Christians, argue that we must simply tell Muslims that the "Allah" to which they are praying sent Jesus, for them.

The God of Muhammed is not the Father of Jesus. We are not speaking of an etymological issue, for the Arabic term *Allah* certainly means "God." But different religions by their nature pour distinctive meanings into terms that can be translated by the English word *God*. Do Muslims mean the same God when they faithfully face Mecca five times a day as Christians do when they bow before the Father? No, they do not. Islam repudiates the Christian concepts of God as *triune* and *personal*, as it repudiates Christianity itself.

Throughout the Qur'an, statements contradict the biblical revelation and make impossible any cohesion between honest disciples of the two religions. The Qur'an teaches that Christians are going to hell because we elevate the status of a prophet to that of a deity. The Bible teaches that no one comes to the Father except through Christ. Islam says that Christianity has abandoned any truth they held of Allah. One need only read surah 5:72 to see that "They do blaspheme who say 'Allah is Christ the son of Mary.' But Christ said, 'O Children of Israel! Worship Allah, my Lord and your Lord.' Whoever joins other gods with Allah—Allah will forbid him the Garden, and the Fire will be his abode. There will for the wrongdoers be no one to help."

This is not a mere modification of the biblical record; it is a complete and utter distortion. History is filled with men and women who, upon reading the biblical record, decided to take the central ideas of the Bible and create a new god, more to their liking. Many of these movements even chose to maintain biblical names and titles. Others have kept Jesus in their religions but molded their view of Him to fit their schematics. One cult calls Jesus the half brother of Lucifer. Another group believes that Christ was a failed Messiah, whose crucifixion left the work of redemption undone. Are we all speaking of the same Christ?

In our estimation, this is the philosophical equivalent of the Tower of Babel (cf. Genesis 11). Sounds may seem similar, but the ideas hurled about with reckless abandon cannot communicate the same concepts. The God of Islam is no more the Father of Jesus than the Mormon Jesus is the authentic Jesus of biblical revelation.

Is Allah personal and intimate?

Muslims believe that Surah al-Ikhlas (112) summarizes their confession of the attributes of Allah. Christian apologists Norman Geisler and Abdul Saleeb accurately reflect the importance of this section when they observe that, "this surah is held to be worth a third of the whole Qurʾan and the seven heavens and the seven earths are founded upon it."[10]

The title *al-Ikhlas* means "the purity of faith," and the succinct chapter says:

> Say: He is Allah
> The One and Only,
> Allah, the Eternal, Absolute;
> He begetteth not,
> Nor is He begotten;
> And there is none
> Like unto Him.

In all of the descriptions of Allah in the Qurʾan, in all of Allah's reported ninety-nine names, in all of his dealings with humankind, the glaring omission is immanence or divine-human intimacy. Allah is never described as personal. A Muslim does not have a "personal relationship with Allah," in the sense that a Christian speaks of having a personal relationship with God. The attributes of Allah ascribed in the Qurʾan present him as transcendent Judge, but never as close Friend. This one-dimensional transcendent separateness is a vital difference between the two religions.

The attributes of Allah are expounded in a number of places in the Qurʾan. Surah 59:22–24 presents one example:

> Allah is He, than Whom there is no other god—Who knows (all things) both secret and open; He, Most Gracious, Most Merciful.
> Allah is He, than Whom there is no other god—the Sovereign, the Holy One, Source of Peace (and Perfection). The Guardian of Faith, the Preserver of Safety, the Exalted

in Might, the Irresistible, the Supreme: Glory to Allah! (High is He) above the partners they attribute to Him.

He is Allah, the Creator, the Evolver, the Bestower of forms (or colors). To Him belong the Most Beautiful Names: Whatever is in the heavens and on earth, doth declare His praises and Glory; and He is the Exalter in might, the Wise.

ʿAli, in commenting on surah 112, expounds upon the nature of Allah in reference to the believers:

The nature of Allah is here indicated to us in a few words, such as we can understand. . . . He is near us; He cares for us; we owe our existence to Him. Secondly, He is the One and Only God, the Only One to Whom worship is due; all other things or beings that we can think of are His creatures and in no way comparable to Him. Thirdly, He is Eternal, without beginning or end. Absolute, not limited by time or place or circumstance, the Reality before which all other things or places are mere shadows or reflections. Fourthly, we must not think of Him as having a son or a father, for that would be to import animal qualities into our conception of Him. Fifthly, He is not like any other person or thing that we know or can imagine: His qualities and nature are unique.[11]

Some Christian apologists have asserted that Islam has no concept of a merciful God. This is not correct. Allah often is called "merciful" in the Qurʾan. The proper distinction between the description of the attributes of Allah in the Qurʾan and the God of the Bible is whether God can be present in the life of the believer. In Islam, Allah is merciful and present in the midst of trial. However, in the Bible, God is not only Sovereign Lord, Judge, and Redeemer. He is also personal. He is not only intimate. He is indwelling. First Corinthians 6:19–20 (NIV) states, "Do you not know that your body is a temple of the Holy Spirit, who is in you, whom you have received from God? You are not your own; you were bought at a price. Therefore honor God with your body."

There is no doctrine in Islam that speaks of having a personal relationship with Allah as a child would relate to a father. To imagine such a relationship violates the sovereign transcendence of Allah. Yet for the Christian, the sacrifice by Christ has done more than purchase our salvation. Through Christ's righteousness credited to our account, we are allowed access to God as our Father. Islam rejects the possibility that Jesus Christ can redeem His people from God's wrath. Likewise, the Islamic definition of Allah cannot allow the concept that any kind of redemption would give access to him. Muslims pray as a step toward salvation, not because they are saved and have a right to come before the Creator of the universe. Hebrews 4:14-16 (NIV) illustrates the vast implications of being declared just before God in the sacrifice of Jesus Christ:

> Since we have a great high priest who has gone through the heavens, Jesus the Son of God, let us hold firmly to the faith we profess. For we do not have a high priest who is unable to sympathize with our weaknesses, but we have one who has been tempted in every way, just as we are—yet was without sin. Let us then approach the throne of grace with confidence, so that we may receive mercy and find grace to help us in our time of need.

What are Allah's defining attributes?

Another former Muslim, who goes by the pseudonym Abdul Saleeb as coauthor of *Answering Islam*, has summarized accurately the Qur'anic portrayal of Allah under six categories:[12]

1. God as the absolute one (His unity). Islam denies any partner or companionship with Allah, but rather His complete unity and uniqueness.
2. God as absolute ruler (His sovereignty). As surah 2:255 states, "There is no god But He—the Living, Self-subsisting, Eternal. No slumber can seize Him Nor sleep." This attribute,

known as aseity, means Allah is self-existent and can sustain all by Himself.

3. God as absolute justice (His equity). Surah al-Imran (3:9) speaks of Allah's precise judgment, which is part of his holiness.

4. God as absolute mercy. *ar-Rahman* is the Arabic term for "the Merciful." It speaks of Allah's willingness to forgive if the Muslim does right.

5. God as absolute will (His volitionality). Many terms and descriptions in the Qur'an depict Allah as ordering existence and all about Him.

6. God as absolutely unknowable (His inscrutability). God is ultimately beyond human comprehension in any meaningful way.

The most succinct way to describe the attributes of Allah found in the Qur'an is that he is sovereign Judge.

Doesn't the Qur'an use the plural *We* when Allah is speaking?

One of the most serious misconceptions we encounter among Christians who have read the Qur'an is that they think they have found a plurality to God, as in the Christian Trinity, when Allah uses the first person plural *We.* For instance, Surah al-Maeda (5:70) states:

> We took the Covenant of the children of Israel and sent them Messengers. Every time there came to them a Messenger with what they themselves desired not—some (of these) they called imposters, and some they (go so far as to) slay.

Does use of the plural *We* indicate that Islam affirms some connotation of a Godhead? Sadly, no; this is simply an example of the "pronoun of regal splendor," which is common to many languages connected to a monarchy. It is a first person plural used by monarchs to convey an idea of majestic royalty. The Queen of England, for example, might say, "We are very pleased" when she is referring only to herself. No trinitarian terminology has crept into the Qur'an.

Is Allah ever described as triune?

Islam unequivocally disavows any attribute of Allah that would bespeak the Trinity. The clarity of this denial is illustrated in surah 5:72-73:

> They do blaspheme who say: "Allah is Christ the son Of Mary." . . .

> They do blaspheme who say: Allah is one of three In a Trinity: for there is no god except One God. If they desist not from their word (of blasphemy), verily a grievous penalty will befall the blasphemers among them.

Earlier, in surah 4:171, the teaching is explicit: "Do not say 'Trinity.' Cease from doing that."

In a series of well-publicized debates, Christian scholar Anis A. Shorrosh and Islamic scholar Ahmed Deedat crossed intellectual swords concerning this central point. Deedat, the Muslim apologist, stated, "He (God) does not beget because begetting is an animal act. It belongs to the lower animal act of sex. We do not attribute such an act of God."[13]

Deedat's statement shows the Islamic misunderstanding of what Christians mean when they speak of the Trinity. Christians speak of God as consisting of three eternal centers of personhood within one being. These centers are described in Scripture as *Father, Son,* and *Holy Spirit* to delineate the command structure within the Triune God. The Son and Holy Spirit were not generated at some moment. Rather Christ is the Son because He submits to the plan of the Father and was sent to earth to serve the Father. The Holy Spirit likewise serves and submits to the plan of the Father and Son.

This has been difficult for Muslims to understand from the beginning. Perhaps because he interacted with unorthodox groups who claimed to be Christian, Muhammed evidently believed that the Trinity consisted of God, Jesus, and Mary. An example is found in surah 5:116:

> And behold! Allah will say:
> "O Jesus the son of Mary!
> Didst thou say unto men,
> 'Worship me and my mother
> As gods in derogation of Allah'?"

To claim a trinitarian view of God is, in Muslim theology, the highest of sins, the Islamic equivalent of blasphemy against the Holy Spirit. Whether the sin is irrevocable is a point of considerable debate. Some Muslims believe such a confession irrevocably and immediately damns the person. Others believe that there is always hope of forgiveness, if the sin is the result of ignorance. Surah 4:116 asserts, "Allah forgiveth not (the sin of) joining other gods with Him." ʿAli comments that this sin is an act of treason against Allah:

> Just as in an earthly kingdom the worst crime is that of treason, as it cuts at the very existence of the State, so in the spiritual kingdom, the unforgivable sin is that of contumacious treason against Allah by putting up Allah's creatures in rivalry against Him. This is rebellion against the essence and source of spiritual Life. It is what Plato would call the "lie in the soul." But even here, if the rebellion is through ignorance, and is followed by sincere repentance and amendment, Allah's Mercy is always open.[14]

How can God be three in one?

Surah 5:73 summarizes the Islamic central belief: "They do blaspheme who say God is one of three, . . . for there is no God except one God." The difficult thing for a Muslim to understand is that any true Christian agrees with surah 5:73. Christianity does not teach that "God is one of three." Nor do Christians believe that

God reproduced a "son" through sexual intercourse with a consort (surah 6:101). Muhammed may well have encountered cults who taught that. Latter-Day Saints, who often identify themselves as Christian but are not in any meaningful sense of the term, teach something of the sort. This idea is as blasphemous to a Muslim as to a biblical Christian. Thus, Islam finds no argument from Christianity when it notes that Allah "has taken no consort (nor has he) . . . begotten any children" (surah 72:3).

Here we find the nexus of the Christian-Islamic dialogue. Shorrosh has explained that most Muslims believe that the Christian doctrine of the Trinity teaches that Mary was a goddess, Jesus her son, and God Almighty her husband.[15] What Christians really do believe is demanded by the full picture God reveals in Scripture. Mary has no part in this teaching and will be covered elsewhere.

First, God is one simple and indivisible unity of divine Being, unchanging and without parts. But second, this simple and indivisible transcendent being exists eternally through a complex nature. A diversity exists within the unity. God teaches most of what we know about His infinite, transcendent being by showing us what He is "like." His Triunity, though, is *like* nothing in human experience. So God reveals Himself through three pictures—Father, Son, and life-giving Spirit. As *Father*, God is Creator and ultimate Ground of all Being, whose presence fills the universe and maintains existence. As *Son*, He proceeds from the Creator-Sustainer to carry out the divine will. In the Son, God was able to set aside His own prerogatives and assume a nature that was both fully human and fully God. The plan of salvation would not have been possible otherwise. As *Holy Spirit* He proceeds from both Father and Son to carry out the divine will, particularly in personally applying the gifts of salvation.

Functionally, God has explicitly revealed these aspects of His being—Father, Son, and Holy Spirit. While all the attributes of God belong to the Father, the Son, and the Holy Spirit, the fatherhood of God relates particularly to His omnipotence and infinity; sonship to His justice and love, and the Spirit to His immanent presence. Here we will give a sampling of what just the New Testament teaches, although the nature of the Trinity can be discerned from all of Scripture.

The Father is God:

[Jesus said,] "For as the Father has life in Himself, so He has granted the Son to have life in Himself, and has given Him authority to execute judgment also, because He is the Son of Man." (John 5:26-27)

Paul, an apostle (not from men nor through man, but through Jesus Christ and God the Father who raised Him from the dead). (Galatians 1:1)

(Who are) elect according to the foreknowledge of God the Father, in sanctification of the Spirit, for obedience and sprinkling of the blood of Jesus Christ. (1 Peter 1:2)

The Son is God:

In the beginning was the Word, and the Word was with God, and the Word was God. He was in the beginning with God. (John 1:1-2)

Then the Jews said to Him, "You are not yet fifty years old, and have You seen Abraham?" Jesus said to them, "Most assuredly, I say to you, before Abraham was, I AM." (John 8:57-58)

For in Him dwells all the fullness of the Godhead bodily. (Colossians 2:9)

The Holy Spirit is God:

[Jesus said,] "You will be brought before governors and kings for My sake, as a testimony to them and to the Gentiles. But when they deliver you up, do not worry about how or what you should speak. For it will be given to you in that hour what you should speak; for it is not you who speak, but the Spirit of your Father who speaks in you." (Matthew 10:18-20)

But Peter said, "Ananias, why has Satan filled your heart to lie to the Holy Spirit? . . . You have not lied to men but to God. . . ." Then Peter said to her [Ananias's wife], "How is it that you have agreed together to test the Spirit of the Lord?" (Acts 5:3-9)

Second, Scripture references all three persons of the Godhead appearing together as distinct, yet equal:

When He had been baptized, Jesus came up immediately from the water; and behold, the heavens were opened to Him, and He saw the Spirit of God descending like a dove and alighting upon Him. And suddenly a voice came from heaven, saying, "This is My beloved Son, in whom I am well pleased." (Matthew 3:16-17)

[Jesus said] "Go therefore and make disciples of all the nations, baptizing them in the name of the Father and of the Son and of the Holy Spirit, teaching them to observe all things that I have commanded you; and lo, I am with you always, even to the end of the age." (Matthew 28:19-20)

Now He who establishes us with you in Christ and has anointed us is God, who has sealed us and given us the Spirit in our hearts as a guarantee. (2 Corinthians 1:21-22)

The grace of the Lord Jesus Christ, and the love of God, and the communion of the Holy Spirit be with you all. Amen. (2 Corinthians 13:14)

Peter, an apostle of Jesus Christ, to the pilgrims of the

Dispersion in Pontus, Galatia, Cappadocia, Asia, and Bithynia, elect according to the foreknowledge of God the Father, in sanctification of the Spirit, for obedience and sprinkling of the blood of Jesus Christ: Grace to you and peace be multiplied. (1 Peter 1:1–2)

If we did speak of three equal gods, as Islamic theology accuses, Christians would follow a view called "tri-theism," but that is utterly incompatible with the teaching of Scripture. The Bible teaches absolute monotheism, for which the theme text is Deuteronomy 6:4: "Hear, O Israel: The LORD our God, the LORD is one!" Neither is it possible that there is one Supreme God and two minor gods. The only option open to those who believe God has revealed Himself truly in Scripture is the Trinity: "three Persons, one Substance." Skeptics have said that Christianity defies logic, making $1 + 1 + 1 = 1$? This is a misunderstanding. The Trinity is not a *triplex* (by addition) but a *triunity* (by multiplication). "His one essence has multiple personalities. Thus, there is no more of a mathematical problem in conceiving the Trinity than there is in understanding 1 to the third power (1^3)."[16]

Is Jehovah, the God of the Bible, actually a physical man?

In contemporary society, one of the more remarkable movements has been the desire to "neutralize" all gender designations for God in Scripture. These "gender-neutral" Bibles are products of a complaint that Christianity is a patriarchal religion because the first person masculine pronouns found in Scripture demean women by portraying God as a "supramale." Muslims occasionally join in this charge, especially to counter a Christian assertion that Islam favors men.

Does the Bible actually portray the Father as a divine model of masculinity, complete with male genitalia? Of course not. God declares in Hosea 11:9, "I will not execute the fierceness of My anger; I will not again destroy Ephraim. For I am God, *and not man,* the Holy One in your midst. And I will not come with terror."[17] So why does Scripture usually refer to God in male terms?

The explanation is that Scripture uses *analogy* to show aspects of

who God is by comparison to things in human experience. How else
could finite language and concepts be used to convey facts about the
infinite and transcendent? Male pronouns used to refer to the Father
do not have *biological* relevance. They have *theological* importance in
distinguishing the God who is from the false gods of other religions.

An example of this is in the Bible's depiction of God as a Father.
Human fathers guard and protect their children with strength and
love in the human ideal. They nurture and give of themselves. God
is like that. The biblical God is described in terms of His relation to
humans as a loving, patient, and ever merciful Parent. The father
concept is a more straightforward picture of how this relationship
works than that of a mother. For example, we learn much about
God as parent by viewing the father-child relationship described in
Romans 8:14-21:

> For as many as are led by the Spirit of God, these are sons
> of God. For you did not receive the spirit of bondage again
> to fear, but you received the Spirit of adoption by whom
> we cry out, "Abba, Father." The Spirit Himself bears wit-
> ness with our spirit that we are children of God, and if
> children, then heirs—heirs of God and joint heirs with
> Christ, if indeed we suffer with Him, that we may also be
> glorified together.
>
> For I consider that the sufferings of this present time are
> not worthy to be compared with the glory which shall be
> revealed in us. For the earnest expectation of the creation
> eagerly waits for the revealing of the sons of God. For the
> creation was subjected to futility, not willingly, but because
> of Him who subjected it in hope; because the creation
> itself also will be delivered from the bondage of corruption
> into the glorious liberty of the children of God.

As God relates to us as His children, we are proffered all the
divine rights, privileges, and standing as heirs of His divine Promise. Therefore, use of the term *He* has nothing to do with physical
characteristics. God is Spirit (John 4:24). Rather God's father-

hood refers to a paternal type of love shown to those who call upon His name.

Is everything in life predetermined?

The issue of whether human beings are pawns in some cosmic game is raised against both Muslims and Christians. Both religions deal with questions of the will of God versus human freedom and what is predestined in the plan of God. The Islamic doctrine is called qadar. Sura al-Anam (6:18) says of Allah,

> He is the Irresistible,
> From above over His worshippers;
> And He is the Wise,
> Acquainted with all things.

As the Irresistible, Allah effectively predestines all belief and unbelief, according to many Muslim scholars. Indeed, al-Ghazzali views this as the logical implication of a God who is Supreme and removed:

> (Allah) willeth also the unbelief of the unbeliever and the irreligion of the wicked and, without that will, there would neither be unbelief nor irreligion. All we do we do by His will: what He willeth not does not come to pass. . . . We have no right to enquire about what (Allah) wills or does. He is perfectly free to will and to do what He pleases. In creating unbelievers, in willing that they should remain in that state; . . . in willing, in short, all that is evil, God has wise ends in view which it is not necessary that we should know.[18]

In the Hadith, Muhammed is recorded as saying:

> Allah's Apostle, the truthful and truly-inspired, said, "Each one of you collected in the womb of his mother for forty days . . . and then Allah sends an angel and orders him to

write four things, i.e., his provision, his age, and whether he will be of the wretched or the blessed (in the Hereafter). Then the soul is breathed into him. And by Allah, a person among you (or a man) may do deeds of the people of the Fire till there is only a cubit or an arm-breadth distance between him and the Fire, but then that writing (which Allah has ordered the angel to write) precedes, and he does the deeds of the person of Paradise and enters it; and a man may do the deeds of the people of Paradise till there is only a cubit or two between him and Paradise, and then that writing precedes and he does the deeds of the people of Fire and enters it."[19]

Do Muslims believe that *qadar* is predestination?

Some Muslims believe that this Islamic doctrine of predestination is overstated. Scholar Fazul Rahman allows for free will when he writes that "to hold that the Qur'an believes in absolute determinism of human behavior, denying free choice on man's part, is not only to deny almost the entire content of the Qur'an, but to undercut its very basis: the Qur'an by its own claim is an invitation to man to come to the right path."[20]

Even popular dictionaries of Islam, written by Muslim *ulema* (scholars) leave room for interpretation:

QADAR [is] often translated as "destiny," "fate," "divine predestination," "divine determination."

Qadar specifically is the divine application of (qada—divine decree) in time, according to the most widespread interpretations.[21]

This is a poorly understood area of disagreement in either religion, with a number of arguments based on nuanced interpretations of biblical and Qur'anic texts, respectively. It is not a subject that promotes fruitful discussion.

Is the Holy Spirit actually the angel Gabriel in Islam?

As Islam denies any doctrine of the Trinity, the very existence of the Holy Spirit is, of course, an enigma. Since Muhammed believed portions of the Gospels had been sent from Allah, and the Holy Spirit is mentioned throughout the Gospels, how did Muhammed deal with His existence?

The Qur²an teaches that the Holy Spirit is actually the angel Gabriel. Gabriel's purpose was to carry the Qur²anic revelations to Muhammed as an emissary or middleman, when Muhammed began having these alleged revelations upon his fortieth birthday. Surah 2:97-98 says,

> Say: Whoever is an enemy to Gabriel—for he brings down the (revelation) to thy heart by Allah's will, a confirmation of what went before, and guidance and glad tidings for those who believe. Whoever is an enemy to Allah and His angels and prophets, to Gabriel and Michael—Lo! Allah is an enemy to those who reject faith.

In Surah al-Nahl (16:102), the text is even more explicit:

> Say, the Holy Spirit has brought the revelation from thy Lord in Truth, in order to strengthen those who believe and as a Guide and glad tidings to Muslims.

As Muslim commentators hasten to note: "(The Holy Spirit is) the title of the Angel Gabriel through whom the revelation comes down."[22] In Arabic, *Gabriel* is transliterated *Jibril*. In *The Popular Dictionary of Islam*, Ian Richard Netton writes:

> [Jibril] is one of the greatest of all the Islamic angels since he was the channel through which the Holy Qur²an was revealed from God to the Prophet Muhammed. He is mentioned by name three times in the Qur²an . . . and elsewhere referred to by names like "The Spirit." Much tradition has accumulated in Islam round the figure of Gabriel: for example, he showed Nuh [Noah] how to build the ark and

lured Pharoah's army into the Red Sea. He pleaded with
God for, and tried to rescue, Ibrahim [Abraham] when the
latter was on the point of being burned to death by Namrud
[Nimrod].[23]

Gabriel does not explain Jesus' reference to the "Comforter" in
John 14–16, the one who would not come until Jesus ascended. As
seen in the section on "Questions of the New Testament," Muslims believe that the comforter to come was Muhammed.

If the Holy Spirit is Gabriel in the Qur'an, are jinn the same as angels?

Actually, in the Qur'an, jinn and angels differ from one another as
entities. Jinn are unseen beings, created from fire, but are not angels.
There are good and evil jinn, some of whom are found in the Islamic
hell, their faces covered with fire (surah 14:49–50). Surah adh-Dhariyat
(51:56): "(Allah says), I have only created Jinns and men, that they
may serve me." In Surah ar-Rahman (55:15), Muhammed says, "And
He created Jinns from fire free from smoke." As one Muslim scholar
notes, "They are spirits, and therefore subtle like a flame of fire.
Their being free from smoke implies that they are free from gross-
ness, for smoke is a grosser accompaniment of fire."[24]

In the Qur'anic depiction of the fall of Satan (Iblis), he is called
an angel, but Muslim commentators note that this is a reference to
jinn. Surah al-Baqarah (2:34) declares, "And behold, We said to
the angels: 'Bow down to Adam:' and they bowed down: Not so
Iblis: he refused and was haughty: He was of those who reject
faith." 'Ali states that there are no fallen angels in Muslim theology. Iblis is spoken of as a jinn. Surah al-Kahf 18:50 bears this out:

Behold! We say to the angels, "Bow down to Adam": they
bowed down except Iblis. He was one of the Jinns, and he
broke the command of his Lord. Will ye then take him as
his progeny as protectors rather than Me? And (the demonic) are enemies to you! Evil would be the exchange for
the wrongdoers!

Some Christian commentators use these verses to expound two perceived discrepancies, first, confusion over whether Iblis is a jinn or an angel, and, second, the statement "progeny of Satan." In our estimation, neither perceived discrepancy is significant.

Notes

1. Timothy George, "Is the God of Muhammad the Father of Jesus?" *Christianity Today,* February 4, 2002.

2. Abdullah Yusuf ʿAli, *The Meaning of the Holy Qurʾan* (Brentwood, Md.: Amana, 1992), n. 5442.

3. Ibid., n. 718.

4. Ibid., n. 1284.

5. An ancient stone structure in Mecca that Muhammed emptied of idols in 630 A.D. It is reverenced by Muslims as a holy shrine, built by Ibrahim (Abraham) and Ismael (Ishmael).

6. For more on Morey's work, contact Faith Defenders in Orange, California, or go to http://www.faithdefenders.com.

7. Ergun Mehmet Caner and Emir Fethi Caner, *Unveiling Islam* (Grand Rapids: Kregel, 2002).

8. George, "Is the God of Muhammad the Father of Jesus?" Dr. George, dean of Beeson School of Divinity, subsequently wrote a book-length treatment, *Is the Father of Jesus the God of Muhammad? Understanding the Differences Between Christianity and Islam* (Grand Rapids: Zondervan, 2002).

9. Ibid.

10. Norman L. Geisler and Abdul Saleeb, *Answering Islam* (Grand Rapids: Baker, 1993), 131.

11. ʿAli, *The Meaning of the Holy Qurʾan,* n. 6296.

12. Geisler and Saleeb, *Answering Islam,* 133–34.

13. Anis A. Shorrosh, *Islam Revealed* (Nashville: Thomas Nelson, 1988), 254. Cited in Geisler and Saleeb, *Answering Islam,* 256–57.

14. ʿAli, *The Meaning of the Holy Qurʾan,* n. 569.

15. Shorrosh, *Islam Revealed,* 114.

16. Geisler and Saleeb, *Answering Islam,* 262.

17. Emphasis added.

18. Abdiyah Akbar Abdul-Haqq, *Dictionary of Islam* (Minneapolis: Bethany, 1980), 147.

19. Sahih al-Bukhari, *The Translation of the Meanings of Sahih al-Bukhari,* trans. Muhammed Muhsin Khan (Medina: Islamic University, n.d.), 8.387.

20. Fazul Rahman, *Major Themes of the Qur'an* (Chicago: *Bibliotheca Islamica,* 1980), 20, as cited by Geisler and Saleeb, 140.

21. Ian Richard Netton, *A Popular Dictionary of Islam* (Chicago: NTC, 1992), 200.

22. 'Ali, *The Meaning of the Holy Qur'an,* n. 2141.

23. Netton, *Popular Dictionary,* 136.

24. 'Ali, *The Meaning of the Holy Qur'an,* n. 5182.

2

QUESTIONS CONCERNING THE
NATURE OF JESUS CHRIST (ISA)

AT VATICAN COUNCIL II, DELEGATES approved one of the most astonishing statements in the history of Roman Catholic theology:

> The Church has also a high regard for the Muslims. They
> worship God, who is one, living and subsistent, merciful
> and almighty, the Creator of heaven and earth, who has
> also spoken to men. They strive to submit themselves with-
> out reserve to the hidden decrees of God, just as Abraham
> submitted himself to God's plan, to whose faith Muslims
> eagerly link their own.
>
> Although not acknowledging him as God, they venerate
> Jesus as a prophet, his virgin Mother they also honor, and
> even at times devoutly evoke. Further, they await the day
> of judgment and the reward of God following the resurrec-
> tion of the dead. For this reason they highly esteem an
> upright life and worship God, especially by way of prayer,
> alms-deeds and fasting.[1]

This seems to set the more than one billion Muslims in the
category of "separated brethren." Is their recognition of Jesus as a
prophet sufficient to merit salvation?

Such questions frequently swirl through the world community of Christian churches. Some mainline denominations are willing to recognize Islam as a hidden, if not orthodox, sect of Christianity, within the stream of religious monotheists. Yet even moderate Islamic scholars heartily disagree with the assessment that they are "closet Christians." Rather, they believe that Christians are wayward Muslims who abandoned the truth of the tawhid (absolute singleness) of Allah. It is their belief that if we do not repent and walk the straight path of Islam, then we shall be consigned to the fifth level of hell, called Laza.[2]

The purpose of this section is to clearly delineate the distinctions between the biblical Jesus Christ as Lord and God, and the Islamic Jesus, called Isa in the Qur'an, who is a prophet and messenger of Allah.

Do Muslims respect Jesus as a prophet?

To the Muslim mind, the answer is unequivocal: They respect Jesus highly as the prophet of Allah. In defending the Islamic concept of *Isa*, Ian Richard Netton writes:

> He is a major prophet for Muslims who has a prominent place in the Qur'an. Islam regards Jesus as purely human and not as the Son of God. Muslims thus have no concept of salvation history with Jesus. . . . Jesus is frequently called "Son of Mary" in the Qur'an . . . (and) eschatological hadith texts portray Jesus coming near the end of time to destroy al-Dajjal (Antichrist).[3]

Muslims have no problem using biblical terminology, as long as they can interpret those terms with their own dictionaries. They can call Jesus the "Word," since they believe this means "communication" in Islam (kalam), and Jesus simply communicated the work of Allah. Surah aal-e-Imran (3:45) begins: "Behold! the angels said: 'O Mary! Allah giveth thee glad tidings of a Word from Him: his name will be Christ Jesus.'" Muslims do not stumble at the term *Christ*, which means "Messiah" to Christians and Jews.

They use the term in a descriptive sense as "the anointed one," rather than as a title. ʿAli wrote in commentary on the aforementioned verse: "*Christos* = anointed: kings and priests were anointed to symbolise consecration to their office. The Hebrew and Arabic form is *Masih* (messiah)."[4] The word, then, is descriptive of Jesus, who was "anointed" to proclaim Allah's truth.

Ironically, Muslims extend more respect to Jesus as a high prophet than do most liberal "Christians." Muslims believe Jesus was born of a virgin; rejection of the virgin birth is a foundation stone of modern theologies. Muslims believe Jesus actually lived in space and time. Liberals proclaim that we cannot know anything substantive about the man Jesus of Nazareth. Muslims believe that Jesus performed miracles (Surah al-Maeda); Liberals scoff at any claim that God intervenes over nature. Muslims believe Jesus is a servant of the eternally existing one true God. Modern theologies believe religions have evolved from polytheism to monotheism over time. The sad truth is that Jesus is held in higher esteem in mosques around the world than in the lectures from purportedly Christian pulpits.

The Islamic Jesus (Isa) is not the Christ of the biblical record, but He is accorded respect as a human prophet in whom Allah has done great things.

Do Muslims believe that Jesus performed miracles?

In Surah al-Maeda (5:112–15), the Qurʾan has a version of a miracle of Jesus rivaling those of the biblical record:

> Behold! the Disciples said: "O Jesus the son of Mary! Can thy Lord send down to us a table set (with food) from heaven?"
> Said Jesus: "Fear Allah, if ye have faith."
> They said: "We only wish to eat thereof and satisfy our hearts, and to know that Thou hast indeed told us the truth; and that we ourselves may be witnesses to the miracle." Said Jesus the son of Mary: "O Allah our Lord! Send us from heaven a Table set (with food), that there

may be for us- for the first and last of us- a solemn festival
and a Sign from Thee; And provide for our sustenance, for
Thou are the best Sustainer (of our needs)."

Allah said: 'I will send it down to you; But if any of you
after that resisteth faith, I will punish him with a penalty
such as I have not afflicted on any among all the peoples.'"[5]

Interestingly, ʿAli's commentary on the Qurʾan observes that the
words spoken by the disciples "suggest the Lord's Supper."[6] Muslims do not deny that Jesus met with His disciples for a final meal on
the night before His arrest, which is usually called the "Last Supper." Nor do they doubt that Jesus performed miracles or that He
was betrayed and arrested. They do deny His crucifixion, burial,
resurrection, and ascension as our High Priest, as we shall see.

Was Jesus born of a virgin, according to Islam?

The foundational teachings concerning the birth of Jesus are
found in Surah al-ʿImran, the third chapter of the Qurʾan. While
Muslims affirm the virgin birth of Jesus, the Islamic narrative differs substantially from the biblical record.

The virgin birth of Jesus, according to Islam, was not a supernatural act of the Holy Spirit infusing the womb of Mary with the
incarnate Lord. Rather, Jesus was created from dust: "The similitude of Jesus before Allah is as that of Adam; He created him from
dust, then said to him: 'Be,' and he was" (3:59). In the creation of
Jesus from dust, Muslims have adopted the "created" Christ theory
of the Arians, who controlled the church through part of the fourth
century. In the words of an Arian slogan, Muslims believe that
"there was a time when Christ was not."

Since the work of the Holy Spirit in the womb of Mary is rejected, the virgin conception of this dust-made child was by divine
spoken fiat. To better understand the difference, Muslims might
compare this to the actual biblical account in Luke 1:26–35:

Now in the sixth month the angel Gabriel was sent by God
to a city of Galilee named Nazareth, to a virgin betrothed

to a man whose name was Joseph, of the house of David. The virgin's name was Mary. And having come in, the angel said to her, "Rejoice, highly favored one, the Lord is with you; blessed are you among women!"

But when she saw him, she was troubled at his saying, and considered what manner of greeting this was. Then the angel said to her, "Do not be afraid, Mary, for you have found favor with God. And behold, you will conceive in your womb and bring forth a Son, and shall call His name Jesus. He will be great, and will be called the Son of the Highest; and the Lord God will give Him the throne of His father David. And He will reign over the house of Jacob forever, and of His kingdom there will be no end."

Then Mary said to the angel, "How can this be, since I do not know a man?"

And the angel answered and said to her, "The Holy Spirit will come upon you, and the power of the Highest will overshadow you; therefore, also, that Holy One who is to be born will be called the Son of God."

Islam explicitly repudiates the biblical story for two reasons. First, the biblical story involves the work of the Holy Spirit internally. Islam rejects a view of the person of the Holy Spirit, other than as the angel Gabriel. That would be redundant if the Holy Spirit is an angel and yet the one speaking to Mary is an angel. Second, Islam can never accept the words of the angel: "He will be great and will be called the Son of the Most High."

In contrast, the Islamic narrative of the birth of Jesus focuses on the decree of Allah, rather than the miraculous birth or Incarnation. Note surah 3:45–47:

Behold! the angels said: "O Mary! Allah giveth thee glad tidings of a Word from Him: his name will be Christ Jesus. The son of Mary, held in honour in this world and the Hereafter and of (the company of) those nearest to Allah; He shall speak to the people in childhood and in maturity.

And he shall be (of the company) of the righteous."

She said: "O my Lord! How shall I have a son when no man hath touched me?"

He said: "Even so:

Allah createth what He willeth: When He hath decreed a Plan, He but saith to it, 'Be,' and it is!'"

Muslims often say, "We respect Mary, even more than do you Christians. In fact, we have an entire chapter of the Qurʾan named in her honor." Chapter 19 of the Qurʾan is named *Maryam*. These ninety-eight verses add a lot of detail not found in the Bible. The chapter begins with the story of Zachariah (ar-Zakariya), verses 1–15. In the Islamic story, Zachariah is struck dumb for three days, until the birth of his son, Yahya (John the Baptist). The story then moves to the impregnation of Mary, with some twists. In surah 19:17, 22–23, we even share Mary's anguish in her childbearing:

> She placed a screen (to hide herself) from them; then We sent to her our angel, and he appeared before her as a man in all respects. . . . So she conceived him and she retired with him to a remote place. And the pains of childbirth drove her to the trunk of a palm tree: she cried (in her anguish): "Ah! would that I had died before this! Would that I had been a thing forgotten and out of sight!"

In comparison, the biblical record emphasizes the birth of Messiah. Even in the text from Luke 1:26–35 quoted above, the focus is not on the instrument God used (Mary) but on the incarnation of "God with us." Isaiah 7:14b predicts, "Behold, the virgin shall conceive and bear a son, and shall call His name Immanuel [meaning "God with us"]." The gospel of Matthew (1:23) quotes this prophecy and shows it as fulfilled in the birth of Jesus.

Did Jesus speak from the cradle, according to Islam?

In the four Gospels, there is no mention that the baby Jesus spoke. The only recorded words from his childhood were at age twelve when His parents found Him in the temple in Jerusalem (see Luke 2:41–50). However, the Qurʾan finds the baby Isa proclaiming from the cradle that he is the prophet for Allah (surah 19:27–33):

> At length (Mary) brought the (babe) to her people, carrying him (in her arms). They said: "O Mary! Truly an amazing thing hast though brought! O sister of Aaron! Thy father was not a man of evil, nor thy mother a woman unchaste!"
> But (Mary) pointed to the babe.
> They said: "How can we talk to one who is a child in the cradle?"
> He said: "I am indeed a servant of Allah: he hath given me Revelation and made me a Prophet; and He hath made me blessed wheresoever I be, and hath enjoined on me prayer and charity as long as I live. (He) hath made me kind to my mother, and not overbearing or miserable; so Peace is on me the day I was born, the day that I die, and the Day that I shall be raised up to life (again)!"

Why would Islam have Jesus speaking from the cradle? There does seem to be an agenda here, for the first words amount to a direct renunciation of the Christian doctrine of His deity.

Does Christ perform any miracles in the Qurʾan that are not in the Bible?

Surah al-ʿImran (3:49) refers to a miracle performed by Jesus as a child that has stirred speculation:

> (Allah will appoint him) a Messenger to the Children of Israel (with this message): "I have come to you, with a Sign from your Lord, in that I make for you, out of clay, as it were, the figure of a bird, and breathe into it, and it becomes a bird by Allah's leave: and I heal those born blind, and the lepers, and I quicken the dead, by Allah's leave;

and I declare to you what ye eat and what ye store in your houses. Surely therein is a Sign for you if ye did believe."

This story is not unique to the Qur'an. It was a tale from a set of spurious Gnostic works that were current in Arabia during Muhammed's lifetime. These works, including *The Infancy Gospel of Thomas* and *The Gospel of Peter,* were condemned as false teachings outside the regions inhabited by the apostate Gnostics. Coptic churches of today's Middle East follow in that theological tradition. By 367, two centuries before Muhammed's birth, these works were declared noncanonical in Athanasius's *Festal Letter.* Still, such works as *The Gospel of Barnabas* have been accepted by Muslims and some modern Christian movements since they do not teach Christ's deity.

Did Christ speak of Muhammed?

John records an extended teaching of Jesus as He prepares His disciples for His imminent betrayal, death, burial, resurrection, and ascension. He promised the disciples that He would send a "Comforter." John 16:5–15 summarizes this teaching:

> But now I go away to Him who sent Me, and none of you asks Me, "Where are You going?" But because I have said these things to you, sorrow has filled your heart. Nevertheless I tell you the truth. It is to your advantage that I go away; for if I do not go away, the Helper will not come to you; but if I depart, I will send Him to you. And when He has come, He will convict the world of sin, and of righteousnes, and of judgment: of sin, because they do not believe in Me; of righteousness, because I go to My Father and you see Me no more; of judgment because the ruler of this world is judged.
>
> I still have many things to say to you, but you cannot bear them now. However, when He, the Spirit of truth, has come, He will guide you into all truth; for He will not speak on His own authority, but whatever He hears He

will speak; and He will tell you things to come. He will glorify Me, for He will take of what is Mine and declare it to you. All things that the Father has are Mine. Therefore I said that He will take of Mine and declare it to you.

Christians have never taught that this "Comforter" or "Counselor" is other than the Holy Spirit, the third person of the Godhead. According to surah 60:6, Muhammed believed Christ was speaking of him:

And remember, Jesus, the son of Mary, said: "O Children of Israel! I am the messenger of Allah (sent) to you, confirming the Law (which came) before me, and giving glad tidings of a Messenger to come after me, whose name shall be Ahmad." But when he came to them with Clear Signs, they said, "This is evident sorcery!"

This reinterpretation of the text may have arisen because of a conjunction of Greek and Arabic terms. The Greek term translated "comforter" is *paraklētos,* which means "the One who comes alongside." A similar looking Greek term, *periklytos,* means "famed," or "praised." The Arabic term that can be translated "praised" is *Ahmad.* This form is similar to *Ahamad,* a variant spelling of *Muhammed.* One Muslim scholar wrote that *Ahmad* "is almost a translation of the Greek word *paraklētos.* In the Gospel of John. . . . The word 'Comforter' in the English version is for the Greek word 'Paracletos,' which means 'Advocate.' . . . Our doctors contend that Paracletos is a corrupt reading of periclytos, and that in their original saying of Jesus there was a prophecy of our Holy Prophet Ahmad by name."[7]

See chapter 5 of this volume for implications of this teaching.

Did Jesus ever say, "Worship Me, for I am God"?

Shaikh Ahmed Zaki Yamani, speaking more honestly than most scholars in these days of "politically correct speech," wrote in *Islam and Christianity Today,*

In the great debate between Christians and Muslims...there are areas of fundamental principles where no amount of logical discourse can bring the two sides nearer to each other and where therefore the existence of an impasse must be recognized. . . . Issues like the Trinity, the Divinity of Christ and the Crucifixion, so central to Christian beliefs, have no place in Islamic faith, having been categorically refuted by the Qur'an.[8]

Muslim scholars have universally denied that Jesus ever called Himself "the Son of God," much less "God the Son." This question is a paraphrase of a Muslim apologist's ever present taunt, which he uses in debates throughout the United States and Britain. In fact, we believe Jesus does call Himself God and is thus worshiped. We offer the following examples, in their textual context, starting with an incident in Jesus' controversy with Jewish leaders, found in John 8:49-59:

Jesus answered, "I do not have a demon; but I honor My Father, and you dishonor Me. And I do not seek My own glory; there is One who seeks and judges. Most assuredly, I say to you, if anyone keeps My word he shall never see death."

Then the Jews said to Him, "Now we know that You have a demon! Abraham is dead, and the prophets; and You say, 'If anyone keeps My word he shall never taste death.' Are You greater than our Father Abraham, who is dead? And the prophets are dead. Who do You make Yourself out to be?"

Jesus answered, "If I honor Myself, My honor is nothing. It is My Father who honors Me, of whom you say that He is your God. Yet you have not known Him, but I know Him. And if I say, 'I do not know Him,' I shall be a liar like you; but I do know Him and keep His word. Your father Abraham rejoiced to see My day, and he saw it and was glad."

> Then the Jews said to Him, "You are not yet fifty years old, and have You seen Araham?"
>
> Jesus said to them, "Most assuredly, I say to you, before Abraham was, I AM."
>
> Then they took up stones to thrown at Him; but Jesus hid Himself and went out of the temple, going through the midst of them, and so passed by.

When the Jewish leaders charged that Jesus was demon possessed, He responded that if anyone followed His word, they would never taste death. The Jews retorted that Abraham was dead, and preceded Jesus, and yet somehow, this son of a carpenter from Nazareth was greater than Abraham? Jesus firmly stated that Abraham had anticipated His advent. In 8:57, the climax of the discussion came: "How could You possibly have ever seen Abraham?" It was a fair question. Abraham had lived two thousand years prior. No man in biblical history had ever lived past 969 years (Methuselah), and certainly this Jesus did not look that old! Jesus' answer froze the crowd. "Before Abraham was born, I AM!" This was a statement of the highest blasphemy. First, Jesus claimed to have existed before the father of the nation, the one to whom the covenant had been given in Genesis 12:1-3. Second, Jesus used the Aramaic word translated "I AM." In Aramaic, this word transliterated the sacred name of God Himself, *YHWH*. This was the name that God gave Moses at the burning bush when Moses asked, "What shall tell them Your name is?" (see Exodus 3:13-14). God revealed His name as *YHWH*. The word was four simple letters in the Hebrew language, so it is called the Tetragrammaton ("four letters").

No Jews ever uttered the Name of God. Ever. It was so holy, that even scribes who were transcribing the Hebrew Scriptures would lay aside their writing instrument when they came to the word, take a fresh unused one, write the four letters, then toss the instrument away. Readers of the text used the word for "lord" in place of the sacred name. Now, this teacher not only uttered the inutterable word *YHWH*, but He ascribed it to Himself and on the very Temple grounds. The Jews picked up stones because there was no other interpretation than that Jesus claimed to be God. The response of the Jewish leaders was inevitable. There is no avoiding the absolute clarity of this statement. Even Muslim scholars admit that the charge leveled against Jesus was the blasphemy of claiming to be God. They believe this charge was later assumed by the disciples as truth, when in fact it was a lie. Notice ʿAli's statement:

> Jesus was charged by the Jews with blasphemy as claiming to be God or the Son of God. The Christians . . . adopted the substance of this claim, and made it the cornerstone of their faith. Allah clears Jesus of such a charge or claim.[9]

This is a remarkable statement. A Muslim scholar, writing a commentary for the English translation of the Qurʾan, admits that the charge brought against Jesus was that of blasphemy—claiming to be God. While the Muslims believe that Jesus never made such a claim, they do not dispute that He was charged with making the claim.

If Jesus actually claimed to be God, then no one—Muslim or pagan—can say they simply "respect" Him. If Christ actually claimed to be God but was not God, then He is not worthy of respect. His disciples, the courts, and the Jewish high counsel unanimously said that Christ made that claim. It seems as well attested a fact as any ancient fact can be. Therefore, one is faced with two options, (1) to reject the claim and confirm that He was a blasphemer, or (2) to revere Him as God. Simple "respect" of Jesus as a prophet simply will not do. If He is not God, He is not worthy of respect; if He is God, then "respect" is not an adequate response.

In the same gospel of John (4:4–26), Jesus encounters a Samaritan woman at a village well. As Jews despised Samaritans and would travel miles out of the way to avoid their towns, she was surprised to find a Jew sitting at the well, ready to engage in conversation with her. She was more surprised when He seemed to be familiar with the details of her sinful life. We pick up the account at 4:19–26:

> The woman said to Him, "Sir, I perceive that You are a prophet. Our fathers worshiped on this mountain, and you Jews say that in Jerusalem is the place where one ought to worship."
>
> Jesus said to her, "Woman, believe Me, the hour is coming when you will neither on this mountain, nor in Jerusalem, worship the Father. You worship what you do not know; we know what we worship, for salvation is of the Jews. But the hour is coming, and now is, when the true worshipers will worship the Father in spirit and truth; for the Father is seeking such to worship Him. God is Spirit, and those who worship Him must worship in spirit and truth."
>
> The woman said to Him, "I know that Messiah is coming" (who is called Christ). "When He comes, He will tell us all things."
>
> Jesus said to her, "I who speak to you am He."

Jesus could have been masquerading as someone He was not. But the woman did not misunderstand the implications of what He had told her. We read later in 4:28–30:

> The woman then left her waterpot, went her way into the city, and said to the men, "Come, see a Man who told me all things that I ever did. Could this be the Christ?" Then they went out of the city and came to Him.

Perhaps the woman is somewhat ambivalent in her rhetorical question, "Could this be the Christ?" Were the people of Samaria confused by the nexus of Jesus' statement? Apparently not, according to their response (4:39–42):

> And many of the Samaritans of that city believed in Him because of the word of the woman who testified, "He told me all that I ever did." So when the Samaritans had come to Him, they urged Him to stay with them; and He stayed

there two days. And many more believed because of His word. Then they said to the woman, "Now we believe, not because of what you said, for we ourselves have heard Him and know that this is indeed the Christ, the Savior of the world."

John not only shows that these people understood Jesus to be the Messiah, but they defined that title as more than a vague anointing by Allah. As Messiah, Jesus intended to be understood as "the Savior of the world." In the context of John's gospel, that can only mean that Jesus was *divine* Messiah—one worthy of worship.

Didn't Jesus refer to Himself as the "Son of Man"?

Yes, Jesus did refer to Himself as the "Son of Man," but this does not negate His claim of divinity. Rather, it is a reference to a very technical prophecy of the Jewish prophet Daniel, made during the Babylonian exile of the Jews in the sixth century B.C. In fact, the term *Son of Man* is part of Christ's testimony of His divine nature. He refers to Himself by that title more than eighty times in the Gospels, for example, these quotations of Jesus in Matthew:

And Jesus said to him, "Foxes have holes and birds of the air have nests, but the Son of Man has nowhere to lay His head." (8:20)

But Jesus, knowing their thoughts, said, "Why do you think evil in your hearts? For which is easier, to say, 'Your sins are forgiven you,' or to say, 'Arise and walk?' But that you may know that the Son of Man has power on earth to forgive sins"—then He said to the paralytic, "Arise, take up your bed, and go to your house." (9:4-6)

"For John [the Baptist] came neither eating nor drinking, and they say, 'He has a demon.' The Son of Man came eating and drinking, and they say, 'Look, a glutton and a winebibber, a friend of tax collectors and "sinners!'" But wisdom is justified by her children." (11:18-19)

We have heard uninformed Christians say that Jesus referred to His deity in references to the "Son of God" and to His humanity in references to the "Son of Man." That seems reasonable, but it just isn't so. The term *Son of Man* carries with it both the presence of the Jewish Messiah and divine authority. Notice Christ's explanation in Matthew 12:3-8 when Jewish leaders complained that Jesus' disciples had broken a rule for keeping the Sabbath:

> But He said to them, "Have you not read what David did when he was hungry, he and those who were with him: how he entered the house of God and ate the showbread which was not lawful for him to eat, nor for those who were with him, but only for the priests? Or have you not read in the law that on the Sabbath the priests in the temple profane the Sabbath, and are blameless? Yet I say to you that in this place there is One greater than the temple. But if you had known what this means, 'I desire mercy and not sacrifice,' you would not have condemned the guiltless. For the Son of Man is Lord even of the Sabbath."

Jesus declares, as the Son of Man, that He is Lord of the Sabbath. He also claims, as the Son of Man, that He can forgive sin against God. How is that possible? It becomes clear when we see how Daniel 7:13-14 sets a special messianic and divine connotation on the phrase:

> I was watching in the night visions, and behold, One like the Son of Man, coming with the clouds of heaven! He came to the Ancient of Days, and they brought Him near before Him. Then to Him was given dominion and glory and a kingdom, that all peoples, nations, and languages should serve Him. His dominion is an everlasting dominion, which shall not pass away, and His kingdom the one which shall not be destroyed.

The "Son of Man" here has explicit authority:

1. He approached the Ancient of Days and is led into his presence. Islam rejects any proximity with Allah.
2. He is given the authority of God.
3. He is given glory. Islam glorifies no one but Allah. If Christ is the "Son of Man," He is worthy of worship.
4. He is given sovereign power. Islam believes only Allah is sovereign. If Christ is given sovereign power, He is worthy of worship.
5. The Son of Man is worshiped. Jesus called on others to worship Him as the "Son of Man."

Was Jesus Christ crucified?

Islam teaches that Jesus was not crucified, nor did He die a natural death later. Surah 4:157 sets out this theory:

> That they said (in boast), "We killed Christ Jesus the son of Mary, the Messenger of Allah." But they killed him not, nor crucified him, but so it was made to appear to them, and those who differ therein are full of doubts, with no certain knowledge, but only conjecture to follow, for a surety they killed him not.

Islamic scholars understand the central importance of the crucifixion of Christ to orthodox Christianity. ʿAli notes in his commentary:

> Christian churches make it a cardinal point of their doctrine that his life was taken on the Cross, that he died and was buried, that on the third day he rose in a body with his wounds intact, and walked about and conversed, and ate with his disciples, and was afterwards taken up bodily to heaven. This is necessary for the theological doctrine of blood sacrifice and vicarious atonement for sins, which is rejected by Islam.[10]

If not Jesus, who was placed on the cross? Some Muslims believe Judas, who was guilty of the treasonous betrayal, actually was the one crucified. Others believe Simon of Cyrene, who carried Christ's cross briefly, took Jesus' place (Matthew 27:32). What then happened to Jesus, if He was not crucified as the Bible teaches? Most Muslims believe that Jesus somehow was assumed into Paradise by Allah, according to surah 4:158: "Nay, Allah raised him up unto Himself; and Allah is exalted in power." A minority of Muslims believe that Jesus did eventually die, but not at the time or in the manner claimed in the Bible. The cross is seen as a death of "disgrace,"[11] so it was unworthy of a prophet of Allah.

How can the death of one man cover the sins of the world?

Islam believes that each person must atone for his or her own sins by outweighing their evil with good deeds. Muslims are confounded by the notion that Christ can stand in for everybody else, with enough righteousness to outweigh all of their evil. Surely one man cannot do enough good works to outweigh all the individual offenses of billions of people. With this understanding of sin and forgiveness, no wonder the idea of the Cross of Christ seems ridiculous. Muslims are not the only ones to stumble here, partly because Christians communicated the reality of the gospel so poorly. Many Christians actually believe this false theology of works. How many medieval Crusaders killed Muslims for the very purpose of adding good works to the death of Christ to outweigh their sins? Miscommunication here only frustrates relations between Christians and Muslims.

To fully understand what the Bible calls Christ's "atonement," we must begin with the concept of radical human depravity. Islam rejects the concept that humanity stands in a state of sin and death in rebellion to the Creator. Individual sins only confirm this larger reality. Christ's death had to have infinite merit before it could confront the penalty for treason against God's infinite holiness. In that sense it would have been easier for Christ to measure out goodness pound for pound to outweigh evil. Medieval Islamic philosophy considered with the Christian Thomas Aquinas the idea that evil is a lack of something and does not have identity in itself. If so, then sins have no existence and so no "weight" in themselves anyway.

Islamic-Christian dialogue must come to grips with the biblical doctrine of *original sin*. Universal human experience would seem to be on the side of Christianity here, for there is palpably a war for supremacy between humanity and God. What is a sin if not an individual's act of defiance, a shot fired against God on the battlefield of a rebellion. Every offense against the Creator of the universe, however insignificant it may seem to us, is an act of treason. The person shakes a fist at the Divine and shouts, "You're not the boss of me!" Muslims bristle at the charge that they have a lower view of divine holiness than do Christians, but clearly Allah is not so picky about total holiness if he can simply measure evil against good on a celestial ledger. He dismisses sins as he wishes when it comes to opening the gates to Paradise. Heaven filled with fundamentally unchanged sinners sounds a lot like human society.

> Then those whose balance (of good deeds) is heavy, they will attain salvation: but those whose balance is light, will be those who have lost their souls, in Hell will they abide. (surah 23:101–2)

Muslims do believe that some sort of human fall took place in the Garden of Eden, but the Islamic doctrine of individual accountability demands that this wrongdoing affected Adam and Eve alone. Surah al-Baqarah (2:35–36) relates:

> We said: "O Adam! dwell thou and thy wife in the Garden and eat of the bountiful things therein as (where and when) ye will; but approach not this tree, or ye run into harm and transgression." Then did Satan make them slip from the (Garden) and get them out of the state (of felicity) in which they had been.

Compare this "semi-fall" with the pervasive effects described in the Bible in Romans 5:12–21:

Therefore, just as through one man sin entered the world, and death through sin, and this death spread to all men, because all sinned—

(For until the law sin was in the world, but sin is not imputed when there is no law. Nevertheless, death reigned from Adam to Moses, even over those who had not sinned according to the likeness of the transgression of Adam, who is a type of Him who was to come. But the free gift is not like the offense. For if by the one man's offense many died, much more the grace of God and the gift by the grace of the one Man, Jesus Christ, abounded to many. And the gift is not like that which came through the one who sinned. For the judgment which came from one offense resulted in condemnation, but the free gift which came from many offenses resulted in justification. For if by the one man's offense death reigned through that one, much more those who receive abundance of grace and of the gift of righteousness will reign in life through the One, Jesus Christ.)

Therefore, as through one man's offense judgment came to all men, resulting in condemnation, even so through one Man's righteous act the free gift came to all men, resulting in justification of life. For as by one man's disobedience many were made sinners, so also by one Man's obedience many will be made righteous.

Moreover the law entered that the offense might abound. But where sin abounded, grace abounded much more, so that as sin reigned in death, even so grace might reign through righteousness to eternal life through Jesus Christ our Lord.

Obviously people have never attained the right to return to the Garden, so can we not agree that to some degree the fall of Adam and Eve did affect all of us? If the Fall only affected Adam and Eve, any righteous person on Islam's "straight path" could regain entrance. No, the human experience is more in line with what the apostle Paul says in the book of Romans. The Bible says that the sin of Adam introduced a controlling principle of depravity into all thought and action (Romans 5:12). Paul speaks for reality when he shows that every corpuscle of every human who has ever been born by natural generation has been saturated with the death of this sin nature. No amount of good could ever weigh in the scales against this crime. This is the fatal flaw with any plan of salvation that depends upon outweighing evil with good. Even the smallest transgression is such an offence that God could not pass it by and remain a holy God. Thus, sin cannot simply be ignored; it must be eradicated.

Christ's work of atonement has a context if human nature is dead and no human being can approach God's perfection. Humans must be given a value and holy perfection that is alien to them. An offended God must be satisfied, and when He looks at the humans in His presence, He must be able to see appropriate moral perfection. Only a human being could answer those two challenges, but no human being could be perfectly holy and offer infinite value to satisfy the infinite penalty for treason against God. A very special intermediary was required.

The incarnation of One who was both God and human was the only way to counter the infinite debt with an infinite payment, the only answer to a state of endemic human depravity. Jesus, an unfallen man because of His unique being, entered a fallen world through the virgin birth. He was the first person since Adam who could freely choose total obedience and remain perfectly righteous. Adam had the capacity not to sin, but he chose to rebel. Christ had willingly emptied Himself of the prerogatives of deity as described in Philippians 2:5–11, so He could have chosen to sin, but He did not. Without sin, Christ, who was fully human and fully God, brought both infinite value and moral perfection to the divine courtroom (John 1:29). In the most stark of contrasts, Adam was born to live eternally in the Garden. Christ was born to die on a barren hill outside Jerusalem.

It may seem unfair that Adam was set apart as the moral representative for every other human being, so his fall infected us all. On the other hand, it seems equally unfair that another representative, a second Adam, could be chosen to pay the penalty for the sins of others. As sin entered by one, so God made a way for eternal life to be purchased by one. Christ on the cross took the place of the guilty. He did not just purchase our forgiveness. Forgiven men must still live with the memory of their evil deeds. The blood of Christ did not just enable God to pardon us. A pardoned man must live forever with the declared sentence of a conviction. The sacrifice of Jesus on Calvary did not just commute our sentence. A commuted sentence is a plea bargain that demands the admission of guilt that remains. The atoning sacrifice of Jesus Christ on the cross actually paid the full and complete debt of our sin. A complete payment is demanded by a righteous and holy God. On the cross, Jesus Christ bore the full and complete wrath of God the Father toward sin in His Being. Jesus Christ, crucified, buried, and resurrected, was and is the One—the Lamb of God:

> Moreover, brethren, I declare to you the gospel which I preached to you, which also you received and in which you stand, by which also you are saved, if you hold fast that word which I preached to you—unless you believed in vain. For I delivered to you first of all that which I also received: that Christ died for our sins according to the Scriptures, and that He was buried, and that He rose again the third day according to the Scriptures, and that He was seen by Cephas, then by the twelve. After that He was seen by over five hundred brethren at once, of whom the greater part remain to the present, but some have fallen asleep. After that He was seen by James, then by all the apostles. Then last of all He was seen by me also, as by one born out of due time. (1 Corinthians 15:1-8)

Notes

1. *Nostra Aetate,* Vatican II.
2. See Section 7, Questions Concerning Eschatology, for descriptions of the seven levels of hell.

3. Ian Richard Netton, *A Popular Dictionary of Islam* (Chicago: NTC, 1992), 124–25.

4. Abdullah Yusuf ʿAli, *The Meaning of the Holy Qurʾan* (Brentwood, Md.: Amana, 1992), n. 386.

5. Formatting has been done by the authors for clarity.

6. ʿAli, *The Meaning of the Holy Qurʾan*, n. 826.

7. Ibid., n. 5438.

8. Ahmed Zaki Yamani, in W. Montgomery Watt, *Islam and Christianity Today: A Contribution to Dialogue* (London: Routledge & Kegan Paul, 1983), ix-x, as cited in Norman Geisler and Abdul Saleeb, *Answering Islam* (Grand Rapids: Baker, 1993), 273.

9. ʿAli, *The Meaning of the Holy Qurʾan*, n. 395.

10. Ibid., n. 663.

11. Ibid., n. 664.

3

QUESTIONS CONCERNING THE NATURE OF THE QUR'AN AND THE BIBLE

CERTAINLY THE QUR'AN LOOKS LIKE a daunting religious document, often five inches thick. Even though the Qur'an contains only 114 chapters, the transliteration of the Arabic and the English makes the printed text quite imposing. Further, many Christians feel somewhat skittish about purchasing a copy. When we encourage Christians to purchase a Qur'an, some of them widen their eyes, as if we are suggesting that they commit an act of idolatry. We believe an intelligent and well read Christian must be exposed to this important work, especially if we are asking our Muslim friends to take the time to read the Bible. We have nothing to fear from other world religions; we must understand what they believe in their own words so that we can both respect them and anticipate their questions.

Is the Qur'an perfect and incorruptible?

The internal evidence of the Qur'an stipulates that it is incorruptible, perfect in every way. Surah 15:9 explains, "We have without doubt sent down the Message; and We will assuredly guard it (from corruption)." Indeed, Muslims believe that the Qur'an is the final and ultimate source of revelation, unlike the Bible, which they say has been corrupted by Jews and Christians. On the other hand, the Qurʾan does not contain miracles, but it is a miracle in itself. To the Muslim, it is the gift of God that has no error and no equal. Allah inspired it and will perfectly preserve it.

There are difficulties with this view, since both internal and external evidence shows inconsistencies and inaccuracies in the Qurʾan.

First, although Muslims claim that there has only been one version of the Qurʾan, facts do not support that assertion. Historically, the Qurʾan of today is a redacted work completed under the third Muslim Caliph, ʾUthman ibn Affan, who came to power in 644. Only after Muhammed's death was the Qurʾan compiled by order of his successor, Abu Bakr. Soon Medina, Mecca, Basra, Kufa, Damascus, and other population centers had developed their individual versions of the writings of Muhammed. These versions evidently varied dramatically. In his monumental work, *Materials for the History of the Text of the Qurʾan,* archaeologist Arthur Jeffery argues that Uthman canonized the Medinan Codex.[1] More important, he ordered that all copies of every other version should be destroyed. This is why only one version is extant.

Even the Qurʾan in Muhammed's day was not guarded from corruption, as shown in the long-standing controversy over the popular passage known as the "Satanic verses" (surah 53:21–23). In this text, Muhammed publicly pronounced that three idols (al-Hat, al-Uzza, and al-Manat) could intercede on behalf of Muslims. Quickly realizing the impropriety of such a view, Muhammed revised the section, canceling any intercession of idols. He explained his lapse by stating that Satan had interjected this text in the divine communication to accommodate surrounding paganism. Allah had prevailed and replaced the "Satanic Verses" with his own (surah 22:52–53).

Even if preservation of the Qurʾan is given all benefit of the doubt, this does not prove that the text is the directly communicated Word of God. It only shows that the words of Muhammed were revered and passed down with care to succeeding generations. Instead, prophecy is the strongest indicator as to whether the Qurʾan (or any other sacred text) is God's Word. Moses explained in

Deuteronomy 18:22, "If what a prophet proclaims in the name of the LORD does not take place or come true, that is a message the LORD has not spoken. The prophet has spoken presumptuously. Do not be afraid of him."

The only significant prophecy in the Qur'an predicted a Roman victory over the Persians (surah 30:2–4), which would take place "within a few years" after the Persians had initially captured Jerusalem (614 or 615). This was an expected and predicable event that would not have surprised anyone who was familiar with the flow of current events. The statement also was hedged by the ambiguous time frame "within a few years." Defeat of the Persians should have been fulfilled within nine years according to Muslim scholars, but it was not fully complete until over a decade after their initial victory (625). One must be charitable to conclude that this was a prophecy fulfilled.

Ultimately, most Muslims believe the Qur'an is guarded from corruption while the Torah, Psalms, and Gospels (Injil) are corrupt. This is inconsistent and dangerous to Islamic theology. For their scenario to be regarded as accurate, Muslims must claim that Allah inspired the Torah and Psalms, after which these documents were tainted by the Jews. Then, Allah inspired the gospel of Jesus Christ, but it was spoiled by Christians. At last Allah was able to write his word in the form of the Qur'an, which has been "guarded from corruption." This theology has two difficulties, beyond the fact that textual studies have found no corruption of biblical content. First, this theory assumes that God is unable to protect His message, so that creation is more powerful than the Creator. Second, it builds its case on the power of Allah to give final and dependable revelation, after Allah had failed at least twice previously. The Qur'anic view of God then has an inadequate foundation on which to build a doctrine of divine revelation.

What does the Qur'an say about the Bible?

Most Muslims assume that the Bible text has been corrupted and therefore is not worth owning or reading. Muhammed said quite the opposite. In surah 29:46, he confessed, "We believe in

the Revelation which has come down to us and in that which came
down to you. Our God and your God is One." He further maintains when speaking to Jews and Christians, "If you were in doubt
as to what We have revealed unto you, then ask those who have
been reading the Book from before you: the Truth has indeed
come to you from your Lord: so be in no wise of those who doubt"
(surah 10:94).

Therefore, Muhammed believed that the Qur'an is not a new
revelation but the final revelation that confirms the perfect will of
God. In fact, the Qur'an acts as a guardian to the previous Scriptures revealed to Moses and Jesus. Surah 5:48 asserts, "To you We
sent the Scripture in truth, confirming the scripture that came
before it, and guarding it in safety." Many Muslim scholars assume
this means that *within* the Qur'an is the preserved older revelation.
This is a misleading interpretation, since Muhammed called the
Torah and Gospels "truth" that cast away any doubt.

The Jewish and Christian Scriptures accepted by Muslims must
then be trustworthy and reliable, including what is written about
Jesus in the four Gospels. Muhammed instructs Christians and
Jews to ask "those who have been reading the Book from *before
you*," and then claims that the revelation is truth "from your Lord."
Within these two phrases lies a principle: The Bible of the seventh
century is considered trustworthy for study and verification of God's
message. Truth cannot be partial. It is either wholly true and from
God, or it is false and is the words of human beings. The Bible
accepted during Muhammed's life is the same as that used by Christians and Jews today.

Muslim scholars hold conflicting views of the Bible. Some say it
has been corrupted *(tahrif)*, while others maintain that it has simply been misinterpreted. The latter view must hold more weight
since Muhammed commanded Muslims to respect and revere the
Torah (Taurat), the Psalms of David (Zabur), and the Gospels
(Injil; surah 5:68-69).

The question remains, however, that if the Qur'an confirms the
Torah and Gospels, why are there discrepancies between the Qur'an
and those books?

Does the Qur'an rely upon other sources for its content?

Muhammed lived in the diverse religious scene of Arabia, where Christians, Jews, and pagans (polytheists) mingled. It is not surprising that Muhammed had some familiarity with the Old Testament and New Testament, the Jewish *Talmud,* and the pseudepigraphical writings by Gnostics and others loosely identified with Christianity. W. St. Clair-Tisdall, in the classic work *Sources of Islam,* identifies sources used by Muhammed in the compilation of stories. Tisdall points out that the Jews living on the Arabian Peninsula did not speak or read Hebrew, nor did they know their own Scriptures. The Jews mainly relied upon tales passed orally from generation to generation for what they knew of the *Talmud,* which they considered sacred and authoritative.

One of the most famous stories related by Muhammed in the Qur'an explains how King Solomon met with the Queen of Sheba (surah 27:22-44). The story from the Qur'an is based on the *Targum,* an Aramaic paraphrase of the Old Testament based on oral translations. In it, the queen tests Solomon until she is utterly impressed and showers him with gifts. Here are some striking similarities between the stories in the Qur'an and in a targum written nearly a thousand years earlier:

1. A bird speaks to Solomon, and the king understands the creature.
2. After extensive travel, the bird returns to tell Solomon of a woman who rules over a beautiful land.
3. The king sends a letter by the bird. The woman receives it and exclaims in surprise that she has received this letter from Solomon.
4. Sheba offers a prayer, which is modified in the Qur'an.
5. Solomon commands the queen's submission. He marshals a force made up of animals, birds, spirits, and demons.
6. After receiving advice she does not trust, Sheba sends an expensive gift to Solomon.
7. The queen goes to meet Solomon in a building she thinks contains water. She tucks up her clothes and so has the embarrassment of showing her legs.
8. After meeting with the king, she praises his God.[2]

Without question, Muhammed trusted the apocryphal gospel stories more than he did the authentic canonical New Testament. Muslim scholars still tend to look to these stories, which were never accepted by orthodox Christians, as they attempt to refute the truth of the real Gospels. The earliest of the false books came later than the lifetimes of the apostles. Most were written centuries later to promote some heretical theological viewpoint.

Another source for the visions also is a possibility that must be suggested because Muhammed did so himself. Muhammed himself expressed the fear that some of his visions were from a demon rather than Allah. When Muhammed first began receiving his visions, he admitted to his wife, Khadija, that he was not certain that they were from Allah and not an evil spirit or jinn. Respected Muslim biographer Muhammed Haykal in *The Life of Muhammad* affirmed that Muhammed needed the assurance of Khadija and her cousin Waraqah to overcome the fear that he was possessed by a demon.[3]

What is the nature of the Bible?

Islamic theology restricts inspiration to the biblical Torah (comprising Genesis, Exodus, Leviticus, Numbers, and Deuteronomy), Psalms of David, and the Gospels. This inspiration is further restricted to versions of these writings that God originally gave. Christians should be well aware, though, that internal evidence speaks for the *complete* Bible's *full* inspiration. Jesus affirmed that the Bible is authoritative, without error, and inspired in its totality by God. God revealed Himself sufficiently through the Bible.

For example, Jesus Christ affirmed the divine and final authority of Scripture and quoted continually from the Jewish Bible (Old Testament). Norman Geisler in *The Baker Encyclopedia of Christian Apologetics* notes that Jesus relied on Scripture to resist the three temptations of the Devil (Matthew 4:4–10). Geisler asserts that Jesus affirmed the Old Testament's . . .

1. divine authority (Matthew 4:4–10);
2. imperishable nature (Matthew 5:17–18);

3. inspiration (Matthew 22:43);
4. unbreakable truth (John 10:35);
5. source in God (Matthew 15:3, 6);
6. ultimate supremacy (Matthew 15:1-10);
7. inerrancy (Matthew 22:29; John 17:17);
8. historical reliability (for example, Matthew 24:37-39 affirms the Flood); and
9. scientific accuracy (for example, the creation of male and female referred to in Matthew 19:4-5).[4]

Jesus testified that the entire Old Testament is authoritative in His quotations from the Torah, the Prophets, and the Writings. His statement in John 14:26 can be taken as a promise that the New Testament would be inspired by the Holy Spirit, although these books were not yet written when He returned to heaven. Jesus said that the *Paraklete*, the Holy Spirit, would teach them "all things" and "bring to your remembrance all things that I said to you." Therefore, to deny the inspiration of the New Testament necessarily accompanies denying the power of the Holy Spirit (as Muslims do; see pp. 43-45) in leading the disciples into truth. Those disciples recognized this promise and claimed divinity for the Old Testament and their own writings that came to be included in the New Testament (2 Peter 1:19-21). Peter included Paul with the Old Testament writers as producing Scripture (3:15-16).

Consequently, the nature of the Bible is inseparably linked with the character of Christ. One who denies the authority of the Bible cannot avoid denying the authority of Christ as a prophet. If we know anything at all about the teachings of Christ as prophet, we know that He declared these things to be true.

Why are there so many versions of the Bible?

Many translations have been made of the Jewish/Christian Scriptures, a sure sign of corruption, according to some Islamic apologists. The Qur'an also has been translated into innumerable languages, but technically these are only interpretations of the real document. The true Qur'an exists only in the Arabic language in which Muhammed first recorded it.

Christians and Muslims historically have differed with one another over the nature of divine revelation. Can something be God's revealed words if it contains the same idea content but isn't expressed in the precise words in which it first appeared? Christians maintain that the concepts penned by the original authors, rather than the pen strokes, make them God's revelation. But certainly the central issue for all of us is whether we can know true, dependable, and authoritative revelations about God in the documents. One who looks closely at the Bible honestly and carefully will not be able to show corruption to its message.

Actually, the numerous English versions have come along only since 1881. In other languages relatively few translations have ever been prepared. It isn't that we have lost some older English or Latin Bible so that we cannot go back and compare.

The real question is how faithful these translations have remained to the thoughts as they were first put onto paper in what are called the "autographs." Theologically, those who argue against the veracity of the Bible because of multiple modern translations are attacking at the wrong spot. Christians readily assume that the work of modern translators is human and flawed, partly because it can be an immense challenge to accurately transfer an idea from 1400 B.C. Hebrew to contemporary German. The issue is whether Christians can know with assurance what went into the first manuscripts or autographs. Only the autographs are held to be directly inspired, without error, and fully authoritative.

Isn't this an easy out, though, since we do not have those original clay tablets, scrolls, and parchment sheets? We do not have those first pages, but we can track and analyze every variation in stroke among thousands of ancient manuscript texts—from the original languages to the very first translations. The earliest New Testament texts available are only a few decades removed from the originals. We can also compare how words were used in the texts with how they were used in contemporary secular documents. Especially since the scholarship of the twentieth century, we can have immense confidence that the words we are reading accurately reflect what Jesus said and Matthew or John recorded.

Historically, there are several reasons why numerous translations have been made over the past hundred years, especially in English:

1. In 1881, B. F. Westcott and F. J. A. Hort published a Greek New Testament text that combined the accumulated knowledge gained from comparing ancient texts. These men made choices among variant readings with which other scholars disagreed, and in spots their work changed the understanding of the standard text of the time, the King James Version. Westcott and Hort depended heavily upon two older manuscripts, which shortened a few passages in the Bible. For example, they chose to exclude a number of verses at the conclusion of the gospel of Mark, arguing that these verses seem to have appeared later. Their scholarship stimulated a lot of debate, which continues.

2. Significant archaeological discoveries have been made during the twentieth century. For example the Dead Sea Scrolls were written in the two centuries before Christ through the middle of the first century. Earlier Scripture texts and contemporary writings are available to compare. Archaeology also has examined the biblical world and its culture.

3. Language use changed dramatically during the social and technological upheavals of the nineteenth and twentieth centuries. Christian leaders called for new translations because they worried that people did not fully understand the Bible's meaning. Most recent English Bible translations have worked most diligently to transfer cultural meaning from the ancient to the modern context. Not all the new versions have equal merit. A problem among English-speaking Christians has been the need to evaluate all these versions and possible translator biases.

Whatever their native tongue, Christians must base their choice of a Bible version and their study of God's Word upon certain standards. First, a translation must be based on the original meaning and literal rendering of the words. Given that some word meanings have changed since Moses recorded the Torah, we must still work to understand those original words. Muslims try to better understand the Qur'an by learning Arabic and studying the text in the original language. Most Christians do not go to that length to learn Greek, Hebrew, and Aramaic, but we expect that anyone who preaches and teaches Scripture has at least a basic understanding of those languages.

Second, although a life of language study will help reveal shadings of meaning, today's Christian can be certain that a good translation can be trusted to be the very Word of God. Norman Geisler summarizes the reasons for our confidence in his work *When Skeptics Ask:*

1. Although there are ten thousand variants among the ancient New Testament manuscripts, most of these are spelling mistakes that have nothing to do with meaning.
2. Of the forty or so significant variant readings, not one of them has an impact on doctrinal beliefs. Geisler explains, "The problem is not that we don't know what the text is, but that we are not certain which text has the right reading. We have 100 percent of the New Testament and we are sure about 99.5 percent of it."
3. The Bible is so well preserved that, even if we did not have a single copy of the Scripture, we could reconstruct almost the entire New Testament from quotations by church fathers of the second and third centuries.[5]

The Bible has been preserved better than any other sacred text. Indeed, it is better preserved than even modern texts of any sort. This includes the Qur'an. Whereas whole versions of the Qur'an were destroyed by Uthman, eliminating what could have been a more authentic copy of Muhammed's words, the Bible has been meticulously copied by diligent scribes. Critics point out that there are no original manuscripts left, but we really do not need them. We unquestionably know, with only an occasional question about nuance and minor detail, what Moses, David, Luke, Paul, and the other writers related from the Holy Spirit.

Don't internal contradictions show that the Bible has been corrupted?

Jesus declared that Scripture has complete inspiration. He taught: "Until heaven and earth disappear, not the smallest letter *[yod]* not the least stroke of a pen, will by any means disappear from the Law until everything is accomplished" (Matthew 5:18 NIV). Jesus here specifically mentions the Torah or the first five books of the Bible, but verse 17 shows that He has in mind all the revelation of God's will in the Law and the Prophets (verse 17). This was a shorthand way of referring to all of Old Testament Scripture. So Jesus testified that everything in Scripture is given by God and will be preserved by God.

If a Christian is willing to say that there are internal errors in the Bible, he must also be willing to say that Jesus was at least misinformed. He wasn't even an accurate prophet, let alone the perfect Son of God. This is not acceptable even in Islamic theology. Muslims are called to accept the words of Jesus (surah 4:171; 5:78).

Yet, many Muslims attempt to point out internal inconsistencies within the Bible. Lengthy books have been written to discuss the various charges of scriptural error and inconsistency, and a full discussion of those charges is beyond the scope of this work. Most of the alleged inconsistencies are just silly or are a matter of misunderstanding what the text says. These can be answered without much effort.

A good example of the kind of problem that is supposed to unnerve Christians was raised in a debate in Birmingham, England, by well-known Muslim apologist Ahmed Deedat. Deedat asserted that two very different genealogies of Jesus are found in Matthew 1 and Luke 3. Obviously both cannot be true, can they?

Actually, both can be true, because they are written to two different cultures, Matthew to Jews and Luke to Gentiles. These groups approached genealogies differently. Jewish culture established birthright through an elaborate structure of tribes, clans, and families. The father of record established kinship. Biology was not a primary concern in the father-child relationship. Through Joseph, Matthew carefully establishes clan ties back to the exile (where Jewish family records tended to get muddy) and then to the monarchy and finally to Abraham. In good Jewish style, Matthew includes the ancestors with whom his readers would be most familiar, including some heroines of the faith. He carefully balances the number of generations in each part of his list. Key persons were noted, not every parent along the way.

More like modern Westerners, Gentiles were less formal in their family trees and more interested in technical bloodlines. Luke argues that Jesus was *supposed* under the natural rules of things to be Joseph's son (Luke 4:23). Because of the unique situation Luke has already laid out, Jesus was biologically of the mother's bloodline alone—and that line also led back to the Davidic monarchy. Greek genealogy excludes women, so Luke does not mention Mary by name. Beyond the David kingship, Luke wants to show the solidarity of Jesus to the entire human race. He is not so concerned with kinship to Abraham as the ultimate ties to Adam and God. He roughly sketches that big picture.

Deedat failed to realize or to accept that Matthew's genealogy was necessary to establish messianic legitimacy, while Luke had to do the same thing through Mary's lineage to show Jesus' legitimacy to Gentiles. Together they show the only way in which Jesus can fully satisfy all of the prophetic expectations. The genealogies prove Scripture's consistency, not a contradiction.

Other reports of inconsistency need deeper investigation. Muslims believe they have found a thematic contradiction when they compare the epistle of Romans to the epistle of James. Paul argues in Romans for salvation through faith alone (Romans 4:1–12), while James stresses the place of works (James 2:14).

This apparent discrepancy has perplexed some Christians over the centuries as well, because they were not carefully thinking through what the two books are teaching. The tension is resolved as we see that Paul and James are speaking about two different aspects of Christian faith and life, and both assume the truth asserted by the other. James is writing to remind his readers that their faith must be practical and living if their testimony is to be regarded as credible and valid. New creations behave in new ways and have actions that reflect the fruits of the Spirit described by Paul in Galatians 5.

Paul has lots to say about living as befits a child of God, but in Romans he particularly lays a foundational understanding about what salvation really is. The recipients of this letter are frequently hearing from legalists who make salvation contingent on rituals and other acts of personal piety. Paul is explaining the theological and eternal reality of salvation, James the temporal *evidence* that salvation is genuine. James wants to make sure that his readers avoid hypocrisy, a false appearance of spirituality that just doesn't ring true in practical living.

Further, Paul describes a believer's positional stance in Christ based on the finished work of the Cross (justification), while James illustrates the Christian's everyday walk (sanctification). Consequently, we are not saved *by* good works but *for* good works (Ephesians 2:8).

Christians must answer any criticism of the consistencies in the Scripture with an attitude of trust and humility. God is our Father and we are His children. No Christian has all the answers, and any of us can be thrown because we don't know some needed piece of information. Nor should we feel superior if the answer to a question asked by another seems obvious. What we know as a Christian depends on a work of God, who has revealed Himself in the Word and His Spirit, so that we will glorify Him, rest in Him, trust His providence, and desire to know more through diligent study. Questions ultimately help us remain dependent on God as we walk by faith.

Don't external inaccuracies prove that the Bible has been corrupted?

The internal consistency and evidence of inspiration is abundant, so that the Christian can trust that the Bible is God's Word. However, many critics look for external fallacies that negate the authority of the Bible. Their charges allow seekers opportunity to look personally at the external evidence and inspect reasonable claims.

Three areas of argument question the truth claims of the Bible: (1) historicity of the text; (2) fulfillment of prophecy; and (3) indestructibility of Scripture as a whole.[6]

First, historicity is investigated as we compare what Scripture alleges with independent confirmation from artifacts and secular documents. Just a century ago, skeptical archaeologists made outlandish claims that they had, or soon would, show the historical misinformation of the Bible. Biblical stories obviously referred to mythical places and events. Even unbelieving archaeologists today have more humility, for this field has become the foremost independent confirmation of Scripture. Of more than twenty-five thousand sites uncovered, not one discovery has ever proven to contradict anything in the Bible. Some sites have purported to, but later work has always shown that it was the researcher, not the text, that had erred.

As we have noted (pp. 76-77), the Bible is the most widely copied and preserved ancient document, yet no scholar has found a single doctrine that could be invalidated or reframed because of copying error or variant textual reading.

Second, prophetic fulfillment is vastly important evidence for judging the validity of any sacred text. The biblical standard is rather strict—100 percent accuracy (Deuteronomy 18:22). Anything less than total accuracy could lead to the execution of the prophet. Yet, hundreds of foretelling prophecies are represented as coming from God. Some of them are quite detailed, and many dealt with precise circumstances that would occur centuries later. Their accuracy is so high that skeptics have tried to redate writings to claim that the predictions were written after the events they predicted had occurred.

Dozens of these prophecies, concerning the incarnation of the coming divine Messiah, were wholly fulfilled in Jesus. These prophecies all were written long before fulfillment, for example:

1. Virgin birth, Isaiah 7:14, written in the second half of the eighth century B.C. See Matthew 1:23.
2. Flight to Egypt, Hosea 11:1, written ca. 755 B.C. See Matthew 2:14-15.
3. Declared to be God's Son, Psalm 2:7, written at latest in 450 B.C. See Matthew 3:17.
4. Sacrificed for the people, Isaiah 53:12, written ca. 700 B.C. See Mark 15:27-28.
5. Pierced hands and feet during crucifixion, Zechariah 12:10, written during Babylonian captivity, ca. 520 B.C. See John 19:37 (see also the prophecy in Isaiah 53:5).

For one of these prophecies to have come true coincidentally in Jesus would be amazing. The odds that dozens of messianic prophecies could have found precise fulfillment in Jesus is mathematically mind-boggling.

Third, the Bible has stood the test of time. As Geisler and William Nix noted in a joint study, "Biblical critics once regarded much of it as mythological, but archaeology has established it as historical. Antagonists have attacked its teaching as primitive, but moralists urge that its teaching on love be applied to modern society. Skeptics have cast doubt on its authenticity, and yet more men are convinced of its truth today than ever."[7]

Indeed, the Bible has been shaken, stirred, and scrambled, yet every time it comes out pure and precise, true to its nature, and trustworthy in its content.

Isn't the Bible corrupt since the men who wrote it were corrupt?

In the Islamic doctrine of revelation, it is forbidden for any prophet to have sin enter his life. He must be the perfect example of honesty and intelligence, before his message can be considered indisputable. This doctrine is foreign to the Christian view for several reasons, foremost of which is that all human beings, including God's ordained prophets, are born sinners. The Christian view is that the sanctity of the writing depends not on the human vessel but upon the Source—God. An omnipotent God can guide the weakest vessels. Further, the fact that we are sinful requires that a perfect Word must be given as the measuring rod.

An important principle must be understood before Christianity as a whole can be grasped: The written Word of God is acceptable for the same reason Christ is the acceptable living Word of God. The Bible is no more corrupt because God guided human authors to write it than Jesus is corrupt because He was placed in human flesh.

Twentieth-century Christian apologist-philosopher C. S. Lewis explained, "The same divine humility which decreed that God should become a baby at a peasant-woman's breast, and later an arrested field-preacher in the hands of the Roman police, decreed also that he should be preached in a vulgar, prosaic, an unliterary language. If you can stomach the one, you can stomach the other."[8] Ultimately, the premise that human frailty or even a sinful past negates God's ability to use a person should be utterly rejected. Prophets were mere men who were open, honest, and repentant. They did not look to themselves for virtue but to God. Indeed, if God were looking for sinlessness in order to use someone, He would be forced to work alone.

Doesn't the Bible have irrational stories that cannot be true?

Someone reading the Bible for the first time may be taken aback by a few stories that seem absurd. In the Old Testament, a donkey speaks (Numbers 22:28–30), and God intervenes in natural processes to lengthen daylight (Joshua 10:12–15). Samson is said to have killed one thousand men with only the jawbone of a donkey (Judges 15:15). In the New Testament, some Muslims find it hard to accept that graves were opened on the day of Christ's death, and some Old Testament believers left their tombs and walked into Jerusalem, presumably in their glorified heavenly bodies (Matthew 27:52–53).

For Muslims, the most difficult story to swallow is Jesus' crucifixion and resurrection. Christians regard the death and bodily resurrection of the Son of God to be the greatest supernatural intervention of God in all human history. After all, if God can raise His Son from the dead, it is certainly plausible that He testified to His great act by opening the graves of other dead saints as heralds of the soon-coming event.

Muslims find such things difficult to believe because they cannot imagine a God who is so interested and involved in human life as to work miracles in our midst. Muhammed did not perform miracles, nor have Muslims seen miracles in their own experience. Islamic theology greatly emphasizes the transcendence and negates the immanence of Allah. He is wholly "other," separate from creation and uninterested in humanity. Christians are accustomed to assuming that God works in ways that are extraordinary and personal. The Incarnation is the ultimate example of His intimacy.

To argue that the earth could not stop rotating for nearly twenty-four hours is to demand that God does not have control and sovereignty over His own creation. Critics claim that halting the rotation of earth would have caused catastrophic consequences. The biblical account does not go into scientific details; we are only told that the daylight hours were lengthened. That might not mean that the earth's rotation actually halted. Perhaps there was a slight dip of the pole or some phenomenon of refraction of the rays of light. W. A. Criswell, in his work *Why I Preach That the Bible Is Literally True*, defends the narrative historically: "It is a remarkable fact that we have a suggestion of this same thing in history outside the Bible. Herodotus, the great Greek historian, tells us that the priests of Egypt showed him a record of a long day. Chinese writings state that there was such a day in the reign of a long-ago emperor. . . . There is nothing of real weight to prove that there was no such event in the history of the world."[9]

Certainly the story is remarkable, but it is also possible given an omnipotent Creator.

Is revelation (*rasul/wahy*) the same as dictation?

Islamic theology believes that Allah alone is responsible directly for the revelation of the Qur'an. Surah 10:37 explains, "This Qur'an is not such as can be produced by other than Allah."

Allah, thereby, dictated his message through the angel of revelation, Gabriel, to Muhammed. To the Muslim, there is no human part in the equation of revelation except the ability to record dictation (surah 39:1-2). This explains why much of the Qur'an is written in the first person voice of Allah. According to Muslim scholars, dictation from Allah grants final confirmation and assurance to the Qur'an.

This theory of revelation and inspiration differs significantly from that accepted by Christian theology for the Bible. Christians believe that the revelation of God came *through* humans who wrote as they were "moved by the Holy Spirit" (2 Peter 1:21). Moreover, what they wrote contained their own personalities while not containing any "private interpretation." Poets wrote poetry, historians recorded history, and sometimes a prophet recorded precise details of a visionary encounter. The Bible is not error free because it was dictated but because the writers were guided by the Holy Spirit as they used their backgrounds, interests, and writing styles.

Prophetic writers occasionally do take down a word-for-word transcription of the words of God. Moses' record of the Ten Commandments is a classic example. Sometimes Jehovah speaks in the first person through the prophetic writings or in visions that have been directly recorded. God's direct address is sometimes signified when a prophet proclaims "This is what the Lord God says. . . ." Most of Scripture, however, has been sifted through human personhood and experience.

Does Islam then propose a stronger view of inspiration than Christianity? It is not stronger, but it is also not the same. To avoid confusion, Muslims and Christians must be very aware that they use similar theological words with different meaning.

The Islamic theory of dictation poses problems. Elsewhere we note questionable ways in which Muhammed seemed actually to rewrite the content of revelation (p. 70). Further, the Qur'an stipulates that it is the *unmediated* words of Allah, but these words were manifested through the vehicle of Muhammed as human scribe. Islamic theology recognizes this difficulty, which is why there is such insistence that Muhammed remained untainted by sin (see p. 95).

Even given a condition of full righteousness, the human element of a copyist means that error is as likely to come about in transcription as through flawed character. The transcendence of Allah actually brings in a second layer of transmission. The angel Gabriel depended upon Muhammed, and Allah depended on the faithfulness of Gabriel to complete his task. No one suggests that angels are without error, since they are not divine. In the end, the question of truthfulness and trustworthiness is not based on any human element but on the sovereignty of God to fulfill His mission of guiding men into truth through His revealed Word. Complete transcendence makes this detailed sovereignty over transmission difficult.

In the final analysis, if the Qur'an is without error, it is because Allah used his power to make sure it stayed that way. Precisely the same can be said of God's preservation of truth in the Bible. The question is not one of full dictation but of discernment (1 John 3:24–4:6).[10]

Notes

1. See Arthur Jeffery, ed., *Materials for the History of the Text of the Qur'an: The Old Codices* (Leiden: E. J. Brill, 1937). The full text of this work is available at http://www.bible.ca/islam/library/Jeffery/ Materials. Islamic response. A brief Islamic response to Jeffery's work by Abu Ammaar Yasir Qadhi can be found at http:// bismikaallahuma.org/Quran/Q_Studies/jeffery.htm.

2. Jameel, "King Solomon and the Queen of Sheba: A comparison Between Targum and Qur'an," http://answering-islam.org/Quran/ Sources/sheba.htm (20 December 2002).

3. M. H. Haykal, *Life of Muhammad* (Plainfield, Ind.: American Trust Publications, 1976), 80.

4. Norman L. Geisler, *Baker Encyclopedia of Christian Apologetics* (Grand Rapids: Baker, 1999), s.v. "Bible, Jesus' View of."

5. Norman L. Geisler and Ronald M. Brooks, *When Skeptics Ask* (Wheaton: Victor, 1990), 160.

6. Norman L. Geisler and William E. Nix, *From God to Us: How We Got Our Bible* (Chicago: Moody, 1974), 57–61.

7. Ibid., 60.

8. Quoted in Clark Pinnock, *Biblical Revelation* (Chicago: Moody, 1970), 175–76.

9. W. A. Criswell, *Why I Preach That the Bible Is Literally True* (Nashville: Broadman & Holman, 1995), 79.

10. It must be noted that there are two primary occasions within the Bible in which God dictated His words to believers: Exodus 20 (Ten Commandments) and Jeremiah 36.

4

QUESTIONS CONCERNING THE
OLD TESTAMENT

EVEN A CURSORY READING OF THE Qur'an will show many similarities to the Old Testament. True, the Qur'an substantially and funda-mentally changes the stories, such as the question of whether Abraham's sacrifice was Ishmael or Isaac in Genesis 22. It is clear that the Old Testament history plays a large role in the formation of the Qur'an. While the Muslim quickly adds that the two docu-ments differ because the Old Testament was changed by the Jews, this is a crossroads where we can meet for discussion.

Does Islam have a creation account?

The Qur'an does not have a lengthy account of Creation such as can be seen in the Old Testament (Genesis 1-2). Instead, passages in the Qur'an speak intermittently about the wisdom and work of Allah on his creatures. However, the Bible and the Qur'an seem to have some similarities when it comes to the origins of the universe. For example, the Qur'an explains that the heavens and earth were created in six days (surah 7:54; 50:38). It is God who both creates and sustains the universe (surah 59:24). Man is given a special place in the order of creation, superior to all other living creatures (surah 95:4). When Adam and Eve sin against God in the Garden, they recognize their nakedness (surah 7:27).

On further review, the Qurʾan has crucial disagreements with the Bible. First, since the Qurʾan does not go into the meticulous detail on the six days of Creation, many Muslims find a theistic form of Darwinian evolution to be compatible with their faith. They note that the Qurʾan does not argue for six literal days since "a day in the sight of thy Lord is like a thousand years" (surah 22:47). Whereas the Bible's detail of Creation (i.e., earth before sun) excludes the theory of evolution, the vagueness of the Qurʾan allows more leeway to accept modern scientific theory without critical analysis.

Second, since Muslims deny the deity of Christ, they also deny His participation in the Creation (John 1:3; Hebrews 1:2). The Qurʾan states, "The similitude of Jesus before Allah is as that of Adam; He created him from dust, then said to him: 'Be'; and he was" (surah 3:59). For that reason, Jesus is equivalent with Adam, who is also considered a prophet in Islam.

The consequences of Adam's sin against God are much different between the two versions of the story. The Qurʾan explains that Adam was removed from Paradise and placed on earth due to his sin (surah 7:24). Whereas the Bible alerts Adam of his future toil due to sin, the Qurʾan affirms that toil and sweat were an intrinsic part of Creation (surah 90:4). Ultimately, Christian theology brought sin and spiritual death upon all humanity. Physical death itself is the result of sin. In Islamic theology, death is natural and intentional in the will of Allah (surah 32:7–11).[1]

Does Islam include the Fall and total depravity?

Similar to the Bible, the Qurʾan declares that Adam was the first person created. He is therefore the father to all human beings (surah 7:27, "O ye Children of Adam"). Ironically, Eve is never mentioned by name in the Qurʾan. In Genesis 2:18–25, God speaks not only of her creation but also of her purpose as the perfect companion to Adam. Also missing from the Qurʾan is the belief that man is created in the image of God (Genesis 1:26). This principle is blasphemous to the Muslim, who repudiates any partnership, even by way of visual representation, to Allah. Islamic theology emphasizes the transcendence of Allah, not his immanence. In Islam, Allah is removed from his creation. In the Bible, God shows Himself to be near to creation.

The key text of Adam's fall in the Qurʾan is surah 2:35-39, which states in part, "And We said: 'O Adam! Dwell you and thy wife in the Garden; and eat of the bountiful things therein as (where and when) ye will; but approach not this tree or you run into harm and transgression.' Then did Satan make them slip from the (Garden) and get them out of the state (of felicity) in which they had been." Though the Qurʾan mentions the Garden, Satan, the tree, the Fall, and their nakedness, there are essential differences from the biblical narrative.

Satan, the agent of deceit, is portrayed without the imagery of a snake. Many Muslims cannot accept the fact that God would create something capable of such evil. Christians can appreciate this aim, though it is unnecessary to protect God from a charge that He created evil in the serpent. Christians readily agree with Muslims that evil is entirely separate from the good creation. For whatever reason, Satan chose the serpent form to delude the humans, and God chose to curse that form in Genesis 3:14 as a reminder to humanity of the evil of sin. The serpent was not evil. What Satan did with the form of the serpent was evil. God did create everything good and is not responsible for causing evil. If Muslims assume He would be responsible for sin with the snake, then He would also be responsible for sin by creating Adam or Satan Himself, who was created to be a holy angel yet instigated rebellion.

Another significant difference comes in the response of Adam and Eve to their sin. In the biblical account, Adam blames Eve (Genesis 3:12) while Eve accuses Satan (Genesis 3:13) for the sin they themselves committed. In the Qurʾan, there is no excusing of sin, only repentance. Adam pleads, "Our Lord We have wronged our own souls" (surah 7:23). Though Muslims claim this to be a purer story, since Adam and Eve unite instead of placing blame on one another, that is not how sin affects a person or a relationship. The Bible presents a realistic story. This is the case throughout the Bible. Biblical critics point out character flaws in the people whose stories are told in Scripture. In this, God is not honoring their sin but allowing the entire truth to be told.

The core difference between the two accounts regards the outcome. In the biblical account, there are awful consequences for all involved. The serpent is relegated to crawling on the ground, not out of punishment to the animal but as an ongoing object lesson, an analogy about the real Serpent. Satan himself is promised ultimate destruction under the heel of a Savior Child who will be a descendant of the woman. Eve and her daughters will be reminded of their loss in the pain of childbirth, and Adam's sons will survive only through hard toil. Because they have become corrupt rebels against God themselves, guilty of infinite treason, they are immediately cut off from God. This is spiritual death, and physical corruption and death will follow for them and for future generations. No such repercussions are in the Qur²an. Allah does not curse the couple in the same way, apparently because they repent. Indeed, it is assumed that death is natural *before* the Fall. Humanity did not fall, only Adam and Eve. The future generations thereby are created with the choice to do good or evil.

Is each human being born sinful?

The Christian understanding of salvation is meaningless unless each person is born with Adam's corrupt and spiritually dead nature, a state of radical depravity. The Bible clearly teaches that when Adam fell, all of humanity was affected by the consequences. The apostle Paul wrote, "Therefore, just as through one man sin entered the world, and death through sin, and thus death spread to all men, because all sinned" (Romans 5:12). Man is tainted with wickedness (Jeremiah 17:9) and is not and cannot be good enough to obtain heaven (Romans 3:10; 3:23; 6:23). Hence, Jesus' death on the Cross was necessary to pay the price that man himself could not pay. Indeed, man is "dead in trespasses and sins" (Ephesians 2:1). Christians have a saying that "Jesus did not die to make bad men good; Jesus died to make dead men alive." Jesus is the second Adam, erasing all of the ramifications imposed by the first Adam.

On the other hand, Muslims believe that all humans are born in a pure, natural state. As they grow in intelligence, each person makes personal choices that set the path of eternal destiny (surah 53:39). According to the Qur'an, Allah will judge each person according to whether the "scales" balance out more good or evil. Salvation is not based solely on faith but on a combination of faith and works. The nature of every human being is such that they can obtain heaven via the mercy of Allah, yet through their own efforts. Sin, therefore, is not intrinsically passed down from Adam to his children but voluntary, for which each person is responsible.

To the Muslim, original sin causes Allah to sin through creation. Muslims believe that Allah not only created but continues to create. Surah 10:4 maintains, "It is He who begins the process of creation, and repeats it, that He may reward with justice those who believe and work righteousness." It is apparent through this verse that the doctrine of salvation is interwoven with the doctrine of the natural state of humanity. If Allah continues to create, he cannot create anything that is sinful, or his image would be marred.

Muslims believe sin is not imputed because both Creation and salvation are a process. In the Christian faith, Creation and salvation are complete, if one will only recognize Jesus Christ, the One who is the Author and Finisher of salvation and true faith.

Does the Old Testament mandate the killing of infidels?

Some Bible critics have tried to equate Islamic *jihad* (holy war) with wars ordered by God in the days of Joshua and the judges of Israel. In the case of the taking of Canaan by Joshua, God does command that entire people groups are to be destroyed (Joshua 6:15-21; 1 Samuel 15:2-3). Consequently, the Christian who says that a God of love would never put anyone to death is biblically illiterate and ignorant of the character of God. Such a romantic sentiment presupposes that the Amalekites (1 Samuel 15), for example, did not deserve such harsh judgment. Yet, these people were so depraved that the Bible states that "the land vomits out its inhabitants" (Leviticus 18:25). God has the right to judge His creation. God is the author of life and thereby has the right to take it as He wills (Job 1:21). It is no more immoral for God to demand the destruction of a people than it is for Him to take away a life naturally. Ultimately, it is a matter of authority, of which God has no equal.

The first difference between this and jihad is that the Old Testament *describes* the slaughter of past peoples as a judgment ordered individually by God in an unusual situation. The Bible does not *prescribe* slaughter. The Qur'an indicates that holy war is not merely historical fact but a present reality (surah 4:101). Second, the Old Testament enemies treated without mercy were evil because of their actions, not because of their religion. The Qur'an defines implacable enmity in religious terms (surah 5:51; 9:29). Third, through the new covenant in Jesus Christ, Christians are commanded to defend the religious liberty of others (Matthew 13:24–30). The only one who has the right to judge someone spiritually is God Himself. This is wholly different from the Qur'an and Hadith, both of which call upon the judgment of unbelievers (kafir). The Hadith reiterates, "If a Muslim changes his Islamic religion, kill him" (9.57).

Sadly, many people quickly point out the Crusades as evidence that medieval Christians were still in the business of slaughter a thousand years after the life of Christ. This is true, not because their killing was supported by the Bible but because they adopted Islamic theology as their own. For example, as early as 833, popes began promising Christian warriors that they would obtain heaven if they died in battle. Such a promise has no support in the Scripture, but it does have backing in the Qur'an and Hadith (1.35). The confusion was natural. The lines of separation were lost between the government, which has the right to wield the sword in civil affairs (Romans 13:1–4), and the Christian, who only has the sword of the Scripture for spiritual affairs (Ephesians 6). To the Muslim, there is no distinction between these two swords.

Weren't Adam, Noah, Abraham, and Moses prophets of Islam?

Islam believes that Allah has sent down a prophet for every people in order to warn them of judgment and guide them to Allah. It is not surprising therefore that Muslims number their prophets in the tens of thousands. Of these, only twenty-five are mentioned by name in the Qur'an. Still, there are a few prophets that Islam honors with high acclaim: Adam (the chosen of God), Noah (the preacher of God), Abraham (the friend of God), Moses (the speaker with God), Jesus (the word of God), and Muhammed (the apostle of God). Adam, created from clay directly by the hand of Allah, is the world's first prophet that is so highly regarded that Allah commands the angels to "bow down to Adam" (surah 2:34).

The character of these prophets is said to be of the highest caliber. They are trustworthy, honorable, and brave. Once the prophet has come with his message, the people are completely responsible for their behavior and must answer to Allah. Though the names correspond with biblical names, many of the stories have changed. For example, whereas the Bible maintains that Noah's wife was safe on the ark, the Qur'an claims that Noah's wife betrayed her husband and went to hell (surah 66:10). Many prophets have unique experiences not allowed outside their dispensation. It is said that Moses spoke directly to God, which contradicts the Qur'an directly (surah 42:51). Muhammed was not ever privy to such conversation.

These prophets differ substantially from the prophets of the Bible. First, the Bible does not gloss over the sins of the prophets. Within Islam, the prophets are required to be sinless, while the Bible portrays the prophets as the mouthpiece of God, yet still fallible, fallen human beings. In fact, Abraham admits his sin in the Qur'an (surah 26:82) while the Hadith narrates three specific lies told by Abraham (Sahih al-Bukhari Hadith 4.578). According to Islamic theology, Abraham could not then be a prophet of Islam. Second, Muslims believe that a prophet will never be forsaken by Allah. This is another reason why Muslims reject the crucifixion of Jesus, as He cried out, "My God, My God, why have You forsaken Me?" (Matthew 27:46b).

Ironically, although Islam claims to revere these men as prophets, Islamic theology declares that their prophetic mantle was distorted by the very men in which the prophets were sent to be messengers. According to Islamic theology, though they wrote voluminously, most of their message is now lost except for that which Muhammed supposedly preserved. Conversely, the Christian continues to revere the words of Moses and the prophets of the Bible, believing that they were given by God and still profitable for instruction and guidance.

Wasn't Ishmael a prophet of Islam?

Since Abraham is considered the father of the Islamic faith (surah 2:130), the question of his sons and their inheritance holds special importance. But before considering the lineage of Ishmael, the student must examine the character of Ishmael and God's promises to him. The Qur'an asserts that Ishmael "was true to what he promised, and he was a messenger and a prophet" (surah 19:54). The Bible too holds Ishmael in high esteem, affirming, "Behold, I have blessed him, and will make him fruitful, and will multiply him exceedingly" (Genesis 17:20b). However, these blessings on Ishmael are not promised without reservation. The Bible acknowledges that Ishmael will be "a wild man; His hand shall be against every man, and every man's hand against him" (Genesis 16:12a). If this is true, he cannot then be a prophet of Islam.

Moreover, the Qur'an greatly diverges from the biblical stories on the relevance of Ishmael. Islam holds that it was Ishmael, not Isaac, who was to be sacrificed by Abraham (surah 37:103). Furthermore, the sacrifice is not a typology of the sacrificial atonement of Christ on the Cross but merely a symbolic gesture in which two men are willing to give their whole lives to Allah. Finally, this act allegedly took place on Mount Mina near Mecca, and not Mount Moriah at what was to become Jerusalem.

Therefore, according to Islam, Ishmael is the perfect son and a noble prophet. Also, Muslims attempt to point out that the Bible, though corrupt, admits that Ishmael was the intended sacrifice when it says, "Take now your son, your only son Isaac" (Genesis 22:2). What Muslims fail to consider is the context of the passage. First, the term "only" may be in reference to your "beloved" son (John 1:18; 3:16). Second, the verse is an affirmation of the inheritance intended for Isaac, the legitimate heir of Abraham, and not

Ishmael, born from a concubine who thereby had no right to the promises of God. It is clear that Isaac is the one God desired to bless (Genesis 21:12).

In regards to the question of equating *beloved* with *only,* Norman Geisler writes, "In addition, the phrase 'only son' may be equivalent to 'beloved son' (cf. John 1:18; 3:16), that is, a special son. God said clearly to Abraham, 'in Isaac your seed shall be called' (Gen. 21:12)."[2]

Aren't Muslims the children of Ishmael?

Muslims center their ancestry upon the lineage of Ishmael, which is essential to Islamic theology and politics. According to the Qur'an, Ishmael is the oldest son by fourteen years and therefore deserving of the land inheritance of Abraham, including that of the Holy Land. The Jews, the descendants of Isaac, would only be blessed if they followed the will of Allah (surah 37:113). However, Muslims believe that Jews have no unconditional covenant with God apart from Ishmael, who is the rightful heir to the promises of God.

Although it is true that Ishmael's descendents settled in the Middle East and Arabia, it is incorrect to say that he is the primogenitor of Islam in Arabia. There is no evidence that Ishmael ever settled near Mecca as Muslim tradition stipulates. Instead, the Bible confirms that Ishmael married an Egyptian woman and settled in the Wilderness of Paran (Genesis 21:21). Second, Ishmael's descendents are not the exclusive ancestors of Arabs. The Bible delineates the ancestral lines of the Arabs back to Joktan (Genesis 10:25–30). The names found in this genealogy have contemporary counterparts in Arabia today. The Arabs are therefore older than Ishmael and not exclusively from the lineage of Ishmael. Anis Shorrosh explains that one strain can be established from Abraham's nephew Lot, whose two daughters gave birth to the Moabites and Ammonites (see Genesis 24). Jacob's twin brother, Esau, was another father, according to Genesis 36. Keturah, Abraham's third wife, gave birth to six sons, who became Arab tribal forefathers.[3]

Finally, one cannot assume that to be Arab is to be Muslim. More than 5 percent of the Arab world claims Christianity as its religion. The great leap of Islamic theology is to assume that Ishmael was a Muslim, so Muslims have the right to the Holy Land via their spiritual father. Yet, the Bible promises that Isaac is the promised son who is given right of land through an unconditional covenant with Jehovah (Genesis 17:18-19).

Didn't the firstborn son deserve the land inheritance?

Muslims are quick to point out that the Bible defends the right of inheritance to the firstborn son (Genesis 38:27-28; Deuteronomy 21:17). The simple conclusion then must be that Ishmael, born fourteen years before Isaac, has first right to the promises and inheritance of Abraham. Spiritually, Muhammed becomes the promised prophet who will succeed Moses (Deuteronomy 18:15-20). Furthermore, he will be the blessing to the nations through Abraham (Genesis 12). Physically, Muslims have rights over the land of Abraham, which they popularly designate as Palestine. Israel's right is subordinate to that of the Muslim, as Isaac's rights were subordinate to Ishmael's inheritance.

Yet, there are several difficulties with the simple conclusions made by Muslims. First, they assume that Isaac is a prophet of Islam and not Judaism (surah 6:84). Second, the Qurʾan places Isaac among the other children of Abraham, and not as the son of promise as the Bible confirms (surah 21:72). In fact, the Qurʾan situates Ishmael, due to his obedience to Allah, in a separate line apart from the other sons of Abraham (surah 21:85). Third, Muslims see the blessings of the Abrahamic covenant as conditional, based on obedience, and not as unconditional, based on God's promises. As Yusuf ʿAli explains in his commentary of the Qurʾan, Ishmael's "steady constancy and submission to the will of Allah were specially shown when he *earned* the title of 'Sacrifice of Allah.'"[4]

However, an examination of biblical passages demonstrates the theological misgivings of Muhammed. First, the firstborn does not have unequivocal rights to the inheritance. This is seen as Isaac blesses Jacob over Esau (Genesis 27:28). Second, Isaac is legitimately the firstborn in the family since Hagar is merely Abraham's maidservant (21:10). Indeed, Isaac is the son of promise, a promise God guaranteed to him without reservation (verse 12). Third, Ishmael received his covenant from God, which was different from the one promised to Isaac. Jehovah, honoring Abraham's compassion for his son Ishmael, granted that "a great nation" would come through Ishmael (verse 18). Finally, this covenant with Isaac is unconditional and eternal (chapter 17). Jehovah has never stopped loving the Jews and still has a plan for them. The book of Revelation promises that they will one day see Christ for who He truly is (Revelation 7). In the end, this covenant finds its fulfillment in Jesus Christ, the Son of God and Savior of the world (Galatians 3:15–18).

Why was Israel chosen to be the "people of God"?

Many today do not believe that the Jews can in any sense be regarded as chosen people of God. There is a strong backlash against such a declaration across much of America, Europe, and the Middle East. But the Bible clearly delineates a position of special honor for the Jews in God's plan. Psalm 135:4 states, "For the LORD has chosen Jacob for Himself, Israel for His special treasure." In Deuteronomy 7:6, Moses says even more strongly, "For you are a holy people to the LORD your God; the LORD your God has chosen you to be a people for Himself, a special treasure above all the peoples on the face of the earth."

Historically, the Jews have been treated harshly by leaders of both Islam and Christianity. Even the Protestant Reformer Martin Luther seemed to carry bitter hatred for the Jews, calling them "beasts that ought to be driven out like mad dogs."[5] Luther, at least, did not pretend to get sanction for his racism from the Bible. Islam, on the other hand, carries hatred founded in the sacred text of surah 5:51. And while the Jews have sometimes been tolerated within Islamic empires, they always are second-class citizens not afforded the same rights as Muslims (see the Pact of Umar).[6] Muslims tend to carry an animosity for Jews, especially Muslims who are closely tied to the Palestinian situation.

By contrast, evangelical Christians tend to be Israel's greatest supporters today. The hatred caused by poor biblical interpretation has been replaced with recognition that God did choose Israel to be His special people. Israel is specially positioned in the lineage from Abraham and Isaac (Deuteronomy 10:15; Isaiah 41:8). The promises of God to the Jews are not temporal but eternal (2 Chronicles 20:7). Those promises are not only spiritual but physical, including the land of Israel today (Genesis 15:18; 24:6; 28:1). God declared that the gospel of Jesus Christ would come through the Jews (Romans 1:16). Christians are grafted into the vine of Israel, though Israel still has a distinct position in the final purposes of God (Galatians 3:29). Finally, God will bring the Jewish people back to Himself as promised. Indeed, the apostle Paul wrote extensively of his passionate desire that his fellow Jews would accept the Messiah, Jesus Christ, and turn to Him for salvation (Romans 9–11).

Therefore, since God has not given up on the Jews despite their disobedience (2 Kings 17:9), the Christian must follow the commands of the Word of God concerning the Jews as God's chosen people.

Has God given up on the Jewish people due to their disobedience?

Closely intertwined with the previous question, this question has special relevance in the realm of Christian theology historically, as well as today. Many Christians, past and present, believe that God has given up on the Jews due to their disobedience, and therefore transferred the promises of Israel to the Church today. The line of reasoning follows in this manner:

1. The Jews were chosen to be the people of God according to the Old Testament.
2. The Jews became disobedient to the point that they did not even recognize the fulfillment of messianic prophecy in the person of Jesus Christ.
3. The Jews, by their rebellion, have forfeited the promises given to them by God.
4. God replaced Israel with "spiritual Israel," otherwise known as the Church.
5. All promises given to Israel now belong to the Church.

There are fallacies within such a belief system. First, historically, the Church only adopted such a position when it discarded a literal interpretation of the Bible for an allegorical interpretation. The great danger of such an interpretation is that it presumes to speak for God. It also assumes that God did not mean what He said, and therefore they have to explain what He means.

Second, the church is different from Israel in several facets. The Church by definition is not a theocratic political unit blessed by God with land but a spiritual living organism based on the death, burial, and resurrection of Christ that is called to share the gospel with the world through the preached Word. Furthermore, the Church does not exist due to Hebrew rebellion as a replacement of Judaism but exists as fulfillment of the prophecy of Jesus Himself (Matthew 16:18-19). In addition, the advent of Jesus Christ is to the Jew first, and then the Gentile. Jews are intrinsically involved in His plan of salvation. Paul himself labored over his kinsmen's rejection of the gospel, which was intended for them (Romans 9:3-5). Moreover, the book of Revelation cannot be understood properly without the distinction between Israel and the Church. God promises that the people of Israel will return to Him and names them by their tribe (Revelation 7).

Ultimately, Christians are grafted into Israel, being considered spiritual Jews. In Romans 11:17, Paul clarifies, "And you (Gentiles), being a wild olive tree, were grafted in among them, and with them became a partaker of the root and fatness of the olive tree." Simply put, the Gentiles (wild branches) are partners of the promises with the native branches (Jews), not usurpers of their promises.

Aren't the Palestinians found within the Old Testament?

The belief that the Palestinians of today are the Philistines of the Old Testament is based on presupposition rather than historical documentation. At the beginning of the thirteenth century B.C., "Sea Peoples" from the Aegean region sailed to the Near East. One of these tribes, the Philistines, settled on the southwest coast of Canaan, known today as the Gaza Strip. The Philistines conquered much of Canaan and were almost successful in eliminating the Hebrew people (ca. 1080 B.C.). In time, King David removed the threat of the Philistines (2 Samuel 5:17-25). Eventually, the Philistines faded from the scene and even their memory was erased except for biblical literature.

Are modern Palestinians direct descendants of the ancient Philistines? If this were the case, the Palestinians have some claim to "Palestine" on their own. There are historical and theological difficulties with the Philistine connection. Historically, there has never been an independent state of Palestine, and a succession of occupying forces have moved people about, beginning with the Assyrians in 722 B.C. This is further supported by archaeological evidence for artifacts as early as 1200 B.C. that disappear nearly five hundred years later.[7]

In reaction to the Bar Kokhba Jewish Revolt in 133 A.D. and encouraged by their own anti-Semitic desires to remove Jewish culture and influence, the Roman Empire decided to designate Judea (Israel) as *Palestine* in 135. Romans seem to have applied *Palestine* to the land and its Jewish inhabitants in derision against the Jewish desire to return to their own government of Israel.

When the Roman Empire fell, the area of Israel was conquered by the Persians (614-29) and by Arabs (638-1077). In 1077, shortly before the start of the Crusades, the Seljuks captured the territory. After a brief period of Arab domination (1187-1244), the Turks took control of the territory and held onto it until the end of World War I. Therefore, there is no valid argument for a Palestinian state according to the history of the land.

The Old Testament Philistine religion also was radically different from Islamic faith. The Philistines sacrificed animals to the Canaanite god Dagon (Judges 16:23). The ancient heritage is immersed in idolatry, one of the chief sins that Allah despises. Philistines were known for their polytheistic worship, the antithesis of what Muhammed desired in worship (1 Chronicles 10:7-10).

Isn't Muhammed the prophet of Deuteronomy 18?

Muslims contend that Muhammed must be the prophet mentioned in Deuteronomy 18:18–19 for several reasons: One is that the phrase "like you" means that a Moses-like prophet would come along, and Muhammed fits that description. Another is that the phrase "from among their brethren" must be referring to the brother of Isaac, Ishmael, of which Muhammed was the only great prophet to come.

Muslims deny that Jesus can fulfill these verses since His character traits were not those of Moses. One Muslim commentator argued that the analogies between Moses and Jesus correspond to "natural birth, the family life, and death of Moses."[8]

Careful study of the Deuteronomy text, however, does not support the arguments that Moses referred to Muhammed.

"Like me" is not referring to the life situation of the prophet but to the specific demand that he function as a true prophet. Moses makes it clear that a false prophet is defined not by family or death but by the words he speaks and the God he serves (Deuteronomy 13:1–6). A true prophet speaks oracles of absolute truth and points to the one true God. The Bible includes prophets such as Isaiah and Micah who spoke of the coming Messiah (Isaiah 7:14; 9:6; Micah 3:1; 5:2). The validation of "like Moses" is also explained in the final verses of Deuteronomy 18. A prophet's prediction must "come to pass" (verse 22) to verify his authenticity as a prophet of God. Not only do the words of Jesus validate His prophethood, but other prophets substantiate His character as the Son of God and Savior. Isaiah prophesied seven centuries before Christ that the Messiah would be virgin born (Isaiah 7:14), rejected by the Jews (53:3), and sacrificed as the atonement for the world (verses 5, 12). Upon this ground alone, Jesus has no equal. On the other hand, Muhammed does not match up and provides no prophecies to demonstrate his own authenticity as a prophet.

Finally, "like me" is referring to the mighty miracles that authenticated Moses' prophetic office. Deuteronomy 34:10–11 states, "But since then there has not arisen in Israel a prophet like Moses, . . . in all the signs and wonders which the LORD sent him to do."

Muhammed never claimed to perform miracles, while Jesus performed countless miracles to authenticate His prophethood. The Qur'an itself, in surah 28:48, differentiates between Moses and Muhammed by declaring, "But (now), when the Truth has come to them from Ourselves, they say, 'Why are not (signs) sent to him, like those which were sent to Moses?'"

The other point of the argument is also incorrect. "From among you" is addressed to the chosen people of God, Israel. The phrase in question is made in reference to other Israelites. That is how it is used in other passages (Deuteronomy 17:14-15). Since the Israelites are in mind, the Gentile Muhammed is disqualified. Jesus of the tribe of Judah fulfills this requirement (Matthew 1:3; Luke 3:33).

Why do orthodox Jews want a temple so passionately?

The Israeli-Palestinian land conflict is not merely a political argument over finding a place for Palestinians to call their own. Part of the land controversy is a theological argument over ownership of sacred property. No piece of land is as controversial as the top of Mount Moriah, which Jews and Christians call the "Temple Mount." It is the third most honored site among Muslims, and the Dome of the Rock is thought to cover all or part of the site of the Jewish temple. Muslims revere this site as sacred since it is where Muhammed allegedly was transported by Gabriel and a horselike creature from Mecca to Jerusalem. There he encountered Abraham, Moses, Jesus, and other prophets. After leading the prophets in prayer, he ascended to the highest heaven where Allah gave instructions for him and his followers (surah 17:1).

Whereas the Dome was built nearly sixty years after Muhammed's death (691), the first temple was built by Solomon more than sixteen hundred years beforehand (957 B.C.) as a sign of Israel's election by God (Deuteronomy 12:5) and the unity of the people of God (Numbers 1-10). The temple provided the Hebrew people a location for the most important sacrifices that would cover their sins (Leviticus 16). It was a reminder to the Jew of God's holiness, wrath, glory, and blessing.

For this reason, many Jews desire to see the rebuilding of the temple today. In fact, the first temple built by Solomon was destroyed by the Babylonians in 587 B.C., only to be rebuilt seventy years later. This second temple was destroyed by the Romans in A.D. 70 after a Jewish revolt was suppressed. As one theologian noted, "The rebuilding is an indispensable token of God's continuing will to bless Israel (Hag. 2:18–19; Zech. 4:9–10)."[9] Orthodox Jews yearn for the day that biblical expectations will come to pass and the Messiah will come and rule from His temple (Isaiah 2:1–5; Ezekiel 37:27). To be clear, the temple is the centerpiece in Orthodox Jewish theology that would complete the puzzle of the final restoration of the Hebrew people. For nearly two millennia, Jews have wandered throughout the world away from their homeland. In that time, they were persecuted, tortured, enslaved, and slaughtered. Now, as Jews are flocking to their homeland by the millions, many know that the land is but part of the picture that cannot be completed without the restoration of the temple, symbolic of the holiness of God, and the unity of His chosen people.

Notes

1. For further details, see David Catchpoole, "The Koran vs. Genesis," *Creation* 24.2 (March–May 2002): 46–51.

2. Norman Geisler and Thomas Howe, *When Critics Ask* (Grand Rapids: Baker, 1992), 52.

3. Anis Shorrosh, *Islam Revealed* (Nashville: Broadman, 1988).

4. Abdullah Yusuf ʿAli, *The Meaning of the Holy Qurʾan* (Brentwood, Md.: Amana, 1992), 813. Emphasis added.

5. David B. Loughran, "Israel . . . The Chosen of God," http://www.atschool.eduweb.co.uk/sbs777/snotes/note0812.html (Dec. 12, 2002).

6. The Pact of Umar was a seventh-century treaty between the Islamic commander Umar and Christians in subjugated Syria. The pact promised toleration and protection for non-Muslims in exchange for a strict code of conduct. Christians would remain quiet, would not repair their churches, would keep Muslim dietary and moral ordinances, and other rules.

7. "Biblical Gath Excavations Reveal Philistine History," http:// www.bridgesforpeace.com/publications/dispatch/archaeology/ Article-8.html (Dec. 12, 2002).

8. I. A. Abu-Harb, *A Brief Illustrated Guide to Understanding Islam* (Houston: Darussalam, 2002), http://www.islam-guide.com/ ch1-3.htm (Dec. 12, 2002). The other point mentioned is used within the same chapter of Abu-Harb's book.

9. S. F. Noll, "Tabernacle, Temple," *Evangelical Dictionary of Theology*, ed. Walter A. Elwell (Grand Rapids: Baker, 1984), 1068.

5

QUESTIONS CONCERNING THE NEW TESTAMENT

DO MUSLIMS BELIEVE IN THE New Testament as a previous revelation of Allah? Do they believe that the disciples corrupted the original manuscripts? Often Christians will begin a gospel presentation by citing one of the Epistles, Galatians for example, only to see the Muslim dismiss that part of the New Testament as corrupted and irrelevant. Christians can be frustrated to find that their favorite Scripture references are rejected out of hand. We believe that a Christian witness should understand this problem at the outset and draw on the Qur'an and sections of the Bible, such as Injil (Gospels) that find some acceptance.

As Paul at the Areopagus (Acts 17), we can stand initially in the unbeliever's frame of reference and proclaim Christ.

How does Islam view the New Testament?

Muslims use much the same arguments as other religious groups who have added to the Bible. First, they attempt to demonstrate the corruption of Scripture through mistranslations or alleged contradictions. Second, they explain that the authority of the Bible is based on another sacred text written hundreds of years after the New Testament. Third, they presume the newer revelation is the final authority and supersedes the Bible. Fourth, they select biblical texts to accept that can be made to fit their theological purposes.

On the issue of corruption, Muslims point out that certain verses have either been added (1 John 5:7-8) or removed (Mark 16:9-20) from the original manuscripts. Ironically, their argument is based on the fact that thousands of copies have been preserved and can be compared for variation. Only a few early copies of the Qur'an have been preserved since variant readings were destroyed by the third caliph, Uthman. Whereas the Christian has the ability to verify which text is correct through manuscript evidence, the Muslim is left to his own presumptions since Uthman was not willing to allow verification of the text through the preservation of variant copies.

Therefore, the Christian looks at the few verses in question with the confidence that the Bible is the most well-preserved book ever written. While a relatively few verses are debated by scholars for authenticity, none of these debates affect any major doctrinal issue. Archaeological evidence continues to confirm more of the historical details mentioned. Also, even earlier manuscripts, such as the John Rylands Papyrus, were discovered during the twentieth century. This fragment of John 18 can be dated to about A.D. 130 and confirms the accuracy of our modern Greek texts. Christians can have utter confidence in the accuracy of their sacred text.

Some of the textual difficulties are the fault of some translator along the way, whose error had to be corrected later. That is the case with 1 John 5:7-8, which was accepted as reliable by the King James Bible translators, even though it could be found in no early manuscript, nor is it quoted by any of the Greek church fathers. On the other hand, the questioned text John 7:53-8:11 has verification both from early manuscripts and historical evidence of its authenticity. Therefore, this is not the problem of the Bible but of one of its translations. Jesus and the apostles promised the preservation of the Bible, not of every translation that may come out.

After Muslims attempt to demonstrate the Bible's fallibility, they argue that the Qur'an was sent from God and has been preserved completely. There is logical inconsistency within this argument. The Muslim believes that the Torah, the first five books of the

Bible written by Moses, and the Psalms of David were inspired by God for the Jewish people. Yet, the Jews corrupted the text from its intended meaning. Then the Christians were given the gospel from Jesus, which was also corrupted over time. Finally, Muslims were given the Qurʾan, which will be guarded from corruption (surah 15:9). How can a person trust that God will guard the Qurʾan from corruption when previous messages of God through the prophets were tainted and lost? Further, how does a finite and mortal man have the power to destroy the words of the Almighty, omnipotent, omniscient God? God must have intended the corruption of the manuscript, or He was less than God.

The Muslim's third argument, that newer revelation supercedes older revelation, seems to follow the rather low view of truth that it is temporary and culturally conditioned. At some point, in that case, the Qurʾan will no longer be true. Assuming that God transcends His creation, and that He reveals what is true, it is illogical to assert that one revealed truth is better than another because it is God's latest thinking on the subject. Muslims and Christians can agree philosophically that newer revelation can add clarity or expand on earlier revelation, but it cannot contradict what came before.

Orthodox Christians do not accept that there has been any new revelation since the New Testament was written, but if God were to send new revelation, it could not contradict authentic older revelation. This is exactly the argument Jesus uses in Matthew 5:17–18. He did not destroy the foundation of the Old Testament, but He was its fulfillment. Consequently, Christians understand that the Old Testament is fully compatible and coherent with the New Testament. Indeed, an unchanging God cannot have an ever changing Word.

After degrading its value, Muslims still attempt to use the Old Testament to promote a theological agenda. This itself is a questionable practice. The Muslim views the Bible as merely another historical document that can be used but not trusted. Ironically, it is not clear that Muhammed shared this low regard for the Bible, which he described as "truth from your Lord" (surah 10:94; see pp. 71–72).

Don't your four Gospels disagree with each other?

The four Gospels, which record the life, death, and resurrection of Jesus Christ, present the Muslim with the most problems regarding the Christian Scriptures. Here are such offensive doctrines as the Incarnation and deity of Christ and the sacrificial atonement of Christ for the world. The doctrines of salvation by grace through faith and the office of Christ as Judge create more complications, for they are antithetical to the teachings of Muhammed found in the Qurʾan.

For these reasons, Muslims do not believe that the four Gospels contain the authentic gospel (Injil) given by Jesus Christ. Instead, they argue, all but a few fragments of the original gospel has been lost. One Muslim commentator explained, "Fragments of it survive in the received canonical Gospels and in some others, of which traces survive (e.g., *the Gospel of Childhood or the Nativity, the Gospel of St. Barnabas*)."[1]

The Muslim argument for the New Testament Gospels can be summarized:

1. Jesus wrote the gospel (Injil), which was unified and only one volume.
2. Just as Moses' message became corrupt, so too did the message of Jesus, the messenger and prophet of God.
3. The four Gospels of today are the invention of the Church, and only contain a minute piece of the true gospel.
4. Since the four Gospels are the creation of Christians, other gospels also must be considered as equally valid in telling the true life of Christ.

Muslims maintain that the four Gospels were not written until the second century and that other gospels were accepted by certain Christians. Muslims point out the widespread controversies over content and authorship in the Christian community. Obviously, Muslims rely heavily upon the views of modernist theologians, who use some radical historical-critical approaches to Scripture study, as sources for their documentation. These critics of the Bible are also critics of religion in general and hold to many beliefs not considered valid by Muslims, including rejection of the supernatural and judgment. Those cited tend to be the older classic liberals of the late nineteenth century.

Most of the old liberal theories have been proven false by archaeological discoveries. For example, a portion of John 18 has survived in John Ryland's Papyrus Greek 457, proving that the gospel was being copied within forty years of the date historically accepted for its composition near the end of the first century. The vast majority of the Church did accept the same books into the Bible. To argue that a few groups denied parts of the Bible does not substantiate the argument. These same groups are infamous for other theological errors.

There were disagreements in the early church about the authenticity of a few New Testament writings, but the Gospels themselves were never the books in question. Early church fathers such as Clement of Rome (30-100) and Ignatius of Antioch (d. 107) quoted frequently from the Gospels. Heretics in the church, such as Marcion (d. ca. 160), were expelled for denying the veracity of the Gospels.

It is easy to see why Muslims flock to *The Gospel of Barnabas* as the most authentic gospel and the only one to be written by a true disciple of Jesus. According to this apocryphal gospel, Jesus did not die on the cross, rather, Judas Iscariot who was substituted for Jesus. Yet, *The Gospel of Barnabas* provides a weak ally:

1. There is no original language text for *Barnabas*, as opposed to nearly five thousand seven hundred original language manuscripts and fragments covering the rest of the New Testament.
2. Though many Muslims use this document today, no Muslim writer refers to it until the fifteenth century.
3. No theologian of the early or medieval church ever quotes or even mentions a gospel by Barnabas.
4. Some Muslims assume that *The Gospel of Barnabas* is synonymous with *The Epistle of Barnabas* (written c. 90), but this is wholly different in content.

5. What this writing says is directly refuted by eyewitness accounts that are hundreds of years older and accepted throughout history.
6. The theology in *The Gospel of Barnabas* is incompatible with Christianity or Islam. In it, Jesus denies that He is the Messiah.

Muslims want to find historical validity for their beliefs about Jesus, yet there simply are none that have credibility. From the beginning, Christians testified to a Jesus Christ who was the Son of God and Savior of the world. The New Testament writings, and especially the Gospels, have affirmed and been authoritative in this confession.

Didn't Jesus turn clay into birds in the Bible?

One of the most popular stories about Jesus from the Qur'an tells that Jesus turned clay figurines into actual birds (surah 5:110). It is possible to find uninformed Christians who assume that this is found in the Bible. However, the fact that Muhammed retells this story demonstrates what sources he is using to claim the life of Jesus as a prophet of Allah. The original story of this miracle is found in *The Infancy Gospel of Thomas,* which appeared in about 150. This was written long after the death of the Thomas for whom it is named and was never accepted as more than a literary fiction. The author wrote:

> This little child Jesus when he was five years old was playing at the ford of a brook: and he gathered together the waters that flowed there into pools, and made them straightway clean, and commanded them by his word alone. And having made soft clay, he fashioned thereof twelve sparrows. And it was the Sabbath when he did these things. And there were also many other little children playing with him.[2]

Muhammed leaves out of his text the dispute over the Sabbath, which is a key theme for the original writer. Muhammed explains that the moral of the story is the power of Allah on his prophets, while the apocryphal texts clearly illustrated the power of Jesus Himself while just an infant. This is further shown in the succeeding verses of *The Infancy Gospel of Thomas* when Jesus kills another boy for simply running into Him.

The narrative is unquestionably a myth, although Muhammed accepts it as the revelation of Allah. Apparently the Christian writings to which Muhammed had access had more to do with apocryphal writings than the New Testament. Muslim scholars admit that not one story of substance is taken from the actual New Testament, but several come from writings that never were accepted by orthodox believers. All of this seems odd, given that Muhammed claimed to have received his revelation directly from Allah, yet it is clear that he used other sources to validate his claims of Christ.

Didn't Jesus say He came with a sword?

Jesus' statement on the sword is found in Matthew 10:34 (NIV): "Do not suppose that I have come to bring peace to the earth. I did not come to bring peace, but a sword." This passage is brought up in some debates as a refutation to Christ's peacefulness or to affirm Christianity's ruthlessness.[3]

Critics who use the text this way always fail to investigate the entire passage to see why Jesus made this provocative remark. The passage, actually six verses contained within one paragraph in the original manuscript, gives an unambiguous explanation of the "sword." The disciples were looking for a political Messiah, but He once again reminds them that He did not come to bring political empowerment. The chapter itself describes the commissioning by Jesus of the disciples to do His will. Jesus explains that "peace" can only come to households that accept the gospel brought by the followers of Christ (Matthew 10:13-14). Jesus warns the disciples that they will be "sheep in the midst of wolves" (verse 16a), hardly a command to act violently. Rather, Christ's message would divide people, and controversy and violence will swirl into persecution. They will fall to the sword at the hands of pagans and pagan governments. Therefore, the disciples should flee to another city when persecution arises (verse 23).

The context of the passage is definitely spiritual and confessional (Matthew 10:32–33), not physical and militaristic. The passage means that faith often divides families (verse 35), something that many former Muslims wholeheartedly understand. The division is real and literal when taken in its intended context. While the world is looking for political peace, Jesus prompts His disciples to count the cost of following Him (verses 28, 38). Knowing the events that will take place soon, Jesus recognizes that the only ones worthy to say they respect Jesus are those who actually follow Him by way of the Cross. The final admonition is given not to take another life, but "he who loses his life for My sake will find it" (verse 39).

Greek scholar A. T. Robertson stresses, "It is no namby-pamby sentimentalism that Christ preaches, no peace at any price. The Cross of Christ's answer to the devil's offer of compromise is world dominion. For Christ the kingdom of God is virile righteousness, not mere emotionalism."[4]

Didn't Jesus come to teach the "straight path"?

The beginning of the Qur'an testifies to the desire in a people's lives for Allah to "Show us the straight way" (surah 1:6). Those who follow the will of Allah may be rewarded with Paradise, while those who follow the crooked way will be judged accordingly (surah 43:61). In fact, chapter 43 in the Qur'an is essential in understanding that the straight way according to Islam is directly linked with the second coming of Jesus Christ who will prepare the way of judgment in the Last Days. This passage also attributes Christ as saying, "For Allah, He is my Lord and your Lord: so worship ye Him: this is a Straight Way" (surah 43:64). Therefore, when Muslims claim that Jesus taught the "straight path," they are asserting that Jesus never desired for anyone to follow Him or worship Him, for judgment and mercy come only from Allah.

Biblical evidence contradicts such a notion. Jesus stated in John 14:6, "I am the way, the truth, and the life. No one comes to the Father except through Me." It is clear through this passage, as well as through many others (for example, John 10:7-9), that Jesus required exclusive allegiance from His followers. He was not *a* way to heaven; He was *the* way to heaven.

Surah 43 argues against the lordship of Christ, but this is exactly the witness Thomas gives as he repents that he had doubted the Savior. We are not told that he ever touched Christ's wounds, yet he proclaimed without equivocation, "My Lord and my God!" (John 20:28). Jesus does not reprimand Thomas for making such a strong statement. Rather, He teaches Thomas that this very confession of who He is will bring greater blessing to those who have not seen Him in person, yet believe.

Paul advances the same message in Romans 10:13: "Whoever calls on the name of the LORD shall be saved." Yet, these are not only the words of Paul but the words of the prophet Joel in reference to salvation in God's name (Joel 2:32).

Perhaps the strongest argument Muslims make is that Jesus never commanded that others worship Him (surah 43:64; 5:116). Jesus could only claim worship if He is God. The Bible clearly teaches that Jesus is God (for example, John 1:1; Colossians 2:9; Titus 3:4; Hebrews 1:8). For a further response to this issue, see pp. 34–39, 55–62.

Jesus also demanded worship in very apparent ways. Jesus instructed people to place their faith in Him, a form of worship (John 11:25). In fact, Jesus required that the disciples pray in His name (John 14:13–14), a sacrilegious doctrine if He were not God. In response, Stephen, while being stoned, prayed *to* Christ in his suffering (Acts 7:59). Jesus Himself accepted worship, which is contrary to the testimony of the Qur'an. For example, when He calmed the storm, those in the boat "worshiped Him, saying, 'Truly You are the Son of God'" (Matthew 14:33).

Peter's confession in Matthew 16:16 (NIV) is unmistakably a confession of worship: "You are the Christ, the Son of the living God." In response to Peter's profession, Jesus declares, "Blessed are you, Simon son of Jonah, for this was not revealed to you by man, but by my Father in heaven" (verse 17). Jesus not only agrees with Peter and commends him for his confession, but Jesus promises Peter that this confession would be foundational to all who gathered to Him (verse 18).

Didn't Jesus speak of Muhammed as the "Comforter"?

Muslim theologians propose that Muhammed is the "Comforter" promised by Jesus in the gospel of John (14:16; 16:7). The Qur'an asserts, "And remember, Jesus, the son of Mary, said: 'O Children of Israel! I am the messenger of Allah (sent) to you, confirming the Taurat (which came) before me, and giving Glad Tidings of a messenger to come after me, whose name shall be Ahmed (Muhammad)'" (surah 61:6).

Using their sacred text, their argument has at least two angles: First, the gospel of John is corrupt in its version because it uses the Greek term *paraklētos* ("one who walks alongside"). The true version should be *Periklytos*, which is a near perfect translation of Muhammed (see pp. 43–45 for a discussion of this argument). Second, even if the word is not corrupt, it would still be referring to Muhammed, since he is "a Mercy for all creatures" (surah 21:107). In fact, it could not be the Holy Spirit as prescribed by Christians "because the Holy Spirit already was present, helping guide Jesus."[5]

A careful study of the text shows that this hypothesis simply will not work unless the entire text is rewritten. The fact is that John explicitly introduces the "Helper" as the Holy Spirit in John 14:14, 26. Jesus promises that this Comforter will come to help the disciples shortly after His departure. In fact, the promise was targeted specifically at the disciples who were with Him at the time. Verse 16 promises the disciples, "You know Him," which could not refer to a man who would not be born for over five centuries. This promise was based on the fact that Jesus would not leave believers without a witness in the person of the Holy Spirit of God.

Beyond these problems, Jesus states that the Comforter "may abide with you forever" (John 14:16). A dead man does not abide with anyone on earth any longer. Finally, there is absolutely no evidence that the text could have said something else at one time but was changed. On the contrary, archaeological discoveries show that this is just how *paraklētos* was used in contemporary documents. There is not one example of *periklytos* found in the entire language of the New Testament, Koine (Common) Greek.

The second argument, that the Holy Spirit was already present, does not negate the promise of the Spirit of God. Jesus' promise was not that there would be an external presence to guide, a characteristic seen throughout the Old Testament. Rather, Christ promised that the Holy Spirit "will be *in* you" (John 14:17). The Spirit's indwelling acts as a reminder to believers of the promise of Christ to never leave or forsake them. Finally, the promise of the Comforter cannot be Muhammed since the Comforter of whom Jesus spoke never calls attention to Himself (verses 13-14).

Is Mary viewed similarly in Islam and Christianity?

Not only is Mary the only woman mentioned by name in the Qur'an, but the references to her in the Muslim holy book are more voluminous than in the New Testament. Although the Bible and the Qur'an both mention the Annunciation (announcement of the coming) of Christ and the visitation by angels to Mary, the Bible and Qur'an have one truly striking similarity when characterizing the life of Mary: Both hold to the virgin birth of Jesus (Matthew 1:23; surah 19:20, 28-29). The Qur'an leaves out important details found in the Gospels including Mary's relationship to Joseph, the journey to Bethlehem, and the manger scene itself.[6] Instead, the Qur'an highlights Mary as a faithful servant of Allah who should be emulated for her devotion and humility (surah 3:42). Chapter 19 of the Qur'an, which is intentionally named after the mother of Christ, makes several additions to the biblical story:

1. The pain of childbirth is mentioned as strong enough to drive her into a palm tree and declare, "Ah! Would that I had died before this!" (19:23).
2. The mother of Mary, though not mentioned in the Bible, plays an important role in reassuring her daughter.
3. Jesus Himself comes to the aid of His mother while still a baby, verbally defending her chastity and honor (19:30).
4. While the biblical story incorporates the worship of the Child, the Qur'an clearly refutes any such notion of deity and attests to Christ's humanity (19:33-36).

Muhammed's deviations from the biblical picture of Mary are similar to apocryphal writings such as the *Protoevangelium of James the Lesser*, a late-second-century document never accepted by Christians. In surah 3:44, the Qur'an enlightens the reader that Joseph earned the hand of Mary by "casting lots with pens" (reeds) for her. The apocryphal text similarly narrates, "After the High-Priest had received their rods, he went into the temple to pray; and when he had finished his prayer, he took the rods, and went forth and distributed them, and there was no miracle attending them. The last rod was taken by Joseph, and behold, a dove proceeded out of the rod, and flew upon the head of Joseph. And the High Priest said, 'Joseph, you are the person chosen to take the virgin of the Lord, to keep her for Him'" (*James the Lesser* 8:9ff.).[7]

As seen in the discussion of the Trinity (pp. 34–35), the Qur'an is confused about Mary within the Christian theology of the Trinity. According to surah 5:116, Christians believe that Mary is the third person of the Trinity, along with Allah and Jesus. Though Muslims dispute that the Qur'an misunderstands the Trinity, the text at least misrepresents what Christianity taught in the Middle East during the time of Muhammed. Though Mary sometimes is called the "Mother of God," and there have been arguments throughout church history about the appropriateness of that title, no church leader ever substituted her for the Holy Spirit. The major Christian sect in Arabia during the life of Muhammed was the Nestorians, who vehemently denied the divinity of Mary. The fact that Muslims incorporated Mary into the Trinity (whether by view of heretical sects or incorrect assumption) demonstrated their view that the Trinity was physical and sensual rather than spiritual and relational.

Did Paul corrupt the teachings of the Gospels?

Muslims who know much about Christianity tend to place the blame for corrupting the true gospel onto the shoulders of one man, the apostle Paul. The author of at least thirteen epistles in the New Testament, Paul certainly worshiped Jesus as the Son of God. His testimony for the deity of Christ is overwhelmingly evident in such texts as Colossians 1:15–20 and Philippians 2:5–11. Whoever wrote the book of Hebrews, Paul certainly would have supported the supremacy of Christ reflected in Hebrews 1:1-8. That he defined for the world the sacrificial atonement of Jesus is also without question, as in Romans 5:6-21; 1 Corinthians 2:1-2; and Ephesians 2:1-10. Therefore, Islam sees Paul as the founder of apostate Christianity. Paul never met Jesus but only desired prominence and power, they argue. That being their view, Paul's writings are not authoritative to Muslims and carry no weight in an argument about the character of Christ.

Muslims attack the character of Paul, asserting that he never met Jesus and so was not a follower. Paul himself maintained that he had indeed met Christ after His resurrection (Acts 9). In every sense, he gave his life for the Savior, so it is hard to imagine that he was intentionally following a lie. Such a charge casts aspersions on the rest of the disciples, who did meet Paul and who would have known what he was teaching (Acts 9:26-28; 15:2, 4; Galatians 2:1-2). They would have to be genuine fools if they were duped so quickly by an incredibly different version of the gospel from the one entrusted to them by their Master. The disciples were challenged to verify Paul to see if his words were genuine (Galatians 1-2). In fact, the mission of Jesus would be a failure if Paul were apostate, since Christ's message would have been erased just a few years after His mission was completed.

Muslims attack the theology of Paul as radically contrary to the theology of Christ. Muslims believe that Jesus emphasized the Law of Moses (Matthew 5:17-18), while Paul negated that very Law. A simple comparison illustrates that Paul's understanding actually was that of Jesus. Both saw the work of the Messiah as fulfilling the Law (Romans 10:4, 9-11 compared to Matthew 5). Jesus and Paul agree on:

1. Human lostness in sin (Mark 3:38; Romans 3:23).
2. The substitution of Jesus to pay the price for sin (Matthew 26:28; Romans 5:8).
3. Salvation by grace through faith alone (Matthew 19:25-26; Ephesians 2:8-9).

We suggest that Paul's problem is not a disagreement with Jesus but rather with Muslims. Since they cannot refute his arguments, they must attempt to refute his apostleship.[8]

Wasn't the New Testament first written in Aramaic?

Many Muslim apologists begin their argument of a corrupt New Testament by supposing that the Gospels (Injil) were never written in the language Jesus commonly spoke, Aramaic. Rather, the disciples chose to write the message in Greek, a language in limited use at the time of Jesus. Some go as far as to contend that Jesus did not know Greek Himself.[9]

Linguistic scholars readily point out that Koine (Common) Greek was the familiar language in the Near East. Historically, this is uncontestable. Alexander the Great captured Jerusalem in 322 B.C. and "Hellenized" the culture, that is, imposed Greek culture on the Jews. Thereby, the Jews replaced Aramaic with Greek as their language of choice. The Jews translated the Hebrew Scriptures into Greek as early as the third century B.C.

It was not that the people of Israel threw away their native tongue, but it was the language everyone used in the common marketplace. Most Jews spoke Hebrew, Aramaic, and Greek. When Jesus spoke in the Temple, He assuredly did so in Hebrew. On the cross, He cried out in Aramaic, "My God, My God, why have You forsaken Me?" (Matthew 27:46). When He cast out the demon in the "Greek" woman, He most likely spoke in Greek (Mark 7:24–30). In fact, Christ's ministry was to all people (Luke 19:10). He was multilingual.

The argument does not center upon the languages Jesus spoke but on whether He promised the inspiration of the New Testament. If so, His words are translated correctly since He superintended the writing of the manuscripts (2 Peter 1:19–21). What is in question, therefore, is not the communication of Jesus but the character of Jesus, for the Living Word has power over the written Word.

Notes

1. Abdullah Yusuf ʿAli, *The Meaning of the Holy Qurʾan* (Brentwood, Md.: Amana, 1992), 292.

2. *The Infancy Gospel of Thomas,* trans. Peter Kirby, http://www.earlychristianwritings.com/text/infancythomas-a-mrjames.html (Dec. 13, 2002).

3. See "Jeremiah McAuliffe v. Abdul Saleeb, A debate from soc.religion.islam," http://www.answering-islam.org/debates (Dec. 13, 2002). Dr. McAuliffe is a former Catholic who converted to Islam while Saleeb is a Muslim turned evangelical.

4. Archibald Thomas Robertson, *Word Pictures in the New Testament,* vol. 1 (Nashville: Broadman, 1930), 84.

5. ʿAli, *The Meaning of the Holy Qurʾan,* 148. See also in the same work, nn. 1461, 5438.

6. George Braswell, *Islam: Its Prophet, Peoples, Politics, and Power* (Nashville: Broadman & Holman, 1996), 250.

7. See http://www.answering-islam.org for further details on the importance and theology of Mary in Islam.

8. Norman L. Geisler and Abdul Saleeb, *Answering Islam* (Grand Rapids: Baker, 1993), 315.

9. See http://www.anwering-christianity.com/jesus_speak.htm for more detail (Dec. 14, 2002).

6

QUESTIONS CONCERNING THE ATONEMENT AND SALVATION

In April 1996, Macksood Aftab, the managing editor of the *Islamic Herald,* wrote an article designed to present a Muslim apologetic against Christian witnesses. He wrote in part:

> One of the basic arguments raised by non-Muslims, especially Christians, against Islam concerns the concept of salvation. They say that in Christianity, one is saved by faith, whereas in Islam one must earn their salvation through good deeds. Unfortunately, many Muslims fall into the trap of defending the position imposed on them by these non-Muslims. This then provides the Christians with a basis for their entire Jesus-Father-Crucifixion-Salvation framework. . . . Many times, Muslims fail to realize that the Islamic concept of salvation is not based upon good deeds, but is primarily upon faith. In the dozens of times Allah . . . talks in the Qur'an about salvation, he always states. 'Those who believe and do good deeds.' Belief is always mentioned before deeds or works.[1]

Concurrent with Aftab's concern for Muslims who misunderstand their doctrines, Christian theologians and pastors have lamented how poorly most Christians understand what the Bible says about the finished work of Christ and salvation. If a Christian is to engage a Muslim with the gospel of Christ, he must clearly understand his own faith, as well as the different mind-set from which the Muslim is operating.

A lack of clarity in this arena is eternally fatal.

Are the scales of Islam reasonable and logical?

Salvation in Islam is not based on God regenerating the soul, since Muslims do not believe the soul is fallen or depraved. Rather, salvation is centered upon the works done by each individual, and whether the good works outweigh the evil works. The Qur'an reports, "Then those whose balance (of good deeds) is heavy,—they will be successful. But those whose balance is light, will be those who have lost their souls; in Hell will they abide" (surah 23:102-3). For this reason, Muslims do not refer to their deliverance as salvation or conversion but as remembering or returning. Islamic theology is clear that each people group has a messenger, and thereby they know the truth and must return to it.

The list of good works necessary to "earn heaven" (surah 39:61) is long. Only those who acknowledge the message and prophethood of Muhammed can merit salvation. The Qur'an explicitly warns that those who reject the message of Muhammed are "in truth Unbelievers; and We (Allah) have prepared for Unbelievers a humiliating punishment" (surah 4:151). The continual recitation of the confession ("There is no god but Allah, Muhammed is the prophet of Allah") is further proof of such necessity. The Muslim daily confesses his belief in the monotheistic God as heralded by Muhammed and then passes it down to his children as he whispers the confession into the ear of each newborn child.

Yet, the Muslim can never be sure of salvation, since it is based on work that must persevere to the end or it will be lost. The faithful Muslim hopes for salvation, but it cannot be obtained on earth. Ironically, believing in the judgment and future life is commanded in order to warrant paradise. Ultimately, the Muslim must be utterly and repeatedly faithful to the five pillars of Islam (confession, prayer, divine tax, fasting, and pilgrimage) to have any possibility of salvation. Any slip can cost weight on the good side of the scales.[2]

Viewed within this perspective, the Islamic doctrine of salvation is untenable in at least two ways. First, if motives, thoughts, and desires are part and parcel to determining an act's value, then people most definitely are not good in their character. Sins are not only wrong acts performed by the individual but righteous acts *not* performed. A person has a difficult time just owning up to the outward commands and prohibitions found in the Ten Commandments and elsewhere. But a holy God also knows the secret things in the heart. And the entire law of God for outward act and inner thought is a unity for acceptable righteousness before infinite perfection. The epistle of James emphatically declares that "whoever shall keep the whole law, and yet stumble in one point, he is guilty of all" (James 2:10).

Second, even if it were possible to be more good than bad, the Qurʾan does not explain how a holy God allows sin to go unpunished (see surah 59:22-24). Though the Qurʾan often speaks of Allah's mercy (surah 4:26; 5:74; 6:12; 10:21), it is unacceptable to think that sins committed are not judged before the One who is responsible for justice. If Allah merely overlooks sin in his mercy, then judgment is not just and forgiveness is arbitrary. Since God is the Lawgiver and the Judge, He enacts punishment on those who break His laws. If a person is judged by a court of law to have murdered someone, it would be unjust if he is suddenly acquitted of the charges for which he is guilty. It would be offensive to the person killed, the victim's family, the community, and to the judge's position. If sins against almighty God go unpunished, then the character of God is flawed.

Without an absolute standard by which to punish sin, Allah's laws are subjective and truly unknowable. Before such a capricious Judge, it truly is impossible to know if one is going to heaven. Islam's view of salvation is illogical and unreasonable.

Did Muhammed doubt his own salvation?

There is no question that Muhammed did doubt his own salvation. In the Hadith, which is considered an authoritative source in Islam second to the Qur'an, Muhammed admits his fear to a woman who is grieving the death of a loved one. When she expresses assurance that the dead person has gone to Paradise, Muhammed reprimands her.

> "How do you know that Allah has honored him?" I replied, "I do not know. May my father and my mother be sacrificed for you, O Allah's Apostle! But who else is worthy of it (if not 'Uthman)?" He said, "As to him, by Allah, death has overtaken him, and I hope the best for him. By Allah, though I am the Apostle of Allah, yet I do not know what Allah will do to me" (Sahih al-Bukhari Hadith 5.266).

Why follow a person who claims to be the greatest prophet but does not know his own eternal destiny? Muhammed was held captive by his own theology. He informed others of the elusiveness of Paradise. He based Paradise not on the work of God but on human effort. He argued that salvation is not something to be grasped here but only something to be acquired in the future. Finally, he explained that the final decision is placed within the will of Allah (surah 14:4). The Muslim must, therefore, do his best and hope for the best.

On the other hand, the Christian is following the One who created the heavens and the earth and has both the authority and a basis for forgiving sin. Jesus told His disciples many times of His departure and return to heaven (John 16:5). He gave others the right to go with Him if they just believed in Him as Savior and Lord. Jesus reassured the thief on the cross, "*Assuredly,* I say to you, today you will be with Me in Paradise" (Luke 23:43, emphasis mine). It is amazing to recognize that Jesus not only promises heaven to every believer but is responsible for preparing heaven for the believer (John 14:2). Ultimately, Jesus was sure of His destination since He is the Creator, Sustainer, Author, Finisher, and soon-coming King. He not only guarantees heaven to every believer; one day He will personally escort them there (1 Thessalonians 4:13–18).

To whom does Christ offer salvation?

Many Muslims view Christianity as an exclusive club in which they are not invited to join. Yet, nothing can be farther from the truth. God's incalculable love for mankind was demonstrated in the sacrifice of His Son Jesus Christ (Romans 5:8). That love was not given selectively but universally. The gospel is clear: "For God so loved *the world* that He gave His only begotten Son, that *whoever* believes in Him should not perish but have everlasting life" (John 3:16). Without question, God's love to the Arab is as strong as it is for the Westerner.

Though the gospel is available in Christ to every person ever born (1 John 2:2), not everyone will be saved since many refuse to accept the way to forgiveness in the blood Christ shed on the Cross for their own sin. They refuse their only Advocate, Jesus Christ, who gave Himself as a "ransom," one who pays the price in order that a condemned man will be free. The Bible speaks of God, however, as the One "who desires all men to be saved and to come to the knowledge of the truth" through "the Man Christ Jesus, who gave Himself a ransom for all" (1 Timothy 2:4, 6).

One must remember that, although God is extraordinarily personal in His offer of salvation, genuine faith must be voluntary. Repentance, the turning from sin to follow Jesus Christ, must be the decision of the one who is sorrowful, or it is not true repentance (Matthew 3:2). Consequently, in God's sovereignty, He allows time, within His larger governing of life, for men and women to turn from sin to the Savior (2 Peter 3:9).

The extent of the atonement is determined by the extent of God's love. Islam teaches that Allah's love and forgiveness is conditioned upon one's righteousness (surah 2:279; 17:25; 19:60). The Bible teaches that God's love and forgiveness is unconditional, based not on how good one has been but on the death of Jesus. Jesus paid the infinite cost of sin on behalf of those who accept that atonement for their own lives (Romans 10:9–10, 13). Salvation is not founded upon the enduring work of each person but on the finished work of Christ (John 19:30). To maintain that Jesus Christ died for the world affects one's theology. To admit that Jesus Christ died for me affects my eternal destiny.

How can the blood of one man forgive everyone?

Two essential denials separate Muslims from the Christian understanding of the sacrifice of Christ for sin. First, Muslims reject any need for *any* sacrifice for sin, much less *the* sacrifice of Christ Himself (surah 22:37). Second, the sacrificial system is rejected as inappropriate, for the individual alone is responsible for earning favor with Allah (surah 22:34–35; 39:61). Indeed, the Qur'an mentions sacrifices only as a means to illustrate man's dominion over animals and Allah's goodness in sustaining humanity with food. Since salvation is integrally connected with the individual and his goodness, there is no need in the Muslim mind to be dependent upon the goodness of a sacrifice for them.

To the Muslim, the sacrificial system that culminated in the Christian belief represents paganism more than true faith. As Muslim commentator Yusuf ʿAli explains, "No one should suppose that meat or blood is acceptable to the One True God. It was a Pagan fancy that Allah could be appeased by blood sacrifice."[3] Therefore, the sacrificial system found within Judaism and Christianity, as much as any doctrine, characterizes the corruption of the two faiths. The point of the sin offering within the sacificial system—the innocent taking on the guilt of the sinner—looked forward to an ultimate reality in the Cross. The significance is misunderstood because it is reduced to an appeasement offering of meat and blood to a god.

One major inadequacy of Muslim theology is in the area that theologians call "anthropology," the understanding of what a human being is in relation to God. The Christian knows that no person can be good enough to earn favor with God (Romans 3:10). Even if goodness outweighed sinfulness (which is not possible), the person still is guilty of breaking the law, and punishment is still prescribed for the criminal acts done against the almighty, holy God. God takes sin seriously and demonstrates this through His wrath. God as Judge is responsible for upholding the Law He has prescribed or He has disqualified Himself as Judge. In fact, if He allows sins to go unpunished, He has made Himself an accessory after the fact.

However, Islamic theology has an even more essential deficiency in the view of salvation. In Islam, salvation is man-centered (humanistic). In Christianity, salvation is God-centered (theocentric). In Islam, people are attempting to gain access to Paradise, a sensual and spiritual abode. In Christianity, everyone has the innate desire to have a relationship with God. Heaven is not created to fulfill fleshly desires but rather as a place where people reconciled to God can be what God intended before sin entered the picture (Revelation 21:1–8).

Therefore, to understand the sacrifice of Christ, one must have a proper biblical view of salvation. The apostle Paul wrote, "that God was in Christ *reconciling* the world to Himself, not imputing their trespasses to them" (2 Corinthians 5:19a). Evangelical Christian theologian Leon Morris explains of the necessity of the Cross, "Other religions have their martyrs, but the death of Jesus was not that of a martyr. It was that of a Savior."[4]

Jesus Christ is a Mediator in the reconciling of God to sinners (1 Timothy 2:5). Only He had the character to make the contribution necessary for salvation. He is the God-Man who, as fully human, can represent the human sinner and as God Incarnate can forgive sin on the basis that He Himself has satisfied justice. Christians agree with Muslims that the blood of an animal cannot be the basis for the forgiveness of sin (Hebrews 10:4). The Old Testament sacrifices portrayed and looked forward to the final, sufficient, and perfect sacrifice of Christ (verses 5–10). Salvation, thereby, has numerous important aspects that are exclusively fulfilled in the person and work of Christ:

1. Christ paid the penalty of sin. As a result, His sacrifice is universal (Romans 3:25–26; Galatians 3:13).
2. Christ redeemed us by paying the price to set us free (1 Corinthians 6:20; Galatians 2:20).

3. Christ manifested the victory of sin and death in the Resurrection (1 Corinthians 15:55–57).
4. Christ, by placing sin upon Himself, turned away the wrath of God (Romans 3:25).
5. Christ removed the barriers between humankind and God, thereby reconciling enemies so that they might become friends (Ephesians 2:16).[5]

Ultimately, a Muslim accepts or rejects the validity of the claim that one man can die for all upon his determination of who Christ is. If He were only a human being, then Jesus could pay only the penalty for Himself. If He is fully God, then He has right over His creation to judge, step in to satisfy justice, forgive, and reconcile to Himself.

Why is the shedding of blood necessary?

Slightly different from the previous question, this often asked question pertains less to the person of Jesus Christ and more to the plan of God to satisfy justice, which demands ultimate payment for an ultimate act of rebellion. The Old Testament is clear about God's plan for salvation. Perhaps God could have chosen another way to redeem humankind, or perhaps not, but He chose a way that was costly to give the greatest gift possible, His Son. Sin offerings of the sacrificial system were closely connected with Jesus Christ. God had ordained before the creation of the world to reconcile those He knew would rebel against Him by offering Himself as a perfect sacrifice. In the blood, there is not only the ultimate penalty of death but the power to overcome death and sin eternally, and so give life. Moses wrote of this aspect, "For the life of a creature is in the blood, and I have given it to you to make atonement for yourselves on the altar; it is the blood that makes atonement for one's life" (Leviticus 17:11). The book of Hebrews continues with this line of thought, stating, "Without the shedding of blood there is no forgiveness" (Hebrews 9:22b NIV).

Most Muslims do not have a problem with capital punishment as a consequence for murder. After all, if a person sheds another's blood, it seems just that the killer's blood should be shed (Genesis 9:6; surah 17:33). The criminal must pay the price for the killing of innocent life. Since sin is as close as a creature can come to murdering the Creator—showing utter disregard for the Creator's being—the ultimate payment of eternal death is reasonable. Even the Muslim who does not believe in original sin certainly believes that all have sinned (Romans 3:23; surah 10:54). God condemned the sinner to pay the penalty for sin, and then stepped in to take the sinner's place. The Incarnation and the spilling of blood on the Cross were both absolutely necessary. His substitution on the Cross demonstrates His willingness to bear man's sin. It is for our scandalous acts and sinful disposition that He put Himself in our place and gave up His life on a thief's cross.

Finally, the blood was necessary as a final and sufficient payment for sin. Muslims worry their entire lives about the scales. Yet, the once-and-for-all shedding of the blood of Christ will relieve all agony to those who believe (Hebrews 10:11–18). The blood is a reassuring reminder to the believer of the sufficiency, love, and grace found in Jesus Christ. In other words, the blood was necessary not only to remove the penalty of sin but to remove the power and presence of sin. Whereas Islam does not adequately explain how people will be guarded from sin even while in heaven, the Bible makes it clear that the blood is an eternal answer.

Is God's mercy contingent upon my changing?

Though both Christians and Muslims speak about the mercy of God, their understandings are diametrically opposed. It is sometimes said that Muslims, like Christians, believe that they can gain the mercy of Allah if they turn to Allah and ask forgiveness (surah 5:74). But Allah only grants mercy conditionally on the basis of future works (surah 6:54). Indeed, Allah's retribution is equal to his promise of mercy (surah 7:167; 13:6). Therefore, mercy is not only contingent in Islam; it is also continual, not because of Allah's love but because of Allah's wrath. The major theological assumption in Islam is that man has the ability to change himself. Although Allah is said to guide the Muslim (surah

6:88; 92:12), the Qur'an does not stipulate that Allah changes the Muslim. Instead, "Allah is swift in taking account" of actions that are either beneficial and merciful or sinful and selfish (surah 24:39).

Alternatively, Christ did not promise mercy on those who *change* but on those who *believe* (John 10:38). Subsequent change is the natural result of God imputing His righteousness upon the believer (Romans 4:6–8) and renewing the image of Himself in the individual that had been marred by sin (2 Corinthians 5:17). This is an ongoing process that is called "sanctification," but salvation of the individual is considered complete and sufficient at the moment God gives it (Romans 8:28–30). The person is free to choose whom to follow, yet one who has been truly changed by God ultimately will choose to freely follow the Lord Jesus Christ. Those who are truly made new may fall into sin and suffer its consequences (Hebrews 6:4–6), but they will be led back to Christ by the Spirit of God who indwells them.

Therefore, mercy is never contingent on change. Belief is the only condition required for mercy to be applied (Psalm 51; Romans 10:13). In Islamic terms, Christian theology believes that mercy by its nature outweighs judgment (James 2:13). It is God's will to show mercy to people, not because they deserve it but because He desires it. God is not looking for people who have cleaned up their lives. None have. God accepts one who surrenders to the Lord and looks to Him to be the Author and Finisher of the faith, able to clean up the dirtiest of vessels (Isaiah 1:18).

Is grace an excuse to sin?

Muslims object that the theological doctrine of free grace will lead to a rampant lifestyle of sin. As proof, some point to the nation that is most identified with Christianity—the United States. This country is guilty of incessant immorality, which must at least be partially a result of this teaching. Muslims also can provide countless individual examples of Christians who say they are saved by grace and live like the devil. Further, if salvation is fully by grace, then an objection is raised that the Law is dead and has no authority over the Christian. Finally, salvation by grace alone leads to a lazy faith.

First, it is absolutely true that the United States and other countries once identified with Christianity are characterized by great immorality. But that moral crisis has not come because North Americans are following Christian teaching but rather because most have rejected the gospel of salvation by grace alone. The United States has lost its moral compass because it does not want to follow principles found in God's Word. The U.S. legislative system historically had at least a philosophical tie to Christianity, but many of the laws of an earlier era have been reversed or removed. Further, even if it were possible to judge a nation by its laws, one must truly judge a nation by its people. The government can force conformity, but it cannot force humility and godliness.

To get an accurate picture of God in Western culture, Muslims must learn that a political system can be separate from religious values. The West does not link religion and politics as inseparably as they are welded within the Islamic community. Ironically, many Muslims readily admit that Muslim cultures can seem moral and pure on the outside but be just as decadent as the West within.

Second, impurity among those identifying themselves as Christians has caused many Muslims to reject the Christian moral compass. They must realize that millions of so-called Christians are living a fraudulent faith. These pseudobelievers have infiltrated the churches and become leaders who now preach a false gospel. False teachers customarily excuse their own depraved behavior by saying that God is love. The nineteenth-century English church leader Charles Haddon Spurgeon once remarked,

> Surely, no intelligent being can really persuade itself that the goodness of God is a reason for offending him more than ever. Moral insanity produces strange reasoning, but it is my solemn conviction that very rarely do men practically consider the grace of God to be a motive for sin. That which seems so probable at the first blush, is not so when we come to consider it.[6]

It should be noted that Christianity is not the only religion with false followers. The percentage of nominal Muslims is also high. In fact, one must look to faithful Muslims or to faithful Christians for an accurate portrait of the respective faiths. Hypocrites are counterfeits. Grace doesn't allow greater sin but leads to the gradual abolishment of sinful patterns. Thus, the grace that saves gives the person power to overcome sin. Sin no longer has the same enticement and fulfillment it had when the person was living under natural law. The Christian is better able to discern what is right and wrong through the indwelling work of the Spirit of God. As the apostle Paul wrote to the Roman believers, "Shall we continue in sin that grace may abound? Certainly not! How shall we who died to sin live any longer in it?" (Romans 6:1b-2).

This makes absurd the notion that Christians are no longer interested in living righteously. Someone who is saved has higher standards of thought and conduct. The difference is that it is no longer the law that points out sin and failure but a new, perfect standard that is rooted in Jesus Christ. In any case, the assumption that keeping the law will save anyone is groundless. The law was given not as a Savior but as a tutor. Its job is to declare guilt and drive a person to the mercy of Christ (Galatians 3:19-25). Muslims will never find a perfect standard for life in their rules. The standard for life can only be found in the One who is the life (John 14:6).

Finally, the Christian walk is anything but lazy. Christians follow a standard that is higher than even that observed by the Muslim. A brief comparison of the five pillars of Islam with the counterpart standards of Christianity illustrate the point:

1. In Islam, confession is to be said continually. In Christianity the focus of regular confession is on Christ (Matthew 10:32). Sins are to be confessed regularly, not as a recitation but in conversation in prayer (1 John 1:9).
2. Muslims pray a ritual prayer five times a day. Christian prayer is to be a continual thought pattern (1 Thessalonians 5:17).
3. In Islam, 2.5 percent of one's substance is to be given to the

poor and needy. Christians are to give at least 10 percent (Malachi 3:8-12; 2 Corinthians 8-9).
4. Muslims are to fast during the month of Ramadan. Christians are commanded to fast in connection with prayer, yet their fasts are not limited to food (Matthew 6:16-18; 1 Corinthians 7:5).
5. Muslims are to make pilgrimage to Mecca. Christians are to take the message of Christ to all the world (Matthew 28:18-20).

It is transparent that grace does not lead to laziness but faithfulness. For this reason, Jesus demanded that His disciples count the cost of discipleship, for it may cost a religious person much, but it costs a Christian everything (Luke 14:25-33).

Will the Jew automatically go to heaven?

One reason for the tension between Islam and evangelical Christianity is that Christians, more than any other group in the world, express support for the nation of Israel. This support should not extend uncritically to every action of the secular government that is now in power in the nation. But generally Christians do believe that God has made an unconditional covenant with the Jews and that the reemergence of a Jewish state in Israel is part of God's plan (Genesis 12:1-3). Some Muslims have questioned whether the seemingly unconditional support for Israel extends to the belief that Jews automatically go to heaven as members of God's chosen race.

Nothing could be farther from the truth. The apostle Paul, an Israelite himself, explained, "I could wish that I myself were cursed and cut off from Christ for the sake of my brothers, those of my own race, the people of Israel. Theirs is the adoption as sons; theirs the divine glory, the covenants, the receiving of the law, the temple worship and the promises" (Romans 9:3-4 NIV). The gospel came through Israel and was first entrusted to the Jewish community, yet the religious leaders as a whole rejected God's special blessings. God gave them His presence in the tabernacle (Exodus 24:16-17), His instruction and call to repentance through the prophets. He prophesied and then fulfilled His promises, but only a minority ever heeded His words.

Israel was judged by God through captivity and oppression. Many of the blessings given first to the Jews are now enjoyed by Christians because the Jewish people refused them. Followers of Christ are adopted by God (Ephesians 1:5), they are part of the new covenant community (Hebrews 9–10), and they have Abraham as a spiritual father (Galatians 3:7). Hence, many Christians have a burden for Jews through these similarities. Moreover, the Bible says that Israel's rejection of the Messiah is not irrevocable (Romans 10). Ultimately, God will bring many of His chosen people back to Himself. Together, many Jews and Christians will celebrate the glory of the Lord in Jesus Christ in the Last Days.

But today, most Jews still reject the Messiah. This does not negate their position in God's program since that is not determined by their goodness but by God's faithfulness. His Word never changes, and His promises are never discarded. However, the only Jews who will be in heaven are those who look to the Christ, the Son of the Living God. In God's plan, there will be many from His chosen people who do so. They will not only be Israel "according to the flesh" but spiritual Israel, "children of God" (Romans 9:8).

How can anyone have eternal security?

When it comes to being sure of one's salvation, insecurity is a virtue in the mind of the Muslim. To be certain of one's eternal abode does not demonstrate confidence but conceit. In fact, Muslim scholars teach that uncertainty leads to obedience, which improves one's chance of reaching Paradise. The overconfident believer in Allah will be lackadaisical in faith and probably lose heaven. Fatalism, the belief that one's eternal destiny is determined solely by the arbitrary will of Allah, also feeds this anxiety. As noted above (see p. 125), Muhammed admitted his own insecurity (Hadith 5.266) and taught his followers to model his example (surah 33:21). In Muslim thought, hell is always much nearer than Paradise. Muhammed believed that in physical illness "fever is from the heat of hell" (Hadith 7.619). Numerous passages in the Qur'an specify the many people whom Allah does not love (surahs 2:190; 2:276; 3:57; 4:360). Every faithful Muslim lives in fear and trepidation, not in faith and tranquility.

However, it is God's will that everyone who desires eternal security can take hold of it with confidence. The apostle John rests in this promise, stating, "These things I have written to you who believe in the name of the Son of God, that you may know that you have eternal life" (1 John 5:13a). Each person within the Godhead takes part in the assurance of the believer. The Father has chosen the believer before the foundation of the world to be His child (Ephesians 1:4). The Son has shed His blood and made all believers "accepted in the Beloved" (verse 6). The Holy Spirit "is the guarantee of our inheritance" (verse 14).

Thus, eternal security is based on God's authority and not on human ability. It is He, the giver of grace, who deserves the glory. To do otherwise would be an insult to God. To be humble in one's own character is a virtue, recognizing human frailty and limitation. To be anxious of God's character is a vice, questioning His reputation and making His honor suspect.

When eternity is settled, faith is freed to be what it is intended to be. The confident believer has full trust in the Lord Jesus Christ to accomplish anything He so desires (Philippians 4:13). Whatever disaster occurs, a believer can remain firm (2 Timothy 1:7). Prayer can be bold (Hebrews 4:16). The Christian walk can be courageous (Philippians 1:14). In the end, confidence in God leads not only to salvation, based on the finished work of Christ, but to glorification, based on the imminent Second Coming of Jesus Christ, who will complete that which He started in every believer (1 Thessalonians 4:13–18).

Isn't fatalism accepted in Islam?

Fatalism, the belief that every event in history is determined arbitrarily by God, is a premise of the faith held by millions of Muslims, though not all. Though some Christians believe that God has determined who will be saved, fatalism assumes that *every* event in time is capricious, so that people are just swept along without hope. In popular terms, this is the usual meaning of the Muslim phrase *Ensh'allah,* translated "if God wills." Muslims draw their rather hopeless acceptance from several passages in the Qur'an, including:

> But Allah does call to the Home of Peace: He does guide whom He pleases to a Way that is straight. (surah 10:25)

> So Allah leads astray those whom He pleases and guides whom He pleases and He is Exalted in power, full of Wisdom. (surah 14:4)

These sentiments were expanded by early Muslim scholars such Ibn Hazn, who asserted, "Nothing is good but Allah has made it so, and nothing is evil, but by His doing."[7] With acceptance of such an interpretation, fatalism has played an integral part in Islamic theology from its formative years.

Fatalism leads to three consequences:

First, humans are given no hope in this life since every single action has been predetermined by the will of a transcendent and impersonal Allah.

Second, hopelessness extends to a low anticipation of salvation, since Allah leads astray whom he chooses. Most people will be damned eternally, and they truly have no choice on this side of hell. Therefore, people are apt to resign themselves to a state of self-defeat. Or, people remove themselves from all personal responsibility of sin, a state of victimization. Ultimately, fatalism leads to anarchy or legalism, while negating any freedom an individual may have.

Third, the heaviest cost of fatalism is that it makes God to be the direct cause of evil. As God is the author of evil, He cannot be defined as absolutely good. Further, if God is the cause of evil and God is eternal, then evil itself has resolution. In the end, God becomes an impersonal force instead of an intimate Father. Sadly, fatalism leads to a god who does not even care enough to save some children. As the Hadith reports, "Aisha, the mother of the believers, reported that a child died and I said: There is happiness for this child who is a bird from amongst the birds of Paradise. Thereupon Allah's Messenger (may peace be upon him) said: Don't you know that Allah created the Paradise and He created the Hell and He created the dwellers for this (Paradise) and the denizens for this (Hell)?"[8]

Notes

1. Macksood Aftab, "Missionary Traps for Muslims," *Islamic Herald* (April 1996).
2. See Muhammed Abul Quasem, *Salvation of the Soul and Islamic Devotions* (London: Kegan Paul International, 1983).
3. Abdullah Yusuf ʿAli, *The Meaning of the Holy Qurʾan* (Brentwood, Md.: Amana, 1992), 831.
4. Walter A. Elwell, ed., *Evangelical Dictionary of Theology* (Grand Rapids: Baker, 1984), 97.
5. Ibid.
6. Charles Haddon Spurgeon, "The Doctrines of Grace Do Not Lead to Sin," http://www.spurgeon.org/sermons/1735.htm (Dec. 16, 2002).
7. Ergun Mehmet Caner and Emir Fethi Caner, *Unveiling Islam* (Grand Rapids: Kregel, 2002), 242.
8. Sahih Muslim, 33.6435.

7

QUESTIONS CONCERNING ESCHATOLOGY (END TIMES)

Eschatology IS A THEOLOGY OF END times or last things. Since about 1840, Western Christians have frequently been intensely interested in the prophecies of Scripture. In recent years, books and novels on the topic are often perpetual best-sellers. Movies with themes about the end of the world, even produced from a secular perspective, post great attendance. Seminars on eschatology and prophecy are well attended, and workbooks, study guides, and charts are in constant demand in certain Christian traditions.

Those looking at the Christian world from outside are naturally bemused by all of this interest, which has developed a language all its own. Some Christian pastors regularly preach sermons on the last days, and their hearers are fed a steady diet of such theological terms as premillenialism, postmillenialism, preterism, amillenialism, and prewrath rapture. None of this is wrong. As a matter of fact, it is greatly encouraging to two theology and church history professors who spend every spare minute writing books!

The interesting dimension, for the purposes of this discussion, is that it is easy, however, to become so inwardly focused that many people who are intimately aware of every minute prophecy in Obadiah are usually ignorant of the eschatological beliefs of Islam. Islamic eschatology greatly affects aspects of Islamic ethics.

With that in mind, we summarize the Islamic views of end times, eternity, heaven, hell, angels, and judgment, with a comparison to Christian theology.

Is Jesus (Isa) the center of Islamic eschatology?

Jesus is not the center of Islamic eschatology, but He does play an integral role. The subsequent questions will delve into the Islamic view of Jesus' return, seen as a type of Elijah or harbinger for the judgment of Allah. One of the seminal texts referencing Jesus the prophet's return is surah 43:61:

> And (Jesus) shall be
> A Sign (for the coming of)
> the Hour (of Judgment):
> Therefore have no doubt
> About the (Hour), but
> Follow ye Me: this
> Is a Straight Way.[1]

In 'Ali's commentary on the Qur'an, one finds a clear statement of the Islamic view of the reason Jesus will return—to bring everyone to faith in Allah:

> This is understood to refer to the second coming of Jesus in the Last Days before the Resurrection, when he will destroy the false doctrines that pass under his name, and prepare the way for the universal acceptance of Islam, the Gospel of Unity and Peace, the Straight Way of the Qur'an.[2]

Certainly such an interpretation of Christ's return would surprise the New Testament writers, yet over one billion people on the planet passionately believe this version. Lest anyone think that this singular verse is an aberration or obsession for a select few Muslims, Abdulazziz Abdulhussein Sachedina has summarized the importance of this modified Jesus:

He will descend in the Holy Land at a place called Afiq with a spear in his hand; he will kill with it al-Dajjal (Antichrist) and go to Jerusalem at the time of the morning prayer. The Imam (Muslim cleric) will seek to yield his place to him, but Jesus will refuse and will worship behind him according to the Sharia of Muhammed. Thereafter he will kill the swine, break the crosses, and kill all the Christians who do not believe in him. Once al-Dajjal is killed, all the Peoples of the Book (i.e. Jews and Christians) will believe in him and will form one single umma of those who submit to the will of God. Jesus will establish the rule of justice and will remain for forty years, after which he will die. His funeral will take place in Medina, where he will be buried beside Muhammed, in a place between Abu Bakr and Umar.[3]

Where shall Jesus return?

In Christianity, Jesus shall return to the same place from which He ascended, according to Acts 1:9–11. In Islam, the return of Jesus Christ is described in oddly specific terms. Hadith Abu Dawud 37.4310 notes: "Jesus (peace be upon him). He will descend (to the earth). When you see him, recognize him: a man of medium height, reddish fair, wearing two light yellow garments."

Many believe that Jesus shall land on a minaret in Damascus, Syria: "Most Muslims believe that Jesus' descent from heaven will be accomplished by resting his hands on the wings of two angels. He will descend onto the white minaret, situated in the eastern part of Damascus. He will invite the whole world to be Muslim including Christians and Jews."[4]

This is in marked distinction to Christ's return to the Mount of Olives, as seen in Zechariah 14:4a NIV: "On that day his feet will stand on the Mount of Olives, east of Jerusalem."

Does Jesus actually kill the Antichrist (al-Dajjal) in Islamic teaching?

Whether Jesus will kill al-Dajjal is a matter of some discussion. The Shi'ites proclaim a teaching of the twelfth imam, Mohammed ibn al-Hanifiyah. In about 875, al-Hanifiyah disappeared. Shi'ites believe he never died but is waiting for the return of Jesus, so he can be the Mahdi ("rightly guided one"), who will kill the al-Dajjal. Ayatollah Khomeini was of this Ithna-ashariyya sect of Shi'ite Islam.

Other Muslims do believe Jesus will personally kill the Anti-christ in a battle on the plains. Sundquist cites Muslim's Hadith Dhikr Dajjal:

> Christ . . . will advance with the Muslims for fighting against Dajjal. The enemy will retreat before the powerful assault of Christ son of Mary, and Dajjal will run away towards Israel by way of the slope of Afiq (a mountain near the city of Fiq in Syria). Christ will pursue Dajjal and destroy him on the . . . field of Lydda. A great slaughter of the Jews will ensue and every one of them will be anni-hilated. The nation of Jews will be exterminated. At the proclamation of truth by Christ, the Christian religion will become extinct. Later the son of Mary will pursue Dajjal and will overtake him at the gate of Lydda and put him to death.[5]

If in fact the majority of Muslims do believe that Jesus will meet the twelfth imam, then an interesting issue develops. The Islamic Jesus actually begins to resemble one of the two witnesses who never died in Revelation 11:3, as neither He nor the twelfth imam ever taste of death. In the Qur'an, Jesus was neither crucified nor died:

> And because of their saying (in boast), "We killed Messiah 'Eesa (Jesus), son of Maryam (Mary), the Messenger of Allah,"—but they killed him not, nor crucified him, but it appeared so to them the resemblance of 'Eesa (Jesus) was put over another man (and they killed that man), and those who differ therein are full of doubts. They have no (cer-tain) knowledge, they follow nothing but conjecture. For

surely; they killed him not: But Allah raised him (Jesus) up (with his body and soul) unto Himself (and he is in the heavens). And Allah is Ever All Powerful, All Wise. (surah 4:157–58)

Obviously, if Christ was not crucified, then He shall not return pierced, as is prophesied in Zechariah 12:10 NIV ("They will look on me, the one they have pierced. . . ."). Thus, Jesus begins to resemble one such as Elijah or Enoch, neither of which died but was translated, according to the Bible.

Does the returning Jesus break all crosses and kill all swine?

According to the al-Muslim collection of *ahadith,* Jesus will break all crosses and kill all swine for two reasons. First, He will end the use of all religious icons, a practice forbidden in Islam, and He will end the use of all the unclean animals, of which pigs are considered emblematic. Muslims have long looked upon the Roman Catholic and Orthodox usage of icons as highly offensive and sinful. Many in the strictest Islamic sects will not even allow their picture taken, for fear of violating this teaching.

> When the Muslims will fall in lines to offer prayers, Christ son of Mary (PBUH ["Peace Be Upon Him"]) shall descend from heaven before their eyes. He will lead the prayers. When the prayers are over he will say to the people: "Clear the way between me and this enemy of God." God will give victory to the Muslims over the hosts of Dajjal. The Muslims will inflict dire punishment upon the enemy. Even the trees and stones will cry out, "O Abdullah, O Abdul Rahman, O Muslim, come, here is a Jew behind me, kill him." In this way God will cause the Jews to be annihilated and Muslims shall be the victors. They will break the Cross, slaughter the swine and abolish Jizya (tax upon unbelievers living in Islamic countries).[6]

Interestingly, Revelation, the last book of the New Testament and the focus of Christian eschatology, most commonly refers to Jesus as "the Lamb." In any case, the cross as a symbol of Christ's death for sin is just that, a symbol. It is not an idol that is worshiped or accorded mystical power by orthodox Christians. The idea that a cross has some magical power in itself is not a biblical concept but the result of pagan influences foreign to the Bible.

Does Jesus become a husband and father upon His return?

In the Hadith of Sahih Muslim, Jesus is said to, "live for forty years during which he will marry, have children, and perform Hajj (pilgrimage)."[7] The meaning of the forty years is unclear in Islamic theology, but many speculate a parallel to the Bible's use of the number, not the least of which was the forty-day temptation of Christ in Matthew 4:1–11.

This stands in stark contrast to Christ's return for His bride, the symbolic name of the church as the spiritual body of Christ in Scripture. "Let us rejoice and be glad and give him glory! For the wedding of the Lamb has come, and his bride has made herself ready" (Revelation 19:7 NIV). This term *bride* is purely metaphorical, a depiction of every believer in Jesus Christ throughout history. Though liberal commentators have speculated that there was something more than a friendship between Jesus and Lazarus's sisters, Mary and Martha, evangelicals are unanimous in asserting that Jesus never courted, married, or even thought of women in a romantic sense. The sovereign Lord of the universe would surely not have had sexual lust nor committed sexual sin as has been suggested by some who would remove all deity from the Lord.

Does the returned Jesus eventually die?

As Sachedina notes, Muslims believe that Christ lives for forty years and even makes a pilgrimage to Mecca. "He will perish all religions except Islam. He will destroy the Antichrist and will live on the earth for forty years and then he will die."[8]

The purpose is to equate Jesus with the rest of the prophets. The importance of this central tenet in Islam cannot be overstated. Christians give supremacy to Christ; so Muslims are zealous to stress His human piety as a humble follower of Allah. Upon Jesus' return, He takes a second place in the prayer time, behind the imam, to show His position. Muslims will often point to Jesus' baptism as a parallel narrative, but remember the words of John the Baptist as Christ approached:

> The next day John saw Jesus coming toward him, and said, "Behold! The Lamb of God who takes away the sin of the world! This is He of whom I said, 'After me comes a Man who is preferred before me, for He was before me.' I did not know Him; but that He should be revealed to Israel, therefore I came baptizing with water."
>
> And John bore witness, saying, "I saw the Spirit descending from heaven like a dove, and He remained upon Him. I did not know Him, but He who sent me to baptize with water said to me, 'Upon whom you see the Spirit descending and remaining on Him, this is He who baptizes with the Holy Spirit.' And I have seen and testified that this is the Son of God." (John 1:29–34)

In His prolonged life and livelihood, Jesus is portrayed as one worthy of honor as a prophet but certainly not as God the Son. Even Jesus' burial between Abu Bakr and Umar places Him in line and equality in Islamic history, rather than in an exalted position upon the throne of David.

Mark the Islamic view in contrast with Christ's own words as recorded in Revelation 1:18 (NIV): "I am the Living One; I was dead, and behold I am alive for ever and ever! And I hold the keys of death and Hades." Christ tasted death for mankind, but His conquest of death means that He is alive forevermore. As Paul writes in Hebrews 7:24 (NIV), "But because Jesus lives forever, he has a permanent priesthood."

Is Armageddon the ultimate jihad?

On occasion, Muslims will point to the Battle of Armageddon as a Christian equivalent of jihad, referring to such passages as Revelation 19:11-16:

> Now I saw heaven opened, and behold, a white horse. And He who sat on him was called Faithful and True, and in righteousness He judges and makes war. His eyes were like a flame of fire, and on His head were many crowns. He had a name written that no one knew except Himself. He was clothed with a robe dipped in blood, and His name is called The Word of God. And the armies in heaven, clothed in fine linen, white and clean, followed Him on white horses. Now out of His mouth goes a sharp sword, that with it He should strike the nations. And He Himself will rule them with a rod of iron. He Himself treads the winepress of the fierceness and wrath of Almighty God. And He has on His robe and on His thigh a name written: KING OF KINGS AND LORD OF LORDS.

Beneath the superficial militaristic description lie some distinct differences, however. Jihad gives merit to the Muslim participant who is trying to reach heaven. At Armageddon, the believers who accompany Christ will have *already* inherited heaven. They are returning not to fight but to simply observe the fulfillment of prophecy. Only Christ is pictured as having a weapon. This final battle is not preparation for judgment but the beginning of final judgment.

Most significantly, the death of the unbelievers is not at the hands of the believers. God alone has the authority to take their lives. Scripture never records Christ's admonition to kill the infidel. Authority over all of life—including death—is found in the hands of God alone.

Does Islamic eschatology depend upon Muslim conquest of the world?

Islamic theologians divide over the goal of world conquest. Many repudiate world conquest as a goal of Islam, while others see the subjugation of all peoples as necessary to prepare for the judgment of Allah. One advocate of the necessity for domination and conquest was the Ayatollah Khomeini, a Shiʾite who came to power in Iran when the Shah was overthrown in 1979. Khomeini spoke with frightening frankness:

> Islam makes it incumbent on all adult males, provided they are not disabled and incapacitated, to prepare themselves for the conquest of countries so that the writ of Islam is obeyed in every country of the world. But those who study Islamic Holy War will understand why Islam wants to conquer the world. . . . Those who know nothing of Islam pretend that Islam counsels against war. Those (who say this) are witless. Islam says: Kill all the unbelievers just as they would kill you all! Does this mean that Muslims should sit back until they are devoured by (the unbelievers)! Islam says: Kill them (non-Muslims), put them to the sword and scatter (their armies). Does this mean sitting back until (non-Muslims) overcome us? Islam says: Kill in the service of Allah those who may want to kill you! Does this mean that we should surrender to the enemy? Islam says: Whatever good there is exists thanks to the sword and in the shadow of the sword! People cannot be made obedient except with the sword! The sword is the key to Paradise, which can be opened only for Holy warriors! . . . Does this mean that Islam is a religion that prevents men from waging war? *I spit upon those foolish souls who make such a claim.*[9]

To add to those who believe world conquest by Islam is inevitable, Mohamed Azad and Bibi Amina have written a terrifying book delineating their beliefs, entitled *Islam Will Conquer All Other Religions and American Power Will Diminish.*[10] The title tells the entire story. If in fact this conquest has eschatological import, then Muslims would be roughly parallel to postmillennialists in their belief that the works of devout men can bring about the end of the world.

Does the Qurʾan support the claims of Islamic world domination?

Does the Qurʾan support such claims of world domination in a geopolitical sense? Those who believe in world domination by Islam cite surah 61:9: "It is He who has sent His Messenger with Guidance and the religion of Truth, that he may proclaim it over all religion, even though the pagans may detest it."

This verse is so central to Islamic ethics that it is repeated thrice, first in surah 9:33, and modified in surah 48:28, which calls Allah to witness the truth. ʿAli adds a fascinating point that illuminates the position of many Muslims:

> There is really only one true Religion, the Message of Allah, submission to the Will of Allah: this is called Islam. It was the religion preached by Moses and Jesus; it was the religion of Abraham, Noah, and all the prophets, by whatever name it may be called. If people corrupt that pure light, and call their religions by different names, we must bear with them, and we may allow the names for convenience. But Truth must prevail over all.[11]

Christians and Jews would vehemently reject this assessment at every turn. Like the Church of Jesus Christ of Latter Day Saints (Mormons) and the Unification Church (Moonies) who followed them, Islam abrogated, adapted, and modified the orthodox faith of Abraham, Isaac, Jacob, and Joseph, and then proceeded to claim that they actually have the true message.

How will Jesus return, according to Islamic theology?

One of the clearest outlines of Islamic eschatology is by Mufti A. H. Elias, in his article "Jesus (Isa) A.S. in Islam, and His Second Coming." He provides thirty blessings attributed to the return of the prophet Jesus:

1. Isa will descend and stay on earth.
2. His descension will be in the last era of Ummat.

3. He will be a just ruler and a fair judge.
4. His ummat will be the Khalifa (deputies) of Rasullah (Muhammed).
5. He will act himself and instruct others on the Qur'an and Hadith.
6. He will lead people in Salaat (prayer).
7. He will stay on earth for a period of forty years after descending. They will be the best era of the Ummat after the first era of Islam.
8. Allah will protect his companions from Jahannam (one of the seven levels of hell).
9. Those who will save the Deen (religion) of Islam by associating themselves with (Jesus) will be amongst the most loved by Allah.
10. During this period all other religions and mazhabs besides Islam will perish, hence there will be no more kafirs (unbelievers) in the world.
11. Jihad will be stopped.
12. No Khiraaj (land tax) will be taken.
13. Nor Jizya (protection tax) money from the kafirs.
14. Wealth and property will be in surplus to such an extent that there will be no one to accept the wealth of others.
15. Receiving Zakaat (almsgiving) and Saadaqa (voluntary giving) will be discarded (as there will be no poor to receive them).
16. The people will love the sajda (kneeling before Allah) more than the world and what it consists of.
17. All types of Deen and worldly blessings will descend on earth (many halal [lawful] things will be created).
18. There will be peace, harmony, and tranquility during the time of . . . Isa's (A.S.) stay in the world.
19. There will be no animosity for a period of seven years, even between two persons.
20. All hearts will be free from miserliness, envy, hatred, malice, and jealousy.
21. For a period of forty years no one will fall ill or die.

22. Venom will be taken out of all venomous animals.
23. Snakes and scorpions will not harm anyone to the extent that if a child put his hand in its mouth, he will not be harmed.
24. Wild animals will not harm anyone.
25. If a man will pass a lion, he will not be troubled or harmed, or even if any girl will open its mouth to test if it will do anything.
26. The camels will graze among lions, cheetahs with cattle, and the jackals with goats.
27. The fertility of the land will increase to such an extent that even if a seed is planted in a hard rock, it will sprout.
28. A pomegranate will be so huge that a jamaat (nation) will be able to eat it and the people will use its peel as shade.
29. There will be so much barakaat (blessing) in milk that a camel will suffice for a huge jamaat, a cow for a tribe, and a goat for a family.
30. In short, life will be most pleasant after the descension of Jesus.

Christians will see parallels in this list to descriptions of life in the millennial kingdom, such as are found in Isaiah and Ezekiel.

Will not all bow before Christ?

Recently, a Muslim called into a radio program on which we were guests, and cited Philippians 2:9-11 as proof of the conquest of the infidels in Christianity: "Therefore God also has highly exalted Him and given Him the name which is above every name, that at the name of Jesus every knee should bow, of those in heaven, and of those on earth, and of those under the earth, and that every tongue should confess that Jesus Christ is Lord, to the glory of God the Father."

Does this text intimate the death of the infidel, and thus is analogous to jihad? True, the text is eschatological in purview, as it means that eventually, every living creature shall bow to Christ to recognize Him as Lord. However, we hasten to add that this shall occur at judgment, after the end of time itself, not in the present age. Neither does it suggest that the infidel is killed, even after judgment. Existence in hell is described as "everlasting" (Matthew 18:8). Philippians 2 is not referring to "forced" conversion but a universal response to the majesty and lordship of Jesus Christ at judgment.

Is heaven described in sensual terms in Islam?

Beyond being the eternal abode of Muslims who have been found on the Straight Way, the Qurʾanic and Hadithic descriptions of heaven seem unusual to those accustomed to the biblical depictions of eternal glory. Surah 56:12–38 gives a clear portrayal of heaven as a sensual abode:

> In the Garden of Bliss: They shall recline on jeweled couches face to face, and there shall wait on them immortal youths with bowls and ewers and a cup of the purest wine (that will neither pain their heads nor take away their reason); with fruits of their own choice and flesh of fowls that they relish. And theirs shall be the dark-eyed houris (virgins), chaste as hidden pearls: a guerdon for their deeds. . . . We created the houris and made them virgins, loving companions for those on the right hand.

ʿAli adds in his Qurʾanic commentary that the "youth and freshness with which the attendants will serve is a symbol of the true service such as we may expect in the spiritual world. That freshness will be perpetual and not subject to any moods, or chances, or changes."[12]

The Qurʾan is replete with references to these virgins, called *houris:*

> They will sit with bashful, dark-eyed virgins, as chaste as sheltered eggs of ostriches. (surah 37:40–48)

> In them will be bashful virgins neither man nor Jinn will have touched before. Then which of the favors of Allah will you deny? (surah 55:56–57)

As for the righteous, they shall surely triumph. Theirs shall
be gardens and vineyards, and high-bosomed virgins for
companions: a truly overflowing cup. (surah 78:31)

Much has been made of the martyrs' anticipation of vestal virgins that are purported to await them in heaven. The belief of
seventy-two virgins is based on hadith 4.2687:

The Prophet Muhammed was heard saying: 'The smallest reward for the people of paradise is an abode where there are
80,000 servants and 72 wives, over which stands a dome deco-
rated with pearls, aquamarine and ruby, as wide as the distance
from al-Jabiyyah (a Damascus suburb) to Sanaʾa (Yemen).'

Is the Devil of the Bible the same as Iblis in Islam?

In general terms, the description of the Islamic devil, called Iblis
or Shaytan, parallels the biblical description of Satan, with a few
distinctions. Muslim writers Azad and Amina write,

According to the Qurʾanic teaching, the being who became
Satan . . . had previously occupied a high station but fell
from divine grace by his act of disobedience in refusing to
honor Adam when he, along with other angels, was ordered
to do so. Since then, his work has been to beguile man into
error and sin. Satan is, therefore, the contemporary of man,
and Satan's own act of disobedience is construed by the
Qurʾan as the sin of pride. Satan's machinations will cease
only on the Last Day.[13]

While we find some similarities, the use of the term *contemporary* when describing Satan's relationship to humanity might bother
students of the Bible. Additionally, Satan's refusal to bow to Adam
is not found in the descriptions of his fall in Isaiah 14:12–15 and
Ezekiel 28:11–19, which traditionally have been seen as Lucifer's
fall from archangel status. Notice the object of Lucifer's derision in
Isaiah 14:12–15:

How you are fallen from heaven, O Lucifer, son of the
    morning!
How you are cut down to the ground, you who weakened
    the nations!
For you have said in your heart: "I will ascend into heaven,
    I will exalt my throne above the stars of God; I will also
    sit on the mount of the congregation on the farthest
    sides of the north; I will ascend above the heights of the
    clouds, I will be like the Most High."
Yet you shall be brought down to Sheol, to the lowest depths
    of the Pit.

His willful disobedience was in direct mockery of God's sovereign reign, not Adam's status. Five times, Lucifer speaks of his desire to stand in God's place, to *be* God. His fall, in the biblical record, was the ultimate idolatry—worship of self.

How is hell described in Islamic theology?

For one who does not achieve a good balance of the scales, a hell of interminable torture awaits. Infidels will be beaten with rods made of iron as they attempt to escape repeatedly, according to surah 22:21: "In addition, there will be maces of iron (to punish) them, Every time they wish to get away therefrom, from anguish, they will be forced back therein, and (it will be said), 'Taste ye the Penalty of Burning!'"

Secondly, the fire will scorch the infidel, as seen in surah 14:49-50: "And thou wilt see the sinners that day bound together in fetters, their garments of liquid pitch, and their faces covered with fire." ʿAli notes that the "pitch" mentioned is the Arabic *qatiran,* a resinlike substance that catches fire rapidly.[14] Additionally, this burning and scorching shall be everlasting and repeated, according to surah 74:27-29.

Surah 40:49 indicates that those consigned to hell will plead with the angels assigned to stand guard to intercede on their behalf, to no avail: "Those in the Fire will say to the Keepers of Hell, 'Pray to your Lord to lighten us the penalty for a day (at least)!'"

The plea is understandable, as the infidels shall also be choking on liquid bacteria. Surah 14:16 notes: "in front of such a one is Hell, and he is given for drink, boiling fetid water." The Qur'an teaches that hell is guarded by the al-Zabaniyya, nineteen angelic guardians, who "thrust violently" against those who attempt to find a hiding place. See surahs 74:30 and 96:18 for more information on these guardians.

In the midst of hell, Islam teaches there will be a Tree of Bitterness, called *al-Zaqqum*. This bitter smelling tree in the pit of hell will resemble demonic heads. The stomachs of sinners obliged to eat from this tree in hell will be badly burned.[15]

One can also see the similarities between the biblical hell and the Islamic hell. Pictures used in the Qur'an, such as boiling springs (surah 88:5), icy darkness (surah 38:57), and a pit (surah 101:9–10) are also found in the biblical record.

Are there levels to hell in Islamic theology?

The similarities between biblical and Islamic depictions of hell, however, end there. The Qur'an teaches that hell is actually compartmentalized in seven levels, which are specifically designed for varying groups of infidels. The seventieth surah of the Qur'an, al-Maarij, is translated "The Stairs." Netton expounds on the chapter:

> It means "The Ascents" or "The Stairs." The surah belongs to the Meccan period and has 44 verses. Its title reflects v. 3 where (Allah) is described as "The Lord of the Ascents" (Thi 'l-Maarij). The majesty of (Allah) is vividly and beautifully emphasized at the beginning of the surah with a reference to the angels ascending to (Allah) in a day whose measure is deemed to be "fifty thousand years." The terrors of the Day of Judgment are described. The wicked will go to Hell while the trustworthy and pious will be honored in Paradise.[16]

So then, what are the levels of hell? The common term *al-Nar* is the literal term for "hell" in Arabic but does not designate any variance between levels. Instead, Islamic tradition has built these levels around the varying Arabic terms used in the Qur'an.

One of the less severe levels is called *Jahannam*, which is the Arabic equivalent to the Greek term *Gehenna*. "The word has connotations in Arabic of 'depth' and is very commonly used in the Qur'an to designate Hell, appearing seventy-seven times. Tradition consigned unrepentant wicked Muslims to this layer of Hell to suffer for a while until their eventual transfer to Paradise."[17] In this one can readily see a parallel to the Roman Catholic doctrine of purgatory, which raises an entirely new set of questions that are not germane to this discussion.

Saqar is a level of hellfire reserved for Zoroastrians. This variant Middle Eastern religion came under special scrutiny by Islamic caliphs for their unwillingness to accept Allah and the Qur'an as the sole revelation and Being. The term, used only four times in the Qur'an, is roughly translated "scorched by the sun."

Sair is the level of hell prepared by Allah as a "blazing inferno," traditionally for the Sabaeans. Though three different groups have carried this title, most Muslims believe them to be a northern Syrian group who taught Neoplatonic thought and Gnosticism. The term is used sixteen times in the Qur'an.[18]

Al-Jahim is the level of hell that is consigned for idolaters. The term appears twenty-five times in the Qur'an.

The fifth lowest level of hell is called *Laza*, which literally means "blazing fire." Ian Richard Netton makes the point that "Laza is one of the seven ranks of Hell to which tradition later consigned the Christians. The word only occurs once in the Qur'an (in surah 70). Here, in v. 15, Laza is described as a great furnace which will burn off the sinner's scalp and swallow up the miser and those who turn their backs on the truth."[19] Surah 70:15–16 reads, "By no means! For it would be the Fire of Hell—plucking out (his being) right to the skull!"

The sixth lowest level of hell is called *al-Hutama*, which means "that which shatters, wrecks or smashes." Netton writes, "Al-Hutama is one of the seven ranks of Hell to which tradition later assigned the Jews."[20] It is described in surah 104:1–9:

Woe to every (kind of) scandalmonger and backbiter, who pileth up wealth and layeth it by thinking that his wealth would make him last forever! By no means! He will be sure to be thrown into that which breaks to pieces. And what will explain to thee that which breaks to pieces? (It is) the Fire of (the wrath of) Allah kindled (to a blaze), the which doth mount (right) to the hearts; It shall be made into a vault over them, in columns outstretched.

The lowest layer of hell is called *al-Hawiya,* which means "the Abyss" or the "chasm." Traditional Islamic interpretation considers this level to be bottomless, reserved for the worst hypocrites. It appears in surah 101:8-11: "But he whose balance (of good deeds) will be (found) light, will have his home in a (bottomless) Pit. And what will explain to thee what this is? (It is) a Fire blazing fiercely."

Is Islam the "whore of Babylon"?

Curious Christians view the onslaught of current events and wonder whether Islam is the evil religious system mentioned in the book of Revelation 17:1-6:

Then one of the seven angels who had the seven bowls came and talked with me, saying to me, "Come, I will show you the judgment of the great harlot who sits on many waters, with whom the kings of the earth committed fornication, and the inhabitants of the earth were make drunk with the wine of her fornication." So he carried me away in the Spirit into the wilderness. And I saw a woman sitting on a scarlet beast which was full of names of blasphemy, having seven heads and ten horns. The woman was arrayed in purple and scarlet, and adorned with gold and precious stones and pearls, having in her hand a golden cup full of abominations and the filthiness of her fornication.

And on her forehead a name was written:

MYSTERY,

BABYLON THE GREAT,

THE MOTHER OF HARLOTS AND OF

THE ABOMINATIONS OF THE EARTH.

I saw the woman, drunk with the blood of the saints and with the blood of the martyrs of Jesus. And when I saw her, I marveled with great amazement.

Is this Islam? Certainly the description of the widespread nature of the system ("many waters") and the bloody persecution they execute upon the martyrs would fit Islamic growth. However, as those who study prophecy attest, the religious system described in Revelation will be a unifying force of peace and love for all peoples. As Roman Catholicism before it, Islam has been accused of being more pervasive than it actually is. It is our opinion that this system of Revelation 17 cannot be just one system but an amalgamation of many systems. It will be an all-embracing buffet that threatens no one and unites every pagan into one soup of "religion."

Is the Christian-Islam conflict a harbinger of the coming of Christ?

Those who believe Islam might be the religious system mentioned in Revelation 17 tend to add that the current chaos is setting up history for the coming of our Lord. Does Scripture bear this out?

Our answer to this question is shaped by our view of how the end times will occur. Christians disagree over what the Bible teaches about the end times, and the authors both accept the position called "premillenial pretribulationalism." Basically, we look for Christ to call the Church home in a sudden rapture before the start of the Tribulation period described in Revelation 6–19. We believe that every prophetic preparation that is to precede the coming of Christ in the clouds has been fulfilled, and He can come at any moment. In sequence, it is our view that the Rapture comes before the Tribulation, followed by the Second Coming, which inaugurates the millennial kingdom and finally the eternal government of God. We recognize that others see another pattern and sequence, and it is beyond the scope of this study to compare the various views or defend ours.

Given that caveat, we do not believe Islam has a central role in this conflict any more than does any other world movement. Each generation of Christians has looked at some world conflict in fear or hope that they were seeing the final crisis unfold. Christ can return at any moment. We do believe that Christ's return is imminent, but we also believe that panic is not the emotion of choice for a believer. We live, pray, and witness as if Christ will return today, but we plan as if Christ will not return for fifty years. This allows a balanced perspective.

Does God rejoice in sending people to hell?

In *Unveiling Islam*,[21] we outlined the stoic nature of Allah as described in the Qur'an. Allah is thought to choose those he wishes to take into heaven, and those he wishes to damn, and his divine pleasure is the sole purpose. One question that came during a television interview turned that idea back upon us as Christians: "Well, doesn't your God of the Bible rejoice when a soul goes to hell? Doesn't an individual consigned to hell somehow give your God some kind of glory and divine pleasure?"

With every fiber of our beings, we repudiate such an idea. One needs only to survey the Bible to see the reason Christ became a man was "to seek and to save that which was lost" (Luke 19:10). In one particular instance, the Pharisees confronted Jesus about His habit of spending time with those considered "unclean" and "impure." Christ emphatically stated, "Those who are well have no need of a physician, but those who are sick. But go and learn what this means: 'I desire mercy and not sacrifice.' For I did not come to call the righteous, but sinners, to repentance" (Matthew 9:12b-13).

The offer of salvation, cleansing, and liberation in Christ is the central message of the gospel. In fact, Peter indicates the heart of God in 2 Peter 3:9: "The Lord is not slack concerning His promise, as some count slackness, but is longsuffering toward us, not willing that any should perish but that all should come to repentance."

Hell is not the choice of God but the choice of rebels against God. Jesus taught that the creation of hell was not for the eternal punishment of human beings but a place of separation from God for Satan and his followers (Matthew 25:41). God does not rejoice when a soul enters hell; neither does He will it. Indeed, the offer of the Father is clear: "Come to Me, all you who labor and are heavy laden, and I will give you rest. Take My yoke upon you and learn from Me, for I am gentle and lowly in heart, and you will find rest for your souls. For My yoke is easy and My burden is light" (Matthew 11:28–30).

Notes

1. Abdullah Yusuf ʿAli, *The Meaning of the Holy Qurʾan* (Brentwood, Md.: Amana, 1992), 1276. All spelling, capitalization, and spacing is in the original text of ʿAli.

2. Ibid., n. 4662.

3. Abdulazziz Abdulhussein Sachedina, *Islamic Messanism* (Albany, N.Y.: SUNY Press, 1981).

4. A. A. Mawdudi, *Finality of Prophethood* (n.p.), 58–61; Sahih al-Bukhari Hadith, 18.814. The authors are deeply indebted to James Sundquist in this section of questions, for his diligent and thorough research. See James Sundquist, *Muslim Jesus Versus Biblical Jesus: Twenty Two Scriptural Reasons Why They Are Not the Same Jesus* (Rock Salt Publishing, 2002).

5. Sundquist, *Muslim Jesus Versus Biblical Jesus.*

6. Ibid. Sundquist adds that Hafiz Ibn Hajar, Fath-ul-Bari (6.450) declares this tradition to be authentic.

7. Sahih Muslim, vol. 1, p. 92.

8. Sunan Abu Dawud, 37.4310.

9. Ibn Warraq, *Why I Am Not a Muslim* (Amherst, N.Y.: Prometheus, 1995), 11–12.

10. Mohamed Azad and Bibi Amina, *Islam Will Conquer All Other Religions and American Power Will Diminish* (Brooklyn: Bell Six, 2001).

11. ʿAli, *The Meaning of the Holy Qurʾan*, n. 5442.

12. Ibid., n. 5231.

13. Azad and Amina, *Islam Will Conquer*, 15.

14. Ibid, 1928.

15. Ian Richard Netton, *A Popular Dictionary of Islam* (Chicago: NTC, 1992), n. 264.

16. Ibid., 154–55.

17. Ibid., 133.

18. Ibid., 221.

19. Ibid., 152.

20. Ibid., 108–9.

21. Ergun Mehmet Caner and Emir Fethi Caner, *Unveiling Islam* (Grand Rapids: Kregel, 2002).

8

QUESTIONS CONCERNING
ETHICS AND POLITICS

AN ETHICAL SYSTEM GOVERNS HOW religious or moral beliefs are applied in everyday circumstances. For example, the Western Christian at this time struggles with applying teachings of the Bible in the context of euthanasia, abortion, the death penalty, social justice, racial relations, poverty, and biomedical advances. In Islam, ethical positions can be deduced from Qur'anic admonitions, but Muslim ethics primarily is prescribed for virtually every scenario directly from the Qur'an and Hadith. As one ethicist has noted,

> Most people in the West believe that Islam is a religion in the traditional sense of the word. However, this is a fateful misconception. Islam is not just a religion. It is much more than a religion. Muslims themselves describe their faith by saying, "Islam is a Complete Way of Life." This is certainly a more apt description, because Islam is a religious, social, economic, educational, health, political, and philosophical way of life. In fact, Islam is an all-embracing socio-politico-religious utopian ideology that encompasses every field of human endeavor.[1]

With that in mind, we endeavor to engage both questions concerning Islamic issues, and questions posed by Muslims within the ethical arena. Our desire is that these answers may serve to enable Muslims and Christians to enter dialogue with more than cliches and "bumper-sticker" answers.

Is there such a thing as "cultural Christianity"?

In the pluralistic context of the West especially, there does seem to be a Christian identification that is more cultural than real. In virtually every statistical report of religious affiliation in the United States, Christianity—and specifically protestant Christianity—seems to be the identification of choice. The Pew Research Council's affiliation survey in 2002 recorded that 82 percent of U.S. respondents considered themselves Protestants.[2] The National Survey of Religious Identification (NSRI) survey in 2001 identified 159 million Americans as "Christian."[3] This is over 76 percent of the U.S. population. More specifically, the Harris poll of April 2000 found 49.5 percent of registered voters polled considered themselves to be Protestants.[4]

This is a tragedy of epic proportions. Let us assume that the mean average of the various polls is true, and half of the U.S. population considers itself Christian. Does that mean that all of them are actually believers in Jesus Christ? Of course not, but for the sake of our discussion, let us assume they are. That many born again believers in a culture would stimulate an amazing revival to rival any movement of God in history. Yet the American landscape seems farther from God than ever before. Why is that the case? Cultural Christianity is counterfeit religion.

Many Muslims form an opinion of Christianity after meeting people who call themselves believers, and may adhere to some intellectual construct of the claims of Christ, but who have never repented of their sin and turned to Jesus Christ as Lord. They may be part of some church organization, but they are not members of the Body of Christ. They are unbroken, unburdened, and unconverted. They resemble the people who joined churches during the American colonial period under the "Half-Way Covenant," when one could become a member of a church due to infant baptism but were not in fact believers in any sense of the word. The tragic effect is that our churches have become filled with unconverted members, who often rise to leadership without a "heart knowledge" of our Lord. This is "cultural Christianity," and it is a fraud.

How have these people found their way into our churches? Why are they allowed to give other religions and skeptics such ammunition against the gospel witness? Among the reasons:

Some are *cultural Christians,* only interested in the things of God as long as it is popular. As long as students restrict their witness to wearing "WWJD" ("What Would Jesus Do") bracelets and praying at flagpoles in high schools on one day a year, they will take part. They buy Christian books that are on the best-seller lists. They want a popular Christianity that heeds trends and takes its place as a cultural phenomenon. This is a counterfeit.

Some are *convenient Christians,* committed to God as long as it fits onto their "palm pilot" schedule around their golf games and quick trips to the coast. They acquiesce to attending church or even occasionally participating in worship. The living sovereign God of the universe must squeeze Himself into their hectic schedules. This is a counterfeit.

Some are *comfortable Christians,* only willing to be part of the community as long as the requirements and expectations do not interfere with their routines or comfort. These people affiliate with felt-need ministries who calm their nerves, tickle their ears, hold their hands, and ease their consciences. Any minister or ministry that challenges them to rise above their lethargy is seen as a threat. They immediately discount any call to sacrifice as unnecessary or superfluous. This is a counterfeit.

Some are *corrupted Christians,* only willing to accept the title of "Christian" as long as it fits within their preconceived notions. These are those who believe that "every religion is right as long as it is sincere." They deny Christ's claim to unique lordship. They want a Jesus of the "buffet line," where He can be sampled alongside other the varieties of religious experience, all of which must be tasted. Again, this is a counterfeit.

This looks pathetic to Muslims who never dare vary from the Qur'anic and Hadithic admonitions because they fear the balance scale. They obsessively follow teachings that dictate how to eat, dress, speak, pray, and live. Then they come to the United Kingdom, Canada, or the United States and see what passes for Christian sanctification. At best it is carnal and at worst an abomination to the call of our Lord. The gospel witness is continually embarrassed by those who call themselves Christians and then proceed to slander His name.

What then is the Christian witness to do when faced with the accusations of Muslims who see this horror? Do not argue and do not defend. Like Daniel, all you can do is follow the Lord with open windows and pray for revival in the land. You must not act as if the Muslims are mistaken, because they are not. What they see is tragically true. They have been exposed to a counterfeit form of Christian ethics, without godliness. To say otherwise insults the Muslim's intelligence and compounds the sacrilege to our Lord.

Instead, point the direction of their gaze to the perfect example of Christian life—our Lord. The Bible is a book written by God that is full of fallible men and faulty acts. Peter denied our Lord. Abraham lied. David murdered. Yet God chose to include these historical events because the essence of Christianity is not Christians but Christ. Everything we believe and everything for which we live is hinged on Him.

Is there such a thing as "cultural Islam"?

Strangely, a recent phenomenon has infiltrated the Islamic world—secular Muslims. The oxymoronic nature of this issue has been seen in recent days. Muslim leaders in the United States estimate that between 6.5 million to 8 million Muslims live in the United States.[5] Yet a study from the ARIS research group in 2001 counted only 1.1 million to 2 million practicing Muslims.[6] An uproar ensued when the Religious Congregations and Membership study was published by the Glenmary Research Center in September 2002.[7] The study estimated that Muslims in America were numbered 1.56 million, a fourth of the number counted by Muslims. The City

University of New York's Graduate Center estimated 1.8 million Muslims, counting children, and the American Jewish Committee reported 2.8 million U.S. Muslims.[8]

The Glenmary numbers actually came from approximately one-third of the 1209 mosques in America, who submitted their active attendees, along with migration statistics and population growth.[9] Since the numbers came from mosques themselves, counting adherents, how does one reconcile these numbers?

One possible explanation could be a striking new development in Islamic history—the advent of a cultural Islam. In virtually every other country with a vast number of Muslims, adherence to Islamic teachings, and specifically to the mosques, was unquestioned. Yet in North America, a new movement has developed among second- and third-generation citizens who still identify with their Muslim family heritage but in practice are nominal at best. Within this "cultural Islam" circle, there is a swelling number of Muslims for Eid al-Fitr, the celebration that breaks the fast of Ramadan, but diminishing attendance at regular Friday prayer times.

The impact of such a seismic shift in adherence cannot be overstated. Reflecting on the numbers, some commentators have chosen to believe that the number of Muslims has been overstated by Islamic propaganda. In fact, the answer may be that both sets of numbers are correct. The population of actual Muslims in the United States may in fact be 8 million, but the actual practicing, mosque-attending population may be closer to 2 million. If this is true, then three out of four Muslims are nominal practitioners at best.

What exactly would a "nominal Muslim" look like? A cultural Muslim would, more than likely, keep Islamic dietary restrictions *(halal)* and perhaps pray five times a day in the privacy of home and read the Qur'an occasionally. The circle of friends would remain predominantly Muslim.

However, this cultural or nominal Muslim works in a pluralistic society and has non-Muslim friends. This person tends to be educated, speaks English fluently, and is knowledgeable of world politics. The encouraging factor, however, is openness. Nominal Muslims feel less threatened by a comparison of ideas and philosophies. They fiercely defend their beliefs when put on the defensive, but they are thoughtful when approached with reason and dialogue.

The cultural Muslim sporadically attends the mosque, usually during the holy days such as Ramadan. Yet such people are well aware that they are a minority in their adopted land, and their exposure to Christians may have changed their preconceived notions. Such a Muslim wants to know what you believe in and whether your beliefs are genuine.

Can't one be both a Muslim and a Christian?

Is it possible to adhere to the absolutes of Islam and Christianity simultaneously? This is the question of *syncretism*. Usually it is asked by well-meaning Christians. The answer is no. Both systems hold to absolute claims of truth, and the Aristotelian law of noncontradiction asserts that one cannot believe in two contradictory truth statements at the same time and in the same way.

Christianity and Islam do stand in abject distinction from one another. Though both religions clearly honor Jesus, their claims concerning Jesus are clearly incompatible with one another. While some mainline denominations have spent a century attempting to redefine Jesus as a wise teacher whose life is open to interpretation, the Bible makes clear that such a Christ does not belong to historical Christianity. In John 14:6, Jesus Himself said: "I am the way, the truth, and the life. No one comes to the Father except through Me." First Timothy 2:5 notes, "For there is one God and one mediator between God and men, the man Christ Jesus."

Islam is clear in its teachings that it is both the culmination of religion and the reconstruction of true faith. In this teaching, it is clear that Jesus, though a prophet sent by Allah, is neither the son of God nor the second person of the Trinity (surah 5:75). Jesus did not die (surah 4:157-58), much less offer atonement for sin.

This redaction of the biblical record is seen in the example of Abraham. Though the Bible calls Abraham the father of the Jewish nation, the Qur'an states he was a Muslim. Christians and Jews are condemned for ignoring this fact:

No, Abraham was neither a Jew nor a Nazarene. He was of pure faith, a submitter (Muslim). He was never of the idolaters. Surely, the people who are nearest to Abraham are those who followed him, and this Prophet (Muhammed), and those who believe.

Allah is the Guardian of the believers. Some of the People of the Book wish to make you go astray, but they lead none astray except themselves, though they do not sense it. People of the Book! Why do you disbelieve the verses of Allah while you are witness? People of the Book! Why do you confound truth with falsehood, and knowingly hide the truth? (surah 3:67–71)[10]

Neither Islam nor Christianity is syncretistic, and neither accepts a "partway conversion."

Quite often this question is asked by those who are actually witnessing to Muslims. Exactly how much of their lives must a former Muslim reject? This is a different question, and it needs some explanation. Those who come from Islam are often shocked by the complete rejection they receive when they become believers. For the former Muslim, conversion to Christ often means the loss of family, friends, home, job, and sometimes their life.

In addition, virtually every venue of life is dictated by the protocols of Islamic teaching, and now that they are liberated by grace, they feel some sense of loss of identity. They need to be assured that it is perfectly acceptable to maintain a cultural heritage. A former Muslim still has a heritage in Middle Eastern history, culture, foods, and languages. These have shaped the individual, just as they have contributed to shaping the world.

The point of contention comes when one's heritage demands a practice that is completely Islamic in nature, such as the fasting during Ramadan. One can turn to Paul's teachings concerning the eating of meat sacrificed to idols in 1 Corinthians 10:23–33. In the text, Paul discusses whether a believer could eat meat sold in the marketplace *(agora)* that had been sacrificed to pagan gods.

The quandary: If I eat it, will I be guilty of worshiping the idol? Paul's answer is to be gracious, especially to the unbeliever who extends an invitation to dinner (verses 25, 27). The believer who eats is not participating in the rituals and is not embarrassing the host by turning down their meal. This is extending grace in the midst of witness for Christ (verse 33).

Therefore, how can a new believer from such a background eat foods that have been slaughtered according to the Islamic methods, or keep the prayer rugs, or listen to his countrymen's music? Tangentially, how does the missionary serving in an Islamic land react when offered such food or stimulus? The Lord tells us through Paul that we use such opportunities and such heritage to reach the Muslim, to build bridges into their lives, and to maintain our cultural identities. Are we intimating that a Christian should participate in the prayer time, going through the al-wudoo (cleansing) and steps in saying the rakats (prayers), but instead of reciting the first surah of the Qur'an, pray to Jesus? Of course not! But we are saying that one should be respectful to the Muslim who is doing so. The Christian should not flaunt disdain for the Muslims saying rakats by stepping over them, nor should the Christian eat openly during the daylight hours of Ramadan. This is how to maintain Paul's demeanor of grace in liberty.

We recommend that new Christians who have come out of Islam should maintain as much cultural heritage as possible, as long as the practices are not intended to hide one's true identity in Christ. Keeping cultural ties strong allows the Father to use a Christian's witness to reach his or her culture and even home country with the Good News of Christ.

Aren't all Christians hypocrites?

Muslims point to the failings of Christians and say, "All Christians are hypocrites." Is this a fair assessment? Perhaps. As fallen men and women, we are redeemed by Christ, but we still struggle with ongoing sin. This struggle is often seen by the unbelieving world and used as to discredit belief in Christ. Certainly countless people who profess to be Christians have embarrassed themselves and their testimonies through thoughtless acts.

Yet even this hypocrisy can be used to explain the gospel. We are saved and born again. The punishment and wrath for our sin was taken by Christ on the Cross, and the debt of our sin has been paid. Yet we still struggle with the presence of sin in our lives and our world. This is not a matter of our salvation but rather of our sanctification. We often encourage believers to be transparently honest with their Muslim friends. Admitting our shortcomings, but not reveling in them, encourages other people with shortcomings to look to Christ. We continuously claim 1 John 1:9, that "if we confess our sins, He is faithful and just to forgive us our sins and to cleanse us from all unrighteousness."

Theologically speaking, we are blameless before God because of our salvation. He is our Father, and we are His children. This relationship is secure. But our sinful acts and deeds affect our fellowship with our Father. We do not always walk as we should. Yet we must be quick to repent before God and ask the forgiveness of those who were watching. This authenticity before others often opens a door to sharing the grace of Christ. This hypocrisy is not a license for the believer to flaunt a sinful nature or to hide behind eternal security. Indeed, we are new creatures in Christ, and the direction of our lives should change when we are saved.

Is "conversion by the sword" justified?

Conversion by the sword is not only not justified; it is not conversion at all. Forced faith is a contradiction in terms. Sadly, both Christians and Muslims have sometimes demanded allegiance under threat of injury or death. During the medieval Crusades period, primarily the eleventh century through the thirteenth century, supposedly "Christian" warriors demanded that Muslims and Jews accept Christianity or die. Some said whatever was required to stay alive, but many more were tragically slaughtered. During the Inquisitions under Tomas de Torquemada (1388–1468), entire populations were tortured in order to force the recantation of some perceived heresy. The Anabaptist leader Balthasar Hubmaier (1480–1528) was tortured twice and recanted once.

Such acts never achieve their ends. The essence of faith stipulates that it is an act of personal will. To choose anything, a person must be given a choice. Even love is an act of volition. Enforcement of Islamic sharia law often amounts to forced adherence to Islam under intense pressure and even the threat of death or torture. This point must be made humbly, with the realization that both religions have been used as an excuse for abuse and injustice. This is true of the distant past and in more recent history.

Did Christ call His followers to die for Him?

Some Christians are called upon to die for their faith. Christ generally asks His disciples to do something far more dangerous. He called us to live for Him. References to "the sword" in the Gospels are often misunderstood to teach that Christ called Christians to give their lives in service to the Lord, not unlike the commitment of the jihadin. The fundamental difference is that the Christian sacrifice is not in violent armed conflict but in personal dedication:

> Now as He was going out on the road, one came running, knelt before Him, and asked Him, "Good Teacher, what shall I do that I may inherit eternal life?"
>
> So Jesus said to him, "Why do you call Me good? No one is good but One, that is, God. You know the commandments: 'Do not commit adultery,' 'Do not murder,' 'Do not steal,' 'Do not bear false witness,' 'Do not defraud,' 'Honor your father and your mother.'"
>
> And he answered and said to Him, "Teacher, all these things I have kept from my youth."
>
> Then Jesus, looking at him, loved him, and said to him, "One thing you lack: Go your way, sell whatever you have and give to the poor, and you will have treasure in heaven; and come, take up the cross, and follow Me."
>
> But he was sad at this word, and went away sorrowful, for he had great possessions. (Mark 10:17-22)

In this narrative, we read of one who was seeking to gain eternal life. Jesus, sensing his true god was his wealth, called him to surrender all, if he was truly willing to follow Jesus. The wealthy man was not and left unconverted.

Yet what can be made of Jesus' statement "take up thy cross"? Did Jesus mean that a true disciple must be ready to kill and be killed in His name? Did He call us to give up our lives in conflict? The answer is far more profound. Jesus called us to follow Him in the complete and total eradication of ourselves. We are called to crucify the flesh. Christ did not call us to kill our enemies; He called us to love them. This love negates any desire for vengeance or "holy war." The cross was in fact an instrument of death only to the one who was carrying it.

Christ calls us to be totally abandoned to His will. Thus, we are truly "crucified with Christ," but that "crucifixion" is different than was His. Our death is to self. The end of our personal ambition does not earn our salvation. Only the death of Christ purchased our salvation, that of the Lamb of God. This is why Paul was able to continue in Galatians 2:20-21: "I have been crucified with Christ; it is no longer I who live, but Christ lives in me; and the life which I now live in the flesh I live by faith in the Son of God, who loved me and gave Himself for me. I do not set aside the grace of God; for if righteousness comes through the law, then Christ died in vain."

If our death could attain any part of salvation, then Christ's sacrifice was useless. This call to die and live on in Christ is our response to our sinful compulsions. We are never called to kill others in the name of our Lord. This crucifixion is our personal desire to be completely given to Christ.

Occasionally in recent years, militants have attempted to kill in the "name of Christ." The bombing of abortion clinics and even the killing of abortion doctors has been perpetrated in our society by some who believe they are "called" to do so. The authors of this book are staunchly "pro-life," believing that life begins at the moment of conception. However, the murder of those who perform these horrific acts is as offensive as is the abortion. This ethic of pragmatism, that the "end justifying the means," is found nowhere in Scripture. Jesus taught us that there is a right thing to do, and a right way to do the right thing. Those individuals who carry out murders stand in direct disobedience to the Christ who called us to *love* our enemies. In fact, the capacity to love our enemies is a proof of our salvation: "You have heard that it was said, 'You shall love your neighbor and hate your enemy.' But I say to you, love your enemies, bless those who curse you, do good to those who hate you, and pray for those who spitefully use you and persecute you, that you may be sons of your Father in heaven" (Matthew 5:43–45a).

Isn't Christian evangelism actually proselytizing?

"We would not mind that you come into our Islamic countries, if you were not so intent on proselytizing our people. You act as if you want to feed and clothe our people, but instead, you only want our people to join your religion." On a university campus, a diplomat for an Islamic country was making the point in private conversation with the authors. His point was that Christians are inherently deceptive, since we offer to give aid but ultimately want to convert the people we are helping to our religion. Our acts of social service are tainted.

In another context, we heard of a missionary society that had, at one time, been a fervent soul winning agency. They changed policy, though, and were criticized for focusing on the social aspects of food, shelter, and medical aid to the exclusion of evangelism.

Caught against such indictments, what are evangelical Christians to do?

In its core mission, Christianity is driven by the commission gave to His disciples in Matthew 28:18–20: "All authority has been given to Me in heaven and on earth. Go therefore and make disciples of all the nations, baptizing them in the name of the Father and of the Son and of the Holy Spirit, teaching them to observe all things that I have commanded you; and lo, I am with you always, even to the end of the age."

The essence of the gospel life is profound. If the sole purpose for salvation was to get the individual into heaven, the best thing that could happen would be to die at the moment following salvation. Certainly at that precise moment, the believer would be both ready and willing to enter eternity. Yet one reason we do not die at the moment of salvation is that we are called to know Him and make Him known.

Does this mean that we are "proselytizing"? The common cultural definition of the term is, "to induce someone to convert to one's religion." Do we enter a country primarily for the purpose of enlisting its people to become a Baptist or a Pentecostal? No. We win them to Jesus Christ, not the Baptist faith, or any denominational title. Our hearts' desire is to see people saved. The only question that determines eternity is not which denominational affiliation or sectarian title one holds but whether you are a believer in the finished work of the atonement of Jesus Christ. We do not come to win them to our denomination; we come to win them to Christ.

Second, acts of justice and mercy such as feeding the hungry and clothing the poor are not just an important introduction to the gospel; they are essential to opening that door. Notice Christ's words about how He regards the importance of serving others:

> "For I was hungry and you gave Me food; I was thirsty and you gave Me drink; I was a stranger and you took Me in; I was naked and you clothed Me; I was sick and you visited Me; I was in prison and you came to Me." Then the righteous will answer Him, saying, "Lord, when did we see You hungry and feed You, or thirsty and give You drink? When did we see You a stranger and take You in, or naked and clothe You? Or when did we see You sick, or in prison, and come to You?" And the King will answer and say to them, "Assuredly, I say to you, inasmuch as you did it to one of the least of these My brethren, you did it to Me." (Matthew 25:35–40)

Yet we cannot mistake the acts of justice and mercy as the end result. It has been said that we can send people to hell on full stomachs and in new clothes. Christian social endeavor without evangelism is only half completed. It treats the symptoms and not the disease. Christian evangelism without social endeavors, or mercy without evangelism, is only halfhearted.

Isn't Christian evangelism inherently racist?

"We do not want the European white man's Jesus."

This complaint is spoken by Muslims and other non-Western faith systems. The logic of this fallacy argues that Christianity is an attempt to sublimate all cultures to a Western perspective. Is Christianity an anglicanized religion used by European land barons to rape other cultures?

Past missionary work has sometimes given credence to this argument. Missionaries identified Christianity with their own Victorian values and so moved to other societies with the decided motive to "bring culture to the unwashed heathen." They set out to overtake the receiving culture, teaching English, etiquette, manners, and sports, until the heathen were civilized. Given this mind-set, mission work stations came to resemble outposts for the missionaries' homeland. This was not then and is not now the gospel.

Again we must differentiate the Christ we serve from the mischief caused by false and ignorant servants. Jesus was not born into Western European culture, and He certainly was not a "white man." Fortunately, most missionaries today understand that, and they are better trained in cultural dynamics. While we still are learning, seldom are the egregious mistakes of the past being visited on nationals by evangelical Christian organizations. Qualified missionaries now see themselves as servants to the work of indigenous churches. The purpose of Christ in any civilization, including the West, is to transform culture to reflect His Word, not someone's paternalistic and imperialistic agenda. Christians should not be oversensitive about justified criticism, nor try to gloss over failures of the past or present. We should learn from them.

The deeper issue is a suspicion that Jesus doesn't really want them, that He died to save certain cultures or peoples, and others who slip in a side door will be second-class citizens of the kingdom. The inherent belief is that Christ only offers forgiveness to the select few and ignores the cries of others. This can be answered quickly from 2 Peter 3:9: "The Lord is not slack concerning His promise, as some count slackness, but is longsuffering toward us, not willing that any should perish but that all should come to repentance." The offer of salvation, eternal life in Christ and eternal forgiveness, peace, and assurance is for everyone. God is willing to accept everyone as His child, and all His children are on equal footing before Him.

Why are there so many "brands" of Christianity?

Great question! Indeed, many Christians also echo this question. A casual survey of the Christian landscape shows hundreds of denominations, small sects, split-offs, and variants. This seems particularly inappropriate in light of Christ's words in John 17:11: "I will remain in the world no longer, but they are still in the world, and I am coming to you. Holy Father, protect them by the power of Your name—the name You gave Me—so that they may be one as We are one."

Denominations within the Protestant movement resulted from many issues, theological, political, and social. The Protestant Reformation normally is counted as beginning when Martin Luther tried to raise questions that needed to be debated in the Roman Church in 1517 until the end of the Thirty Years War in 1648. In the early years of this period, most Reformers intended to fix the problems of the Catholic Church and remain within. They wanted to "reform" the church. But there were already other groups of disaffected Christians who wanted only to leave the Catholics and go their own way.

So, from the start, the Reformers all saw the evils and aberrant doctrines that had to be corrected, but they split into two distinct groups over how to do it. The radical Reformers, such as the Swiss Brethren, believed that Rome was beyond repair, and they wanted to begin afresh. Therefore, even at the beginning, denominations were formed from the differences between the purpose of the continental movement. Each group had specific differences that caused them to develop their own communities. Europe was beginning to solidify its modern national governments, and the political climate encouraged divisions along regional or national boundaries. More recent splits occurred because some Christians wanted a more emotional expression of their faith, and others left denominations that were being infected with unbelief.

Local churches, of course, split over less profound matters, some of which are embarrassingly petty.

Lest the Muslim feel too smug over this splintering of the Christian world, they should remember that Islam itself is not monolithic. The civil wars between Shi²ite and Sunni Muslims in the Iran-Iraq conflict of the 1980s is but one example of open and bloody warfare that still occurs within the Islamic community. Ayatollah Khomeini persecuted the Sufi Muslims, just as some Reformers hunted the Anabaptists.

A cursory survey of Islamic sects would also show varying groups, some of which regularly declare each other to be ghulat (cults). In addition to the main three sects, Shi²ite, Sunni, and Sufi, there are also Wahhabi, Kharijites, Alawites, Ahmadiyyas, Azalis, Druze, and many subgroups. Indeed, Islam is just as splintered as is Christianity, which speaks more to the human condition than to the call to unity of each movement's leaders.

Doesn't the Qur²an say that there is no coercion in religion?

When Muslim speakers quote from surah 2:256, they are in fact citing a tremendous rationale for the support of religious liberty, even in Islamic republics: "Let there be no compulsion in religion: Truth stands out clear from Error: whoever rejects Evil and believes in Allah hath grasped the most trustworthy handhold, that never breaks."

²Ali's commentary on the verse makes a lucid point:

Compulsion is incompatible with religion: because (1) religion depends upon faith and will, and these would be meaningless if induced by force; (2) Truth and Error have been so clearly shown up by the mercy of Allah that there should be no doubt in the minds of any persons of good will as to the fundamentals of faith; (3) Allah's protection is continuous, and His Plan is always to lead us from the depths of darkness into the clearest light.[11]

Were this the complete position of the Muslim populace, one could anticipate comparative peace between the various religions and Islam. Recently this verse often has been quoted against those who would question the peacefulness of Islam. How does one answer this clearly pacifistic verse?

Unfortunately, other verses seem to disagree with this one. A simple perusal of the subsequent chapters finds three sections in the three following chapters that are quite militant:

> If anyone desires a religion other than Islam (submission to Allah), never will it be accepted of him, and in the Hereafter he will be in the ranks of those who have lost (all spiritual good). (surah 3:85)

> When ye travel through the earth, there is no blame on you if ye shorten your prayers for fear the Unbelievers are unto you open enemies. (surah 4:101)

> O ye who believe! Take not the Jews and the Christians for your friends and protectors. They are but friends and protectors to each other. And he amongst you that turns to them (for friendship) is of them. Verily Allah guideth not a people unjust. (surah 5:51)

The Muslim apologist will immediately say that these verses have been taken out of context. For the sake of clarity and fairness, we shall examine the context of all three elsewhere (pp. 249-52).

The very chapter from which the "no compulsion" quote comes also includes verses that work against the "religious liberty" implication one hears when the verse is recited:

Fight in the cause of Allah those who fight you but do not transgress limits; for Allah loveth not transgressors. And slay them wherever ye catch them, and turn them out from where they have turned you out; for tumult and oppression are worse than slaughter; but fight them not at the Sacred Mosque, unless they first fight you there; but if they fight you, slay them. Such is the reward of those who suppress faith. (surah 2:190-91)

What then is the argument? The Muslim will say that this is a passive position of war, or only in the context of war, but that is certainly a different position than the "religious liberty" interpretation of surah 2:256.

Doesn't the Bible also call for a veil on women?

Strangely, many women's rights leaders of the West remained silent when Muslim women were brutalized in Afghanistan, kept from education, and oppressed in such a heinous manner.

The evangelical Christian must here be emphatic. The first purpose of a veil, according to the Muslim man, is modesty. Certainly many of us who attend church in our culture can appreciate modest dress when faced with immodest dress that we occasionally find in church. We would never disagree with the desire for both men and women to present ourselves in such a way to honor God and act respectfully.

Scripture certainly seems to indicate the use of the veil at first glance in 1 Corinthians 11:1-12:

Imitate me, just as I also imitate Christ. Now I praise you, brethren, that you remember me in all things and keep the traditions as I delivered them to you. But I want you to know that the head of every man is Christ, the head of woman is man, and the head of Christ is God. Every man praying or prophesying, having his head covered, dishonors his head. But every woman who prays or prophesies with her head uncovered dishonors her head, for that is one and the same as if her head were shaved. For if a woman is not covered, let her also be shorn. But if it is shameful for a woman to be shorn or shaved, let her be covered. For a man indeed ought not to cover his head, since he is the image and glory of God; but woman is the glory of man. For man is not from woman, but woman from man. Nor was man created for the woman, but woman for the man. For this reason the woman ought to have a symbol of authority on her head, because of the angels. Nevertheless, neither is man independent of woman, nor woman independent of man, in the Lord. For as the woman came from the man, even so man also comes through the woman; but all things are from God.

Does this mean that we should begin to demand that women should wear head coverings in church? The answer is no. It is important to read the entire text. The veil, in Paul's admonition, is symbolic of the protection of the husband, not his superiority over her. Indeed, the final verse indicates that we are given to our spouse as an honor of God as well. At the heart of the matter, we have to understand the context of Corinthian culture. In the first-century world, a woman who exposed her head in public often did so to proclaim her promiscuity. Paul says that a woman might as well shave her head, as a woman who had been publicly disgraced or was flaunting cultural mores. If we were to take this verse at face value, and preach from our pulpits that women should have their heads covered in public, would we also complete the teaching and proclaim that short hair is a sin as well?

We continue following the analogy Paul presents. As Christ was to God the Father, so is the wife to her husband. Is Christ, as the second Person of the Godhead, any less God than the Father? Is He somehow a "lesser" god? Of course not. Neither is the wife subsumed under her husband before God. The key is that Christ, as God the Son, willingly submitted Himself to the work and will of the Father, and upon His incarnation, temporarily laid aside His divine prerogatives. Therefore He was able to say, "I have come to do the will of the Father." So too does the wife willingly submit herself to her husband, not as a lesser creature but as one completely equal to the husband in every way. Christ is as much God as God the Father, and the wife is on equal ground with her husband.

For the Christian, the wearing of a veil by a woman is descriptive, meaning it presents a specific instruction that gives a contemporary principle. Does the fact that we see the text to have a specific meaning to the Corinthian church in any way negate the admonition to our day? No. We find in the text the principle that is universally applicable, regardless of culture or context. In every culture and in every culture, believers are called to present ourselves as children of God and thus modest. In the Ukraine, Christian women often wear a head wrap to show modesty. In some American cultures, women regularly wear hats as a symbol of submission. Regardless of the cultural context, we would be well served to remember our worship is in the presence of God, and we bring our best to Him—our best attitudes, our best service, our best sacrifice, and our best clothes.

For the Muslim community, use of the veil by women is *prescriptive*, meaning absolute and without interpretation. It is required and literal, so Muslims view Western women as lascivious:

> And tell the believing women to lower their gaze and be modest, and to display of their adornment only that which is apparent, and to draw their veils over their bosoms, and not to reveal their adornment except to their own husbands . . . or their sons . . . or their brothers. . . . And let them not stamp their feet so as to reveal what they hide of their adornment. . . . (surah 24:31)

Muslim countries cannot agree as to the extent to which women should wear the veil. Some use the full covering, including the full face, called a *burqa*. Others use a *niqab* to cover the left eye and the bridge of the nose or the *hijab* to cover everything but the face and hands. In addition, the ornamentation on the veil has come under scrutiny. Some sects allow varied colors and designs, and others allow only a single color and no decoration whatsoever.

Isn't pork forbidden in the Bible?

Leviticus 11:1–47 and Deuteronomy 14:3–21 gave the children of Israel a strict dietary code, which excluded such foods as pork:

> Nevertheless these you shall not eat among those that chew the cud or those that have cloven hooves: the camel, because it chews the cud but does not have cloven hooves, is unclean to you; the rock hyrax, because it chews the cud but does not have cloven hooves, is unclean to you; the hare, because it chews the cud but does not have cloven hooves; is unclean to you; and the swine, though it divides the hoof, having cloven hooves, yet does not chew the cud, is unclean to you. Their flesh you shall not eat, and their carcasses you shall not touch. They are unclean to you. (Leviticus 11:4–8)

Jews still abide by most of the dietary instructions God commanded, which are variously called "kosher" and "allowable." In Islam, similar restrictions of diet are also explicit. The Muslim is taught that all foods are "halal, haram, or mushbooh."[12] *Halal* is the Arabic term for "lawful," and includes such foods as milk, honey, fish with scales, vegetables, fruits, nuts, and grains. *Haram* (prohibited or sinful) foods include alcohol, pork, and foods that have not been prepared correctly. *Mushbooh* foods are suspect or questionable, such as whey and food additives.

These restrictions are drawn from both the Qur'an and the Hadith, such as surah 2:168, "O mankind! Eat of that which is lawful and wholesome in the earth, and follow not the footsteps of the devil. Lo! He is an open enemy for you." Surah 5:88 also invokes, "Eat of that which Allah hath bestowed on you as food lawful and good, and keep your duty to Allah in Whom ye are believers."

Do these laws still apply? Though some Adventist or Sabbatical

Christian sects would insist that the Levitical laws are still in effect, the vast majority of Christians believe that God cleansed those foods when speaking to Peter in Acts 10:9–16:[13]

> The next day, as they went on their journey and drew near the city, Peter went up on the housetop to pray, about the sixth hour. Then he became very hungry and wanted to eat; but while they made ready, he fell into a trance and saw heaven opened and an object like a great sheet bound at the four corners, descending to him and let down to the earth. In it were all kinds of four-footed animals of the earth, wild beasts, creeping things, and birds of the air. And a voice came to him, "Rise, Peter; kill and eat." But Peter said, "Not so, Lord! For I have never eaten anything common or unclean." And a voice spoke to him again the second time, "What God has cleansed you must not call common." This was done three times. And the object was taken up into heaven again.

What was this cleansing of the food? Was God saying that the dietary restrictions, including pork, were now obliterated by God, and no longer in practice? Was God saying that the restrictions were a mistake, or man-made? No. Instead, Christ Himself spoke to the need for the Levitical laws. In Matthew 15:10–11 (NIV), "Jesus called the crowd to him and said, 'Listen and understand. What goes into a man's mouth does not make him "unclean," but what comes out of his mouth, that is what makes him "unclean."'"

The law, in all of its strong and explicit instructions, could never save, but it could show how far we stood from a holy God. Christ fulfilled the law and became the only path by which anyone could reach God (Matthew 5:17–18). The heart (in the Bible the "inner person") is the most important element of worship, not the outer acts. The cleansing of food in Acts 10:9–16 was also a precursor for another profound event—the work of evangelism. Peter continues with an astonishing teaching, given the culture of the day: "Talking with him, Peter went inside and found a large gathering of people. He said to them: 'You are well aware that it is against our law for a Jew to associate with a Gentile or visit him. But God has shown me that I should not call any man impure or unclean'" (Acts 10:27–28 NIV).

Those without Jesus Christ, of whatever race, were no longer to be avoided; rather they were to be engaged and reached. Christ called believers to touch their lives, reach into their worlds, and share with them the precious Good News.

Isn't polygamy commanded in the Old Testament?

The Qur'an teaches that a Muslim man may have two, three, or four wives (surah 4:3), as long as he can care for them. Muslims say that the Old Testament teaches that many of the patriarchs and leaders of God's people had multiple wives, so God must sanction polygamy.

The first mention of a man having multiple wives is found in Genesis 4:19 (NIV), "Lamech married two women, one named Adah and the other Zillah." Lamech was the son of Methushael, and the great-great-great-great grandson of Adam. Esau married multiple wives, to the displeasure of his father, Isaac (Genesis 28:6–9). Isaac's other son, Jacob, was tricked into marrying two women, as he was working to earn the hand of Rachel. This is hardly a ringing endorsement, especially when the Pentateuch includes God's prohibition of kings marrying multiple wives, especially pagan ones:

> When you come to the land which the LORD your God is giving you, and possess it and dwell in it, and say, "I will set a king over me like all the nations that are around me," you shall surely set a king over you whom the LORD your God chooses; one from among your brethren you shall set as king over you; you may not set a foreigner over you, who is not your brother. But he shall not multiply horses for himself, nor cause the people to return to Egypt to multiply horses, for the LORD has said to you, "You shall not return that way again." Neither shall he multiply

wives for himself, lest his heart turn away; nor shall he greatly multiply silver and gold for himself. (Deuteronomy 17:14-17)

The portrait of a man who had manifold problems because he failed to obey this ruling was Solomon. As his power and legacy grew, so did Solomon's greed for women. These women, often daughters of foreign kings, led Solomon's heart away from God:

But King Solomon loved many foreign women, as well as the daughter of Pharaoh: women of the Moabites, Ammonites, Edomites, Sidonians, and Hittites—from the nations of whom the LORD had said to the children of Israel, "You shall not intermarry with them, nor they with you. Surely they will turn away your hearts after their gods." Solomon clung to these in love.

And he had seven hundred wives, princesses, and three hundred concubines; and his wives turned away his heart. For it was so, when Solomon was old, that his wives turned his heart after other gods; and his heart was not loyal to the LORD his God, as was the heart of his father David. For Solomon went after Ashtoreth the goddess of the Sidonians, and after Milcom the abomination of the Ammonites. Solomon did evil in the sight of the LORD, and did not fully follow the LORD, as did his father David. (1 Kings 11:1-6)

The essential point here can be lost as we look at a man with a thousand wives and mistresses: God never told anyone to ever marry more than one person. Nor does the Bible ever show a multiple marriage to have had a good result. In fact, the Bible describes marriage as the analogy for Christ and His church (Ephesians 5:22-33). The intense devotion and singular loyalty is lost in a home established by multiple, simultaneous marriages.

Why do Christians use Christmas trees and Easter eggs, which are pagan in origin?

The question of whether Christians can or should use pagan images and symbols is a good one, for our practices are often regarded rightly as world centered by unbelievers. Holiday celebrations include customs and symbols that have absolutely nothing to do with the commemoration of our Lord's incarnation, nor His crucifixion, burial, and resurrection.

Some of these elements, including the use of eggs at Easter and trees at Christmas, have pagan origins. Evergreen trees date back to ancient Scandinavian mythology. The rabbit and eggs symbolized eternal fertility and prosperity in parts of the ancient world. So Christians disagree as to how far we should go in allowing these symbols into our holiday commemorations, and whether they involve unholy syncretism with the unbelieving culture.

Many Christians have refused to use holiday symbols with non-Christian connotations, and some reject totally the celebration of Christmas. The fundamental issue that transcends Easter bunnies is how to focus on giving glory to God in these holidays, rather than on the pageantry of these traditions, whatever their origin. The panoply of activities that surround the holidays can become an affront to the acts of God we celebrate. How exactly does going into debt to purchase gifts celebrate the advent of our Lord? How do children celebrate the resurrection of Christ in the defeat of death, hell, and the grave by looking for eggs after the morning service?

Christians can get distracted from the essence of the holy moments we celebrate. We become consumed by our desire to provide memorable moments for our families, so that Jesus and even fiscal responsibility are forgotten. Most tragically, we forget that others, including Muslims, are watching.

In the midst of the Christmas gaudiness and commercialism, Muslims gather for Ramadan. For over one month, they fast during the daylight hours, even denying themselves a sip of water. Families gather each night for the evening meal. If gifts are given at all, they are simple. The family joins to read a significant portion of the Qur'an, so the entire book is completed during the holiday. In the midst of this commemoration of sacrifice, simplicity, and unity, the excesses of Christians seem hollow and irritating. Perhaps following the model of Islam in concentrating on the purpose of the holy days would allow us to enjoy the spirit of the seasons.

Notes

1. "Islamic Law and Its Challenge to Western Civilization," http://www.Muhammadanism.com (May 18, 2002).
2. Pew Research Council, "Americans Struggle with Religion's Role at Home and Abroad," report released March 20, 2002.
3. This survey was conducted in conjunction with the American Religious Identity Survey (ARIS), under the leadership of sociologists Barry A. Kosmin and Seymour P. Lachman at the Graduate School of the City University of New York. These numbers are skewed in that they include members of the Church of Jesus Christ of Latter-Day Saints (Mormons) and Jehovah's Witnesses as "Christian."
4. Statistics can be deceptive, yet these polls are examples of American religious affiliation. The Harris poll was conducted over the Internet, and not all Americans have Internet access. In this case, the sample included 13,224 registered voters who chose to be in the survey.
5. Aly Abuzaakouk, American Muslim Council, 1999.
6. Glenmary Research has a similarly low estimate.
7. Art Toalston, "U.S. Muslims, Tallied at 1.56M, Far Below Leaders' 6-7M Claims," in *Baptist Press* 27 (September 2002).
8. Ibid.
9. Ibid.
10. Translation from Shaykh Ahmad Darwish, *The Holy Koran: Its Meaning Rendered into English,* Mosque of the Internet, version 1.0 (2001). See http://www.allah.com.
11. Abdullah Yusuf ʿAli, *The Meaning of the Holy Qur'an* (Brentwood, Md.: Amana, 1992), n. 300.
12. Such lists can be found from Islamic dietary schools, including the Islamic Food and Nutrition Council of America and the Islamic Halal Food Monitor of Canada.
13. Christians officially ended the dietary laws in the ruling that accepted

Gentiles into the church as full members (Acts 15:23-29). While Peter interpreted his vision in Acts 10 as instruction that the Gentiles were acceptable before God and was not literally about food, the Jerusalem Council obviously saw that accepting the Gentiles implied dropping the clean food commands.

9

Questions Concerning Culture and Pluralism

In its "Year in Review" for 2002, *World* magazine counted the clash of cultures as a defining conflict of our time. The tensions of polarization between groups with contrary worldviews have escalated. As Gene Edward Veith noted, 2002 "was a bad year for multiculturalists, relativists and people who insist that all religions are equally valid. And yet, they remained true to their assumptions and did not let the facts get in their way."[1]

Veith means that, more than ever before, those who believe in absolute truth are regarded as racist warmongers. If the West has a pluralistic society, must we dispense with all claims to exclusive truth? This section will raise some of the pertinent issues related to this question, matters that concern Christians, Muslims, and our multiculturally minded friends.

Aren't all religions the same?

"Unite or perish!"

This motto was the mantra at a Parliament of the World's Religions. Six thousand people who attended heard the words repeated until they were imbedded as a fundamental doctrine of faith. Erwin Lutzer, pastor of the Moody Church in Chicago, observed, "The group most often targeted for criticism—the folks who could not be expected to buy into this united agenda—were those who belonged to the historic Christian faith."[2] The parliament represents just a fraction of a growing population of religious pluralists, who believe that all religions are essentially the same socially, historically, morally, and theologically.

At this point, faithful Muslims and Christians alike shake their heads in frustration.

This modern movement has its basis in tolerance not in truth. In fact, tolerance is only a stepping stone to the ideal of acceptance. Pluralists are quite willing to sacrifice the claims to exclusive truth of Jesus Christ on the cross of unity. Jesus consequently becomes an enlightened individual, comparable but never superior to Buddha, Muhammed, and a pantheon of past and current mystics.

This involves a paramount shift in the way people think of themselves. As relativists redefine or dispense with the need for salvation, they imagine some spark of the divine in their own psyches. If all are partakers of God, then any intolerant claims of exclusivity selfishly denies what is relatively and uniquely beautiful in each individual.

Such belief in the equality of all religions is inconsistent in its demands. First, ecumenism in its belief system becomes the exclusivist's ideal for the world to follow. This is the height of hypocrisy to condemn out of hand anyone who disagrees with the philosophy of relative truth. Indeed, many ecumenical groups are striving for mandatory acceptance, an oxymoron. To disagree with another religion becomes tantamount to a high crime. What is left after the removal of "bigotry" is a palatable pablum acceptable to all. There is no room for passionate faith.

Ecumenism is illogical in that it allows no critical analysis, only undivided allegiance. It asks the disciple to accept a way that cannot be known, a truth that cannot be found, and a life that cannot have universal meaning. Ecumenicists mandate that any teaching critical to another must be considered unacceptable. The way of ecumenism is thereby the way of the mindless, not the thoughtful. Yet, one who is not seeking to find is not seeking at all. Pilgrims are called to wander aimlessly through a neverland of meaninglessness.

In the end, all religions are the same if they all are man-made and man-centered. Christians, on the other hand, know that religious traditions never satisfy the soul. Only a relationship with the Living God can satisfy the longing of having a Heavenly Father (Isaiah 9:6). Pluralists of whatever religious label can respect Jesus of Nazareth, but only a true Christian worships Him.[3]

Why do Christians care what anyone believes?

Imagine that someone you've met has a heart condition that will soon prove fatal if not treated. Imagine further that you personally know the only cardiologist in the world who can perform this necessary surgery. Would it not be callous—in fact, immoral—not to refer the sick person to the one who could help? In a world permeated with spiritual heart disease that leads only to death and destruction, Christians can refer the sick and dying to Jesus Christ, the only One who can relieve their pain, suffering, and disease. For Christians not to care under such circumstances would be unthinkable.

Christians must be willing to go to places they have never been, to people they have never met, in order to bring the gospel to people who desperately need it. Many of those to whom the witness goes are not open to the message at first. The witness for God expects this, for the Bible speaks of the life of the unbeliever as blind to the light and dark (John 12:35–36). Part of this darkness comes from long-held religious traditions that lack eternal truth (Acts 17:22–34).

It is universally evident that all except the most hardened desire a relationship with God, although they usually do not understand their longing and try to fill the vacuum with other things. Therefore, Christians, who themselves were once in darkness, are called to share the message of hope that someone in the past shared with them. This is not an "us-against-the-world" mentality. The thoughtful Christian sometimes makes cultural mistakes out of ignorance, but takes the chance of making mistakes because he or she does respect the one with whom they share and empathizes with the need for spiritual truth. Witness to Christ has been described as "one hungry man telling another hungry man where to find food."

Another essential reason for caring, even if the attitude is not reciprocated, is that beliefs have consequences. Those who wish to malign the missionaries who come to their countries as intolerant also malign truth as relative. Many defenders of tolerance do not believe there are any eternal repercussions to this life, so this life is all that matters. Christians acknowledge that a person's response to the revelation God gives them affects the person's eternal destiny.

If the pluralist or agnostic is right that there are no consequences, then we should be tolerant, for life is individualistic, random, and meaningless. But if the Christian is right, then the "virtue" of tolerance is actually the worst possible way to treat others. If Jesus is the only way to heaven, as He Himself claimed to be (John 8:58), then the highest call in life is to share Jesus with someone who needs to know Him (John 1:29).

Aren't Christians and Muslims both exclusivists?

To be sure, Christianity and Islam, which between them account for more than 3 billion followers of varying levels of commitment, both claim a message with exclusive truth. The Qur'an teaches that only those who accept the message of Muhammed will earn heaven. Polytheists, among whom they count Trinitarians, will have their place in Hell (surah 98:6). Likewise, Christianity demands exclusive obedience to God in one person, Jesus Christ (John 14:6; Acts 4:12). Anyone who rejects Christ's sacrifice for them on the Cross has no hope of heaven and are "without excuse" (Romans 1:20).

Although many assume that the two religions have much in common, it can be demonstrated that they agree on very little aside from their monotheism. Among the essential differences:

1. *Christians have a different God.* He is personal and relational, and at the same time He is Trinity (One God in three Persons). Allah is transcendent and unreachable.
2. *Christians have a different view of salvation.* One can only be saved by believing in Christ for the forgiveness of sin. Islam believes works can earn favor with Allah.

3. *Christians have a different view of humanity.* Christians believe all are sinners and unrighteous, in need of the Savior.
   Islam teaches that everyone is born Muslim and is only corrupted later by individual actions.
4. *Christians have a different view of the Bible.* Evangelical Christians believe the Bible is the inerrant, infallible, inspired Word
   of God. Muslims believe the Bible is thoroughly corrupt, only
   worthy of acceptance when it is confirmed by the Qurʾan.
5. *Christians have a different view of Jesus.* Christians identify
   Jesus as the Christ or Messiah for all, the Son of God who is
   the Savior of the world. Christians thereby honor Him by
   praying to Him, calling upon Him for salvation, and worshiping Him. Muslims believe that Jesus is a mere man who only
   deserves respect, not worship.

These two world religions cannot be the same, since they are
based on mutually exclusive claims. They are different not only in
terms of theology but in the way of morality. Whereas a Muslim
sees the highest model for life in the "greatest prophet" Muhammed,
the Christian looks to the example and teachings of God in the
Savior, Jesus (Philippians 2:5).

The most significant distinction is in the conflicting views of the
person of Jesus Christ. He is either a mere man (surah 5:75) who
has no right to be called the Son of God (surah 5:116; 19:88), or
He is the One and only Savior (1 Timothy 2:5).

Doesn't *Islam* mean "peace"?

After the horrors of the terrorist attacks of September 11, 2001,
the world news media went into complete politically correct mode
and allowed Muslims to distort the actual meaning of *Islam. Islam,*
they say, is derived from *salam,* the word for "peace." This reflects
the tranquil nature of the religion. As an example, *USA Today*
posted a brief appraisal of Islam that asserted, "God's message was
reaffirmed and finalized by the Prophet Muhammad. Islam is a
religion of peace, mercy and forgiveness."[4]

This assessment overlooks some important details of the word

Islam. First, the word is not rooted in the word peace *(salam)* but in the infinitive word *Salama,* which can be translated as either "the stinging of a snake" or "the tanning of the leather."[5] The root word, from which *peace (salam)* also comes, is then modified. This changes the meaning emphatically. Hence, the term *Islam* has traditionally been translated as "submission, surrender, and resignation."

Second, there is no historical evidence that Islam ever had the connotation of "peace." This explains why Muslim apologists have never substantiated their argument that Islam means peace. On the other hand, Muhammed himself clearly explained his intention by the word. When the founder of Islam sent letters to Arabian tribal leaders asking them to become Muslims and surrender to God, he would sign the letters, *Aslem, Taslam,* "Surrender and you will be safe." Therefore, Muhammed's use of the word meant surrender within the context of military conquest, not spiritual submission to Allah.

Do good Muslims go to hell?

Faithful Muslims commit their entire lives to doing the best they can to earn the favor of Allah. More than any other religion in the world, Islam is based on works. As seen through the five pillars, devout Muslims continually repeat the confession, pray five times daily, give a portion of their income to the poor, fast for a full month during Ramadan, and travel across the globe to make their mandated pilgrimage to Mecca. In addition, most Muslims are moral people in general. They provide for their family and participate in community affairs, while rejecting social ills prevalent within the culture.

None of that is enough to appease a holy God. Good works no more cover bad works than an act of kindness can take away the guilt of a murderer.

To be clear, the authors are exclusivists of the strongest standard. Not only do we believe that "good Muslims" go to hell; we believe "good Baptists" go to hell. We belong to the Christian theological tradition that goes by that name, so we have warm regard for Baptists. But anyone who rejects the mercy of God is not entitled to the mercy of God, whatever they call themselves and however kindly they live. As they reject the compassionate sacrifice of the Savior, they reject any hope of heaven. Indeed, unbelievers must recognize that they are not merely rejecting a truth. They are rejecting truth found in the person of Jesus Christ, whose desire is for all men to be saved. Yet, Christ will not force anyone to Himself, for true love is voluntary, not mandatory. It is a choice and not coercion. But, the unbeliever must recognize how much is rejected by the one who says no to the open arms of the Lord:

1. The unbeliever rejects the Lamb of God who takes away the sin of the world (John 1:29). Without Christ, one must bear personal responsibility for offending the perfect and infinite God.

2. The unbeliever rejects the Great Physician, who can heal wholly and eternally the effects of the human state of death (Luke 18:35-43). In effect, the unbeliever must personally cope with with a spiritual cancer that eats away at the soul.

3. The unbeliever rejects the Chief Shepherd. The metaphor of sheep and shepherd are foreign to most of us, but we can understand complete helplessness and dependence on one who protects. Christ as Chief Shepherd protects His sheep from the dangers and temptations of the wolves (1 Peter 5:4). Without such a Defender, the unbeliever must fend for himself or herself against all the darkness of the world.

4. The unbeliever rejects the High Priest who can sympathize with the plight of man since He "was in all points tempted as we are, yet without sin" (Hebrews 4:15). The picture of a high priest comes from Judaism, in which the high priest was appointed as chief mediator between the people and God. Without such a go-between, the unbeliever has to endure the trials and temptations of life alone, without the understanding love of God.

5. The unbeliever rejects the Savior from the penalty for sin,

who will save His people from their sin (Matthew 1:21). Without Jesus, the unbeliever attempts the impossible, satisfying the perfect standard of God in order to get to heaven.

If anyone is "good enough" to go to heaven, there is no need for Jesus to fulfill these five roles for us. Sadly, it is not only "good" Muslims who reject the payment for sins by Jesus; many "good" people who adopt the label *Christian* do likewise. In the end, the argument about goodness is unbiblical. People are not born good but depraved. Moreover, no one can be considered good who rejects the finished work of the Cross, for that is the one and only sin that sends a person, no matter their religious affiliation, to hell (Matthew 12:31).

Can Islam and Christianity agree on anything?

In recent days, many Christians have searched for common ground with Muslims. Some liberal Christians have gone so far as to deny that there are essential theological differences. For example, Pope John Paul II issued a statement of solidarity with Muslims, exclaiming, "Though they do not acknowledge Jesus as God, they revere him as a prophet. They also honour Mary, his virgin mother; at times they call on her, too, with devotion. In addition they await the day of judgment when God will give each man his due after raising him up."[6]

As this book has shown, such a judgment lacks a theological foundation, but it is true that Muslims and Christians have some common ground. Morally, Islam and Christianity condemn many of the same social evils. Muslims adamantly oppose therapeutic abortion as an offense against God, the Giver of life.[7] The Qur'an states, "O people, if you have any doubt about resurrection, (remember that) we created you from dust, and subsequently from a tiny drop, which turns into a hanging (embryo), then it becomes a fetus that is given life or deemed lifeless" (surah 22:5). Likewise, in similar manner to the Bible, the Qur'an unequivocally condemns homosexuality (surah 29:29), suicide, and euthanasia (surah 4:29). As one scholar notes concerning the morality within Islam, "Islam does not condone frivolous pleasures, lying, slander, arrogance, boasting, scheming, obscenity, insult, spite, envy, and inconstancy."[8]

The Muslim and Christian share some theological ground. Both agree that God is One (Deuteronomy 6:4; surah 2:255) and that He is the Creator of the universe (Genesis 1-2; surah 13:12-13). Both agree that God is all-knowing (omniscient) and all-powerful (omnipotent). Unlike Eastern religions, the two religions agree that God is to be worshiped (John 4:23; surah 11:123). This is not to say that Muslims and Christians worship that same God, but the two faiths have a few similarities between their respective theologies that can act as a primer for discussion.

Indeed, with such commonality, it is easy to open a conversation with a Muslim. Yet, unlike ecumenical Christians who end the discussion with a warm comparison of shared beliefs, evangelical Christians seek the opportunity to speak about the things that matter most in life. Commonality also demonstrates that truth is truth wherever it is found, and some truth is found within each worldview. God has never left people without a witness (Romans 1:18-32). He has manifested the truth to each, even if unbelievers choose to suppress it. Indeed, since His "invisible attributes are clearly seen" (Romans 1:20), the Muslim has the chance to seek and find the God who is.

Aren't theological discussions harmful because they are divisive?

Modern rationalism and postmodern relative truth have not been kind to the discipline of theology. For different reasons, the two philosophies relegate spiritual study to a place of less importance than the "pure" sciences. Philosophy and religion generally are considered peripheral at best. In this era of technology, men and women have demoted the importance of theology below improvements to their physical comfort. Convenience has replaced confession. Psychological self-helps have supplanted earnest repentance. Furthermore, the theological, social, and hard sciences are so compartmentalized that their "truths" are considered completely unrelated. Alongside this mentality, the late twentieth century ushered in an era of tolerance and diversity. Therefore, the only palatable spirituality does not offend anyone. It must accept and integrate other faiths. Hence the question is asked whether the Christian-Muslim dialogue should continue or whether it does more harm than good.

Unlike Western pop culture, Muslims recognize the importance of theology. In fact, Muslim theology drives most Middle Eastern societies. The Christian has far too long allowed conversation about God to be restricted to its own gatherings. U.S. citizens must remember that their nation in particular was founded upon a concept of freedom *of* religion. That meant that uninhibited discussion about God was to be allowed in the public square as well as the private worship center. Even founding fathers of the United States who were not Christians appreciated the importance religion played in society. Though anyone is free to believe as he or she wishes, this does not mean that religion is to be swept away from the marketplace of ideas. Other generations in the English-speaking world called theology the "queen of the sciences." It was a driving force within other areas of specialty.

Muslims looking at the West have difficulty understanding why the subject of theology is the only arena truly regarded as taboo. One can speak publicly about any topic so long as there is no reference to God in the discussion. Once divinity comes up, the venue is expected to move to the place where the church meets, away from the ears of others. *However, theological discussion is needed and necessary to aid the situation at hand.* It is ignorance, not intellect, that leads society to push away the answers to its dangerous situations. One need not be afraid that passionate disagreement will lead to violence so long as people understand that they have the right to believe as they wish.

Furthermore, debate over even the most emotional issues can lead to truth, which is the announced objective of free speech, press, and religion. Some people still point to the Reformation wars as an illustration of what can happen when there is too much bantering in religion. This straw man must be laid to rest. What caused the bloody conflicts between 1530 and 1648 was not the freedom of religion but the lack of freedom, as various European

princes tried to consolidate political power around a single unifying religious system. There was little or no distinction between
church and state, so Catholics and Protestants alike persecuted each
other through their respective government power centers. Only in
Roman Catholic areas and in parts of the Eastern Orthodox world
are there any remaining semblances of church-state oligarchy related to Christianity.

Are public theological discussions helpful or harmful? Replace
the word *theological* with the name of some other discipline. Not
many Germans would say that the removal of *political* debate would
lead to a more peaceful unity between the eastern and western
parts of the nation. Not many Canadians would say that the elimi-
nation of intellectual debate would solve the intercultural tensions
in Quebec. Then, no Christian should buy into the fallacy that
stifling theological discussion will lead to a more spiritual society.

Isn't sincerity the measure of religious truth?

Since the rise of German liberal theology in the early 1800s,
there has been a growing notion among the elites of the historically Christian areas of the world that spirituality is a matter of
sincere experience, rather than absolute truth. The idea became
endemic over the twentieth century, so that countless philosophers
and theologians now assert that it is meaningless and irrational to
speak of a "supernatural" reality. This ideology has left human beings to their own devices. It is no wonder that people look to their
own experience as the ultimate gauge of right and wrong.

Only evangelical Christianity testifies that one can have a real
experience in relation to spiritual realities, but that experience alone
may not involve God and His truth. One can be utterly sincere in
religious feelings yet absolutely outside truth. In the end, all truth
should be experienced, but not all experience is truth.

Traditionally, both Islam and Christianity reject the notion that
sincere feelings can measure the validity of religious truth. The all-
out assault on the trustworthiness of the Bible over the past two
hundred years has created a paradigm shift within Christendom.
Millions of Christians have attempted to hold onto a "relevant"

faith by giving up the complete reliability of the Bible. They exchange its truthfulness for emotion and unfettered experience. In
many circles, Christian experience is no longer measured by right
belief but by a set of acceptable behaviors. Unacceptable behavior
is justified at the same time by arguing that experience in Jesus
Christ is the ultimate measure of truth.

Make no mistake by believing that this is true Christianity. Jesus
did not hold to this deviant position. He taught that the Bible is
fully reliable propositional truth (John 17:3). Truth is not found in
feelings but in relating to the person of Christ as He is revealed in
the Bible (John 14:6). Sincerity may reveal whether someone truly
cares, but it does not prove that someone is correct.

Muslim theology also vehemently rejects subjective sincerity as
the basis for religious truth. Islam is not based on experience but
on the argument that the Qurʾan is the ultimate revelation from
Allah, a set of propositional truths that can be understood and
followed (surah 23:90). Islam does not allow a sincere Christian
who believes in the Trinity to go to heaven since belief in monotheism is categorically demanded. The key passage in the Qurʾan
that negates the superiority of sincerity, states,

> Those who disbelieve among the People of the Book and
> among the Polytheists were not going to depart (from their
> ways) until there should come to them clear Evidence, Mes-
> senger from Allah, rehearsing scriptures, kept pure and holy;
> wherein are books rights and straight. . . . And they have
> been commanded no more than this: to worship Allah,
> offering Him sincere devotion, being Truth (in faith). (surah
> 98:1-3, 5)

One should note the importance of the Qurʾan as evidence that
is the measuring rod ("right and straight"). In Islam, sincerity is
the outcome of faith, not the originator of faith. In the end, how
can one argue that either Islam or Christianity must be right because the people are sincere, when either faith itself contradicts
such an idea?

Must Christians attack Islam and its prophet Muhammed to present Christ?

When a prominent Southern Baptist pastor referred to Muhammed, the founder of Islam, as "a demon-possessed pedophile who had 12 wives, and his last one was a 9-year-old girl,"[9] the outcry from much of the American public, along with leaders within the Muslim community, was venomous. Groups such as the Council on American-Islamic Relations decried the comments as hate filled, bigoted, and deplorable. Muslims called for an apology to the Islamic community for the offensive remarks. Mainline Protestant and Jewish groups joined the protest against such statements as being unloving, harsh, and unnecessary. Jesus Himself, they said, would never have been guilty of such abhorrent attacks. Even some evangelicals worried that the critical comments might put Christian missionaries in harm's way in countries with large numbers of Muslim radicals.

In our view, the comments were both necessary and appropriate. No one seemed much concerned about whether the statements were accurate. According to the Hadith, Muhammed was married to a nine-year-old girl with whom he had sexual intercourse (7.64). By modern standards at least, such an act would be seen as a mark of pedophilia. Muhammed himself expressed belief that at times he was demon possessed. The speaker was making a judgment about facts that until recently were accepted by all in the Muslim community. Ironically, few commentators used the occasion of the remarks to raise questions about the controversial behavior of Muhammed, only the controversial nature of the statements. In a politically correct culture, it has become more offensive to criticize a sinful act than to take part in sinful behavior.

Would Jesus ever speak in such an insensitive and unloving way? Let's review some of Jesus' statements that are recorded in the Gospels:

1. Jesus characterized the Pharisees as the offspring of poisonous snakes. "Brood of vipers! How can you, being evil, speak good things? For out of the abundance of the heart the mouth

speaks" (Matthew 12:34). Jesus used the politically incorrect term on at least two occasions (Matthew 3:7).

2. In one message recorded in the gospel of Matthew, Jesus characterized both Scribes and Pharisees as "blind guides" (23:16), "fools" (verse 17), "hypocrites" (verse 25), and "whitewashed tombs" (verse 27). Indeed, the last remark, comparing the two groups to tombs that are beautiful on the outside yet full of stinking and rotting flesh on the inside, is probably the most offensive term used by Christ. Jesus declared, "For you are like whitewashed tombs which indeed appear beautiful outwardly, but inside are full of dead men's bones and all uncleanness" (verse 27).

3. Jesus characterized the Pharisees as children of the Devil. "You are of your father the devil, and the desires of your father you want to do" (John 8:44).

The Apostles also were guilty of divisive language in reference to other religious groups:

1. The apostle Paul characterized some men as "blasphemers," "traitors," and "despisers of good" (2 Timothy 3:1-9). He warns weaker members of the faith not to be taken in by them.

2. The apostle Peter described false teachers as "brute beasts" (2 Peter 2:12) and "wells without water" (verse 17). Finally, he explains the end result of such teachers, "A dog returns to his own vomit" (verse 22).

3. The apostle John described false teachers as "antichrists" (1 John 2:18) and "liars" (verse 22). In fact, he says that whoever denies that Jesus is the Christ is a liar.

The problem ultimately resides in how one is "offended." In today's psychologically driven culture, offense does not deal with factual inaccuracies but with emotional irritation. Yet, Jesus' definition was that an "offense" was an enticement to sin (Matthew 18:7). In this meaning, harsh language cannot be offensive unless it is inaccurate.

We are always concerned about dangers faced by missionaries. But it would seem to be an indictment of Muslim culture if a statement by one preacher thousands of miles distant causes people to react violently to innocent parties. If Islam truly is a religion of peace, then certainly those who peacefully represent another religion should be in no danger because of such a statement. Christians have not reacted in violence at the maligning of Christ's name. Rather they have tried to answer the attacks with reasoned evidence that the attacker was incorrect.

The reality of Christian life today is that the act of presenting the gospel in a predominantly Muslim culture in itself will stir animosity that can spill into violence. The statement that raised all the ruckus will not make much of a difference in that fact of life. Yet, God never promised that Christians would be protected from tribulation, only that He would be with them in the face of danger.

The gospel is offensive since it convicts people of sin and asks them to discard their religious baggage for the true gospel found in Jesus Christ and Him alone. Indeed, those who bear the most fruit in evangelism are not those who worry about offensive remarks but those who are bold in their speech, proclaiming the truth in love. Christians are called to be bold in pointing to the Savior while refuting those who speak lies and blind followers from the truth. Christians are called to be loving in that they see the individual as a person for whom Jesus died. They recognize that the most unloving act is to refuse sinners a chance to accept the Savior.

Aren't all religions flawed?

There is a famous Buddhist analogy given by numerous religion professors who attempt to justify how all religions in the world are equal. The scenario, popularly known as the parable of the blind men and elephant, goes as follows:

> Once upon a time there was a certain raja who called to his servant and said, "Come, good fellow, go and gather together in one place all the men of Savatthi who were born

blind . . . and show them an elephant." "Very good, sire," replied the servant, and he did as he was told. He said to the blind men assembled there, "Here is an elephant," and to one man he presented the head of the elephant, to another its ears, to another a tusk, to another the trunk, the foot, back, tail, and tuft of the tail, saying to each one that that was the elephant.

When the blind men had felt the elephant, the raja went to each of them and said to each, "Well, blind man, have you seen the elephant? Tell me, what sort of thing is an elephant?"

Thereupon the men who were presented with the head answered, "Sire, an elephant is like a pot." And the men who had observed the ear replied, "An elephant is like a winnowing basket." Those who had been presented with a tusk said it was a ploughshare. Those who knew only the trunk said it was a plough; others said the body was a grainery; the foot, a pillar; the back, a mortar; the tail, a pestle, the tuft of the tail, a brush.

The moral of the story as stated by the teacher is twofold. First, virtue is found in accepting truth as relative and partial. Second, one of the greatest vices is to quarrel with one another over different perceptions, yet ultimately the same God.

The analogy, however, is false. First, the conclusion to this parable is not that all religions are equally right but that all religions are equally wrong. An elephant is an elephant, not a pot, tail, or brush. The blind men are wrong. Period. This would demonstrate that no one in this world actually has a true grasp of God, which means we are only left with false perceptions and knowledge.

Second, this analogy is actually a good picture of natural, finite man attempting to find his way to an infinite, holy God. The truths reached are inevitably incorrect.

This analogy assumes that God did not in any way reveal Himself in history. If God does not care and left blind men to their own struggles and limitations, then blindness is a virtue since it leads to unity. But that is not what happened, and this form of religious pluralism ignores what God has done, even as it presumes that Jesus Christ is no better than any other human being.

One other question arises. How do we know that the elephant is truly an elephant in the first place unless one puts his trust in Buddha? The answer to this parable may have less to do with the story and more to do with the narrator. The difference between the Christian and other religionists is not only in the story line but in the Author.

On what criteria are countries designated Islamic states?

Islam prides itself as being a "cradle-to-grave" religion that encompasses spiritual aspects of life, as well as economic, political, and social aspects. Hence, after independence was declared from their colonial governments, many Muslim countries looked immediately to shar'ia Islamic law. Though there are significant differences in the way these governments are run, they have features in common:

1. *Religious Supremacy.* Islam is the official state religion. Other religions are either tolerated or persecuted, depending upon the interpretation of law. At best, those with different faiths are deemed secondary citizens.
2. *Moral Codes.* Laws are based on the Qur'an and Hadith. Laws that may seem archaic in the West are introduced, including amputations and beheading. These laws also cover daily habits, including laws guiding dress and forbidding financial institutions from collecting interest.
3. *Religious Codes.* Crimes include religious offenses as well as criminal violations. Any offensive speech against Islam, Muhammed, or the Qur'an is considered blasphemous and punishable.

Anything that is forbidden (*haram*) in the Qur'an is illegal in the country.

At this writing, there are twenty-four Islamic states, five of which are particularly strict in enforcing religious laws—Iran, Saudi Arabia, Pakistan, Egypt, and the Sudan. In recent years, the Sudan has most egregiously violated the right to life and liberty. The Sudanese government, flanked by *jihaddin* (holy warriors), have Islamicized its citizens through forced conversion, systematic starvation, enslavement, torture, and imprisonment. In the twenty years after the Sudan declared itself an Islamic state, an estimated 3 million Christians were enslaved or slaughtered. Similarly, Iran has religious apartheid that forbids religious minorities from handling food to be eaten by Muslim and outlaws Muslim business owners from hiring religious minorities. In Saudi Arabia, home of the two holiest sites in Islam, all non-Islamic worship is forbidden, even in private homes. In Pakistan, a blasphemy law passed in 1986 outlawed any language critical of Muhammed or the Qur'an. Since its inception, thousands have been executed.

Other counties accepting Islamic law include Afghanistan, Algeria, Bahrain, Comoros, Djibouti, Iraq, Jordan, Kuwait, Lebanon, Libya, Mauritania, Morocco, Oman, Qatar, Somalia, Syria, Tunisia, United Arab Emirates, and Yemen. Malaysia is the most recent country to implement Islamic law into its political system. Now, a person caught drinking alcohol will receive forty to eighty lashes, while anyone guilty of adultery will be stoned to death.

Doesn't Western culture breed immorality?

Muslim disdain for U.S. culture in particular and the West generally is encouraged by the perception that the culture has encouraged immorality domestically and internationally. Looking at the American scene in particular, one cannot disagree that America has become an increasingly immoral nation. Lying, stealing, cheating, and abortion are rampant within the population. Muslims especially center their criticism on the sex-obsessed promotion of pornography, homosexuality, and general sexual promiscuity. Television, movies, and music fuel such criticism. The term *Great Satan* has even become a popular designation for the United States in some Muslim circles.

While founded upon much evidence, Muslim criticism of

immorality is based on the premise that freedom is a vice, not a
virtue, since it is an open door to the cesspool of sin. Moral sins such
as adultery and homosexuality must be punished and so deterred.
Such religious rituals as prayer must be enforced by law in order to
encourage faith. The fallacy in this argument is obvious: to many
Muslims, the state has responsibility over the soul of the individual.
Democracy, held as the greatest form of government by Westerners,
is disparaged across much of the Middle East as inferior to theocracy.

In part, Muslims misunderstand Western history and government. Democracy is not by nature anarchical rule that accepts any
type of behavior as normal and tolerable. Until recent times, the
United States held to the sanctity of life, self-control of sexual rela-
tionships and support of monogamous marriage, and other high
moral values. The reason for the advance of sinful behavior is not
the system but the breakdown of laws within the system. This began as a philosophical shift that argued that truth is relative and life
is accidental. In fact, history proves that all governments are prone
to failure when the people become self-centered and sinful.

The Muslim should not make the mistake of equating the United
States with Christianity. The United States is not a Christian nation, although it owes much to Christian principles for its founding and long prosperity. Many Christians have fought against the
vices that Muslims list in their barrage against the West. Christians
recognize that sins such as abortion should be outlawed, but Christians are vehemently opposed to a theocratic government since faith
must be voluntary, not coerced. For example, if one forces people
to pray, then prayer still has meaning only for those for whom it is
genuine.

This is not to say that Christians are without fault in failing to
stem the advance of immorality. Churches for the past century
have shifted from a focus on purity to a focus on peace. In its wake,
morality was sacrificed for individuality, and the Church was weakened at its core.

Yet, before branding the United States in particular as completely
immoral, consider the following examples of virtue since about
1950:

1. The last seven military actions in which the United States participated have had as a major goal the freedom of Islamic peoples or countries.
2. Even before the overthrow of the Taliban, the United States led the world in humanitarian aid to Afghanistan.
3. America's generosity after World War II brought Germany, Britain, Italy, and France into economic prosperity. In fact, the United States never required these countries to pay back their loans. In 1956, America once again came to the aid of France, saving it from financial bankruptcy.
4. The Marshall Plan and Truman Policy after World War II pumped billions of dollars into discouraged countries.
5. American persistency helped lead to the end of the old Soviet Union, freeing millions of Muslims from the tyrannical rule of communism.
6. American medicinal advances have raised the level of health across the globe.

Being in the spotlight, blemishes of United States and Western culture are readily in view. But one should ask a final question: Would we prefer forced conformity leading to political and religious oppression or would we rather have freedom, despite its societal sicknesses?

Notes

1. Gene Edward Veith, "Culture Year-in-Review," *World* (28 December 2002), 42.
2. Erwin W. Lutzer, *Christ Among Other Gods* (Chicago: Moody, 1994), 11.
3. Ibid., 12.
4. "Q & A on Islam and Arab-Americans," http://www.usatoday.com/news/world/islam.htm (Dec. 17, 2002).
5. See Hans Wehr, *Dictionary of Modern Written Arabic* (New York: French & European Publications, 1985) for details. This source is considered authoritative not only by major universities but by Muslims in general.

6. Alex Kirby, "What Muslims and Christians Share," http://news.bbc.co.uk/1/hi/uk/1762359.stm (Dec. 17, 2002).

7. George Braswell, *Islam* (Nashville: Broadman & Holman, 1996), 137. See also, http://www.submission.org/pro-life.html (Dec. 17, 2002).

8. Ibid., 120.

9. Todd Starnes, "Southern Baptists Leaders Affirm Vines in Wake of National Attacks," 19 June 2002, at http://www.baptistpress.org/bpnews.asp?ID=13645 (Dec. 18, 2002).

10

QUESTIONS CONCERNING
RELIGIOUS LIBERTY

ON APRIL 28, 2002, TWELVE CHRISTIANS were killed in a predawn
attack in Ambon, Indonesia. A press report described the appalling
event:

> (The twelve Christians) were brutally murdered and another
> six were injured in a deadly attack on the village of Soya
> during the early morning hours. . . . The attack on the Prot-
> estant Christian Soya village near Ambon was carried out by
> armed attackers around 4 a.m. Sunday morning. Black-clad
> Muslims "went from house to house while proclaiming Allah's
> greatness, murdering anybody they could lay hands on, not
> sparing women and children, including a nine month old
> baby that was killed by bullets," according to the Crisis Cen-
> tre Diocese of Amboina. Six of the victims were stabbed or
> shot while another six were burned to death.[1]

Is this incident an aberration, part of a cultural civil war that
only used religious terminology, or something more? Such stories
rarely find world press coverage, yet the persecution of Christians
has reached epic proportions. Is this seemingly systematic
extermination prescribed by Islamic doctrine, or are Muslims defying

Islamic teachings of tolerance? Does the history of Protestant-Catholic fighting in Northern Ireland excuse those who defend violence in the name of Allah? This section will examine the doctrines and prescriptions of Christian and Islamic responses to diversity.

Does Islam espouse religious liberty?

No Islamic republic or nation governed by Islamic law espouses religious liberty—not one. This has always been the case. Though some point out medieval Christian groups who sought shelter in Islamic countries from Roman Catholic persecution, the historical record portrays little peaceful coexistence. *The Pact of Umar,* a seventh-century document prepared for the second Muslim caliph, tackled the problems of governing a growing number of conquered peoples. *The Pact* develops the policy that non-Islamic religious minorities are second-class citizens who should not be afforded the same rights as Muslims. In exchange for protection, Christians and Jews would surrender their religious rights and promise:

> We shall not build, in our cities or in their neighborhood, new monasteries, Churches, convents, or monks' cells, nor shall we repair, by day or by night, such of them as fall in ruins or are situated in the quarters of the Muslims.
> We shall not teach the Qur'an to our children.
> We shall not manifest our religion publicly nor convert anyone to it.
> We shall not prevent any of our kin from entering Islam if they wish it.
> We shall show respect toward the Muslims, and we shall rise from our seats when they wish to sit.
> We shall not display our crosses or our books in the roads or markets of the Muslims.
> We shall use only clappers in our churches very softly.
> We shall not raise our voices when following our dead.
> We shall not show lights on any of the roads of the Muslims or in their markets.
> We shall not bury our dead near the Muslims.[2]

In general, one can see the jihad of Islam most clearly within the depletion of Eastern Orthodox Christianity. In areas that had Orthodox majorities as high as 80 percent when Islam came to power, the Christian community was obliterated by massacre, enslavement, and humiliation under Islamic law.

Persecution has remained constant or expanded in modern times. Just a few of the more serious recent examples of mistreatment of religious minorities includes:

1. Since implementation of Islamic government in the Sudan in 1980, millions of Christians have been killed, enslaved, raped, tortured, and kidnapped.
2. Saudi Arabia has sanctioned the death penalty for belief in any faith other than Islam.
3. Pakistani converts to Christianity lose rights to housing, jobs, and inheritance.
4. Morocco imprisons anyone found guilty of proselytizing his or her faith.
5. Kuwait prohibits any teaching about non-Islamic religions.
6. Qatar forbids the construction of a church.
7. Mauritania requires that all of its citizens be Muslims. Mauritanians are forbidden to own any sacred texts from other religions.[3]

Some Muslim-led countries, such as Morocco, have a measure of religious *toleration*, but none allow religious *liberty*. Official and institutionalized persecution has long been a blot upon Islamic societies. When one thinks about the level of suffering caused and the degree of hatred and violence expressed, these countries practice a form of domestic terrorism on their own citizens. Muslim apologists have difficulty defending the peaceful nature of their religion, when its leaders sanction such violence even inside their own borders.

Don't Christians have a terrible track record on religious liberty?

Utter disregard for human life and freedom frequently has been perpetrated by persons in power who waved the Christian banner. The difference is that these acts are unjustifiable from the Bible or any accepted teaching of the faith. These violent periods can only be regarded as horrific crimes by false teachers and false or misled ignorant believers. Most identify the Crusades (1095–1291) as one of the most bloody misuses of Christianity, although Muslims bear some responsibility for the brutality of those wars. Medieval Islam and Christianity shared a parallel hatred for Jews, and both suppressed dissenters with extreme cruelty. However, although there are similarities, the reasons for their violent tendencies in persecution have differed in essentials.

Islam succeeded during its first one hundred years through military conquest. Christianity succeeded during its first two and one-half centuries (about 61–312) by surviving intermittent periods of intense persecution. Caliphs Abu Bakr and Umar sharpened their swords for battle, but the apostles Peter and Paul prepared their bodies for beatings and martyrdom. Warriors of Islam crossed North Africa in hopes of political conquest. Witnesses for Christ scattered throughout the Roman Empire hoping for spiritual awakening. This difference in viewpoint is based on the teachings of Christ. His disciples have been willing to shed their blood so that others could live in Him; the disciples of Muhammed have been willing to shed other people's blood for the sake of Allah. Nor have many Christian martyrs been motivated by an understanding that they would receive sensual pleasures in heaven.

Christianity left this Christ-centered ideal under the reign of the Roman emperor Constantine, who converted to Christianity from paganism in 312. While the political motivations for his faith make its reality open to dispute, he testified that he had seen a vision in which a flaming cross accompanied the Latin legend, meaning "In this sign conquer!" Constantine credited his subsequent victories in battle to his Christian belief. Those victories secured his place as undisputed emperor, and he immediately set out to maintain power by uniting all his subjects under the same church doctrines. In Constantine, political sword merged with the spiritual sword, perverting Christianity. Not until 1648 would this unholy union be broken.

During these centuries of alliance, governments vied with church leaders for the right to install bishops, build churches, and settle theological disagreements by fiat. True faith grew weaker as the church was no longer an organism based on voluntary membership but rather an organization based on citizenship. Secular rulers and politicized popes became the norm, and churchmen were accorded great privilege and stature.

Protestant Reformers inherited this church-state political philosophy. Governments and churches continued to demand that all of their citizens share one religious system, and dissent was regarded as treasonous. This also is why Jews continued to suffer in Christian lands after the decline of the Roman Catholic inquisitions. Politicians were less interested in a pure faith than with the societal status quo. Vestiges of this alliance existed in Europe after the end of the Thirty Years War in 1648, but the philosophy lay in ruins. Unfortunately, it was replaced by a secular backlash against any religion in the Western Enlightenment, until all believers in God were objects of destruction in the French Revolution of the 1790s. A more positive democratic reaction to church-state persecution transformed the American colonies and culminated in the revolution that founded the United States. Over many generations, Christians demanded freedom of religion and defended it as the biblical model. Though it took over thirteen hundred years, Christians returned to their roots of religious freedom.

Is religious liberty taught in the Bible?

Most Christians believe strongly in religious liberty because it is explicitly biblical. The key passage in the New Testament concerning this doctrine is found in Matthew 13:24–30:

Another parable He put forth to them, saying: "The kingdom of heaven is like a man who sowed good seed in his field; but while men slept, his enemy came and sowed tares among the wheat and went his way. But when the grain had sprouted and produced a crop, then the tares also appeared.

"So the servants of the owner came and said to him, 'Sir, did you not sow good seed in your field? How then does it have tares?'

"He said to them, 'An enemy has done this.'

"The servants said to him, 'Do you want us then to go and gather them up?'

"But he said, 'No, lest while you gather up the tares you also uproot the wheat with them. Let both grow together until the harvest, and at the time of harvest I will say to the reapers, "First gather together the tares and bind them in bundles to burn them, but gather the wheat into my barn."'"

Later Jesus explains the characters and plot of the parable. The world, known as the "kingdom," will have believers (wheat) and unbelievers (a wheat look-alike weed sometimes called a "tare"). The wheat belongs to the Lord (man who sowed good seed) and the tares belong to the Devil (his enemy). In the end times (harvest), the servants will want to destroy the sons of the Devil, but Jesus will not allow it lest believers also be hurt. In the end, justice will come by way of God's judgment through Christ.

Only Jesus Christ has the right to judge the soul of a person. We might deduce from that principle that civil government has no right to "bear the sword" in theological matters (Romans 13:4), and even church authorities had better be very careful in judging others. Whatever their places of authority, Christians who attempt to persecute others can leave damaged brothers and sisters in their wake. The history of the Christian church is littered with massacres of Christians by Christians who intended to purify the church of error. Truth and error intermix throughout the world, and Jesus reminded His disciples that the wheat and the tares will grow together since Satan works in all societies. It isn't the Christian's responsibility to deal violence against unbelief.

Other biblical passages agree. The apostle Paul reminded the church in Ephesus that the Christian only has one sword, the Word of God (Ephesians 6:17). The apostle Peter emphasizes the long-suffering of the Lord, recognizing that God does not desire that anyone should go to hell (2 Peter 3:9). Why would someone hasten His judgment? Indeed, violence leads people away from the loving arms of the Savior.

In an age of relativity and confusion, one must have a plumb line to measure what is right and wrong. In our own country, the United States, the constitution has provided a balanced democracy that has held up for more than two hundred years. But constitutions come and go. The Bible is the only unchanging source of authority. As Balthasar Hubmaier (1480–1528), a Reformation Christian advocate of religious liberty, stated, "The greatest deception of the people is the kind of zeal for God which is invested without Scripture in the interest of the salvation of souls, the honor of the church, love for the truth, good intentions, usages or custom, episcopal decrees, and the indication of reason, all of which have been begged from the light of nature. These are lethal errors, when they are not led and directed according to Scripture."[4]

What is the difference between religious liberty and toleration?

In 1689, the English parliament ended a bloody period of war and persecution by passing the Act of Toleration. This document allowed freedom of worship for Protestants in England, Wales, Ireland, and Scotland. Although it was a vast improvement that ended a time of intense suffering for thousands of dissenters, the law still showed a high degree of arrogance. Membership in the state-controlled episcopal national churches was encouraged. Some groups, such as Roman Catholics, still could gain no legitimacy at all. The act also set out obligatory religious duties that every citizen had to obey. For example, although people were free to tithe to their respective denominations, they still were required to pay a tax for the established national church. Dissenting churches were treated like stepchildren who had to register with the government for certification.

The most important principle inherent in such *toleration* laws was that the best and most lenient of them insisted that the state retained the wisdom to instruct people in a set of beliefs that they "should," and in some cases "must," share. What right has any secular government to set standards for doctrinal acceptability in religious organizations? If the government truly has the right to legislate for one's soul, *de facto* government is usurping prerogatives of deity. Toleration stipulates that government has the authoritative right to control, certify, grant permission, and exploit religion as it sees fit.

Liberty specifies that government has the indisputable duty to protect the rights of each person or religious group from legislative or judicial control. Examples of toleration in Islam include countries like Turkey, where the Orthodox Church has the right to exist but not expand. The ecumenical patriarch, Bartholomew I, is denied the right to reopen his seminary in order to train men for the priesthood. In Brunei, the significant minority of Christians are forbidden to meet in groups of more than five people.

In the end, toleration is a tactic used to put up with people while hoping for their gradual extinction or removal from society. On the other hand, liberty does not hold that all religions are equal in truth, but it ensures equality in entitlement to be heard. Members of society can then choose their faith. Toleration guarantees the political superiority of an official religion and relegates dissenters to the pile of outcasts. It operates out of political pragmatism or the superiority complex belief that, since it is right and all others are wrong, it deserves special treatment and privileges.

Yet, people who are securely confident in their faith do not need special favors from government to back up their claims. They will allow God to defend Himself and allow the truth to stand on its own merit against counterfeits.

Why are some Christians treated differently from other Christians in Islamic countries?

On a visit to Morocco, a group of Christians were allowed to discuss religious liberty with leaders within the Islamic community.

During the conversation, an Islamic cleric expressed approval for freedom of religion so strong that it astonished several of the Christians. One Christian asked him, "So you do not mind when a Muslim becomes a Christian?"

He responded, "Religious liberty allows a Christian to become a Muslim, not the other way around."

This is part of the reasoning behind a double standard in some Islamic societies. Christians are more tolerated if they were born to Christianity than if they are former Muslims who have been "re-born" to Christ. To be a Christian by birth is acceptable; to be a Christian by rebirth is damnable. The people in the most danger within Islamic states are those who have converted from Islam to another faith. Not only is conversion unacceptable (surah 3:85); it is punishable by death (hadith 9.57). The apostate commits the unforgivable since of either associating Allah with a partner (shirk) or trading the fundamentals of the faith for falsehood.

Traditionally, the Christian by birth, or dhimmi ("protected person"), is a second-class citizen who paid extra taxes in order to receive protection from Islamic rulers (surah 9:29). One author noted the humiliation involved in this perpetually lower status, "The law required from dhimmis a humble demeanor, eyes lowered, a hurried pace. They had to give way to Muslims in the street, remain standing in their presence and keep silent, only speaking to them when given permission. . . . Any criticism of the Koran or Islamic law annulled the protection pact. In addition the dhimmi was duty-bound to be grateful, since it was Islamic law that spared his life."[5] Consequently, the dhimmi is always vulnerable, because at any time tolerance to his existence can change to outright persecution.

One must remember that Islam is a missions minded faith that looks for ultimate submission by the world to Allah. Even when Muhammed was in the midst of battles, he took time out to tell his followers why they should protect an infidel: "If one among the Pagans asks you for asylum, grant it to him, so that he may hear the Word of Allah" (surah 9:6). Many Muslims believe the ultimate purpose of any act that protects an unbeliever is conversion.

Why is the United States always at war with Islam?

Since the September 11, 2001, attack on the World Trade Center in New York City, President George W. Bush and other U.S. government leaders have gone out of their way to emphasize that they have not declared war upon the religion of Islam. Bush went so far as to partake of the celebration meal at the end of Ramadan to show his respect for America's Muslims. Some Muslims still believe that the U.S. government is anti-Islam. The United States seems intent on attacking Islamic governments and it has long expressed solidarity with the nation of Israel. Moreover, Muslims believe that America's interest in the Middle East is purely economic and self-serving and that holy lands such as Saudi Arabia are being exploited.

The U.S. perspective is a lot different. Even before the New York City and Pentagon attacks, citizens of that country felt that they were not out to war on Islam, but Islam had declared war on them. Middle East tensions are hardly new to the era of oil. Muslims blame Western colonization of the eighteenth and nineteenth centuries for their disastrous economies today. Imperialism placed political, social, and economic control in the hands of infidels who exploited the people and resources of the Middle East and Africa. Worse, the governments mandated a modified form of Islamic government to create a caricature of democratic rule. After World War II, Westerners were forced out, and the former colonies were independent.

From the 1980s, many of these countries were installing strong Islamic governments. The Islamization occurring across the world does not reflect a new model of fanaticism but a renaissance of sorts. Though many in the West call these Muslims extremists, they are actually traditionalists. They look to their past with admiration and nostalgia, hoping to reclaim the glory days of Islam. One must remember that before European colonialsts took control of much of the world, Islam was the colonizer. The first hundred years of the faith saw an incredible expansion through the Middle East into Asia, Africa, and Europe. It took Charles Martel to stop the advancing jihad and push back the Muslim warriors to Spain.

There they settled until they were ousted nearly 750 years later. Muslims also ruled India for hundreds of years.

The conflict of the late twentieth and early twenty-first centuries war is not about politics but religion. The ideological confrontation of the Cold War is now theological in the Confessional War. A range of Muslims, buoyed by oil-produced wealth, once again believe that Islam can advance into new territories and set up Islamic law. This confidence has turned into success in Malaysia, while the fighting is expanding in places such as Nigeria. One similarity between the new Confessional War and the Cold War should be kept in mind: In either rivalry, the citizens who live within the regimes may desire peace. A party with great power and a passionate confessional agenda is acting to change the course of history.

Are Muslims persecuted in their own countries?

Since Islamic law governs with an iron fist and different sects carry mutual grudges, it is not unheard of for Muslims to persecute other Muslims who come under their control. The prime example of such persecution is found in Saudi Arabia. The Saudi monarchy has dictatorial power and a long-standing desire to remove the dissention within Islam stirred by the Shi'a sect. Shi'a adherents are forbidden to have their own mosques. They must pray in private homes or out in the forests. The government has demolished cemeteries sacred to the Shi'a and forbidden any teachers or professors to come from Shi'a families. One Sunni teacher was so strong in her belief that the Shi'a sect was false that she told her elementary age school class that Shi'a Muslims worship stones and not Allah.[6]

The more strictly a country observes Islamic law, the more likely that Muslims will persecute other Muslims. The minority groups are more likely to be persecuted if they are feared as a political threat. This is why Christians are persecuted in Iraq no more intensely than are Shi'a Muslims. To Saddam Hussein, the relatively few Christians were not political rivals. He was more worried about those capable of causing a legitimate religious uprising.

The most radical Muslims in the world are the Saudi-supported Wahhabis, who are attempting to reform all of Islam according to their own radical bent. This sect forbids its members from using the name of Muhammed in any prayer. They prohibit visiting a Muslim grave at a cemetery and demand that other Muslims obey their principles or risk violence in a jihad. A number of splinter groups and factions have arisen within the last century, leading to the observation that Islam is going through its own reformation era, comparable loosely to what occurred in Christianity in the 1500s. At stake in the internal conflicts is the future direction of the religion. The world will have to wait to see what shape Islam will finally take.

If Christians are called to love, isn't it a sin for them to go to war?

Christians have always struggled with the issue of pacifism. When, if ever, is it defensible for a follower of the Prince of Peace to take up arms on behalf of a nation? The theologian Augustine (354–430) developed strict guidelines for waging a "just war" in which Christians might participate. Rules of the "Just War Theory" still govern many Christians.

Within the Reformation of the sixteenth-century, a group of dissenters emerged who vehemently opposed any justification for war. These pacifists would not take up arms even during the raging Turkish onslaught that threatened Europe from the East. Michael Sattler (1495–1527), a leader of these "Anabaptists" (given that name because they rebaptized adults after their conversion experience), contended, "The sword is an ordering of God outside the perfection of Christ. . . . But within the perfection of Christ only [church discipline] is used for the admonition and exclusion of the one who has sinned."[7]

Sattler was not opposed to the government going to war, for God had ordained the government to wield the sword (Romans 13:4). Rather, he maintained that Christians cannot legitimately go to war since they are citizens of the kingdom of God. Sattler did not merely replace political justice with the virtue of universal love. He instituted a stricter judgment of church discipline. To the average Anabaptist, discipline ("the ban") was the most severe punishment that could be placed on them.

Sattler's Anabaptist colleague Hubmaier disagreed with this view and countered with a more positive view of government and Christian involvement in war. First, Christians are not simply citizens of the coming kingdom but are also sojourners in this world. Therefore, they should pray for the perfect kingdom to come (Matthew 6:10), while admitting the reality of the current situation. There are two swords in this world (the sword of secular rule and the sword of the Word of God). Each of these has its distinct place in God's rule, and Christians are called to take part in both. Government is directly ordained by God and therefore worthy of Christian service. Subsequently, if a Christian refuses to defend the helpless, he in turn will be judged by God. Hubmaier stated, "Whoever now does not want to help the government save widows, orphans, and other oppressed ones, as well as to punish vandals and tyrants, resists the order of God . . . for he acts against the mandate . . . of God, who wants the righteous to be protected and the evil to be punished."[8]

Hubmaier articulately gave biblical yet simple arguments for Christians to follow when it comes to deciding whether to go to war. First, a Christian has a right, and in reality a duty, to fight in war, assuming that the government is good, and the cause is virtuous (peace and/or protection). Those who truly love God and love their neighbor will do what they can to bring about peace, prosperity, and protection in this world. If the righteous do not participate in government, only the wicked and tyrannical will rule.

Aren't Jordan and Turkey examples of Islamic moderation?

As there is an ever increasing tide of militant Islam emerging, defenders of Islam repeatedly proclaim the virtues of moderate Islamic-led nations such as Jordan and Turkey. After all, Jordan is home to nearly two hundred thousand Christians—5 percent of Jordan's population. Jordan's moderate monarch succeeded in implementing Christian religious education for Christian children. In 1994, Jordan signed a peace treaty with Israel, a move condemned through much of the Islamic world. The only other Arab country to make a similar agreement with Israel was Egypt in 1979.

Turkey has long sought to be a part of the community of nations as well as the Islamic world. Turkey became a signatory to the North Atlantic Treaty Organization (NATO) in 1949 and allied with the United States against both the USSR in the 1962 missile crisis and Iraq in the 1991 Gulf War. Turkey also stands alone as an Islamic democracy that is willing to join alliances with Western interests, such as the European Union. Unlike Jordan, Turkey does not have any significant Christian minority.

To understand how these two countries emerged as examples of moderate Islam, one needs to look at their historical distinctives. A scarlet thread connects Jordan to the Palestinian situation in Israel, for Jordan once controlled parts of what is now Israel. Although a supporter of the United States against Iraq, Jordan still has close ties to Iraq, its sole supplier of energy. Moreover, it is known that individual members of the royal family sympathize with militant Islamic groups.[9] In fact, the militant Islamic party known as the Muslim Brotherhood has gained momentum in Jordan. Probably the best picture of the volatile situation in Jordan today can be seen by its geographical location. Wedged in between Israel, Syria, Saudi Arabia, and Iraq, the Kingdom of Jordan is in a most precarious situation. The situation within its borders does not get any easier.

On the other hand, Turkey has a terrible track record, which it is not always willing to admit. While the world was at war in 1915, Turkey planned the systematic execution of all Armenian Christians. In one day, April 24, 1915, the Turkish government was responsible for killing six hundred thousand Armenians. Within the next three years, the total number massacred grew to nearly 2 million. In the 1990s, the Turks used the campaign against the Kurds as an excuse to wipe out whole Christian villages in the southeast part of its country.

Turkey has also banned the Assyro-Chaldean Christian minority from building new churches and holding public office.[10] In 2002, the Islamic-based Welfare Party won a landslide victory sweeping them into leadership positions.

While Jordan has shown some moderation under trying circumstances, Turkey remains a more violent and repressive regime than it superficially appears to be.

Should the West grant religious liberty to Muslims from Christian-persecuting countries?

Some North Americans have reacted harshly to the threat of terrorism and to reports of oppressed minorities in the Islamic nations and would favor restricting freedoms for Muslims in countries such as the United States. Indeed, it is ironic that our father assisted in building a mosque in Columbus, Ohio, while his sons could never assist in planting a church in Istanbul or Ankara. This is not fair, but it is a reality with which Christians should be familiar.

Across the globe, Islamic countries are moving toward a more radical form of political Islam, and in its wake, precious freedoms are surrendered to the strict structure of Islamic law. But this is not only the case in Muslim-led nations. Former Eastern Bloc governments such as Belarus still restrict religious freedoms, prohibiting private meetings and requiring permits for evangelistic endeavors. The state-supported Eastern Orthodox Church in Belarus lobbied for the law and is working with the government to obtain a separate agreement with the state.[11]

Christians will continue to meet oppression, even as they herald religious liberty to anyone, anywhere in the world who will listen. A strength of Christianity is that Christians are called to a biblical ethic that seeks the good even of those who abuse us. Therefore, American Christians must be careful that bitterness and pain shared with our suffering brothers and sisters does not take us from this sacred principle and make us vindictive. Christians must also keep in mind that some Muslims come to the West because they have been the target of discrimination.

We should consider that Saul, one of the greatest persecutors of the church, was miraculously changed and became the Paul who wrote more than one-third of the New Testament. America's freedom allows this nation to be one of the greatest mission fields in the world. We would not have it otherwise.

Notes

1. This and many more stories can be found at persecution.org, along with other Web sites that track the persecution of Christians worldwide, including voiceofthemartyrs.com (May 12, 2002).
2. "The Pact of Umar," at http://www.fordham.edu/halsall/source/pact-umar.html (Dec. 19, 2002).
3. Paul Marshall, *Their Blood Cries Out* (Dallas: Word, 1997), 17-69.
4. Balthasar Hubmaier, "On Heretics and Those Who Burn Them," in *Balthasar Hubmaier: Theologian to the Anabaptists*, ed. H. Wayne Pipkin and John H. Yoder (Scottdale, Pa.: Herald, 1989), 64-65.
5. Mark Durie, "The Dhimmitude of the West," August 2002; http://www.dhimmitude.org/archive/dhimmitude%20of%20the%20west%20aug02.html (Dec. 19, 2002).
6. Saudi Institute, "Religious Freedom in the Kingdom of Saudi Arabia—Focus on Citizens," 15 October 2001, at http://www.shianews.com/hi/articles/politics/0000151.php (Dec. 19, 2002).
7. Michael Sattler, *The Schleitheim Confession*, in *The Life and Thought of Michael Sattler*, ed. C. Arnold Snyder (Scottdale, Pa.: Herald, 1984), 119.
8. Balthasar Hubmaier, *On the Sword*, in Pipkin and Yoder, eds., *Balthasar Hubmaier*, 521.
9. Christopher Slaney, "Jordan Seeks Peace in Sea of Troubles," *Middle East Times*, 19 July 2002, at http://www.metimes.com/2K2/issue2002-29/reg/jordan_seeks_peace.htm, (Dec. 19, 2002).
10. Marshall, *Their Blood Cries Out*, 50.
11. Felix Corley, "Belarus Official: Permission Required for Religious Meetings of More Than 10," *Baptist Press*, 16 December 2002, at http://bpnews.net/bpnews.asp?ID=14862 (Dec. 19, 2002).

11

QUESTIONS CONCERNING
WORLD HISTORY

FOR MOST PEOPLE IN THE WEST, the controversy between Islam and the rest of the world seems a new phenomenon. The conflict, however, has affected the world radically since the first invasions into the Mediterranean, African, and European worlds. It is a footnote of history that there likely would be no Protestant Christianity as we know it if the Turks had not threatened the region around the Austrian Alps in the 1520s. Faced with a revolt of peasants at home and the threat of Islam, the Roman Catholic governments were distracted from moving against the Protestants until they had a chance to become established. Islam and Christianity have long interacted within the larger context of world history.

Why is Jerusalem so important to Muslims?

As we have been called upon to explain current international events on television and radio, one of the most common questions from Christians is why Muslims care so much about Jerusalem, a city that Muhammed did not even visit. For example, to those outside Islam, it seems that Muslims simply built the Dome of the Rock on the temple mount to deny Christians and Jews this real estate that is so sacred to them.

Islamic claims to the land of Israel must be understood by

Christians if we are to comprehend the deep and complex conflict unfolding in the Middle East. That Muslims believe the land is holy is beyond dispute. Jerusalem has been *al-Kuds* ("the holy one") and *al-Kuds al-sharifa* ("the noble holy one") among Muslims since the medieval period.[1] It remains one of the three holy sites of Islam, along with Mecca and Medina.

However, Islam teaches that in Jerusalem Muhammed had Miʾraj, one of his most profound experiences with Allah. Surah 17:1 tells of Muhammed's miraculous night journey from Mecca to Jerusalem and then on to heaven on the twenty-seventh night of the month of Rajab:

> Glory to Allah Who did take His Servant for a Journey by night from the Sacred Mosque to the Farthest Mosque (in Jerusalem), whose precincts We did bless—in order that We might show him some of Our Signs: for He is the One Who heareth and seeth (all things).

ʿAbdullah Yusuf ʿAli's *The Meaning of the Holy Qurʾan,* he provides detail to the Islamic tradition that surrounds their holy day:

> It opens with the mystic Vision of the Ascension of the Holy Prophet: he was transported from the Sacred Mosque (of Mecca) to the Farthest Mosque (of Jerusalem) in a night and shown some of the Signs of Allah. The majority of Commentators take this Night Journey literally. . . . Even on the supposition of a miraculous bodily Journey, it is conceded that the body (of Muhammed) was almost transformed into spiritual fineness. The Hadith literature gives details of this Journey. . . . The Holy Prophet was first transported to the seat of the earlier revelations in Jerusalem, and then taken through the seven heavens even to the Sublime Throne, and initiated into the spiritual mysteries of the human soul struggling in Space and Time.[2]

ʿAli continues that medieval European literature reflects the story of the influence of the Night Journey, including Dante's *Divinae Commedia* (c. 1300).[3] Allusions to the Night Journey are found throughout the Qur'an. Surah 53:1-11 provides an Islamic proof of Muhammed's qualifications to be the final prophet:

> Your companion is neither astray nor being Misled nor does he say (aught) of (his own) Desire. It is no less than Inspiration sent down to him; he was taught by one Mighty in Power, endued with Wisdom: For he appeared (in stately form) while he was in the highest part of the horizon. Then he approached and came closer, and was at a distance of but two bow-lengths or even nearer; so did (Allah) convey the inspiration to His Servant—(conveyed) what He meant to convey.
>
> The (Prophet's mind and) heart in no way falsified that which he saw.[4]

The chapter continues to describe the vision of heaven as a garden. The angel Gabriel appeared to Muhammed. These two texts merged with surah 81:19-29 to describe the Night Journey and provide the hadithic writers with a foundation for their additions.

The ascension story propelled the Muslim army toward Jerusalem after Muhammed's death. By 638, Caliph Omar captured the city, and Jerusalem became part of the heritage. Omar apparently built a temporary mosque near the supposed sakhra ("rock"), and approximately fifty years later, in 691, the Umayyad Caliph Abd al-Malik ibn Marwan built a mosque. Either al-Malik or his son, al-Walid, built or renovated the large mosque later, and it came to be known as the "Far or Remote Mosque."

In addition to these factors, Jerusalem has eschatological implications for the Muslim, as described on pages 141-42.

Why is Jerusalem so important to Jews?

The spiritual and geographical dimensions of Jerusalem in the Jewish faith are so extensive and profound as to defy adequate description. This center of Judaism resonates both as a symbol of God's covenant and the literal manifestation of His promise. From the site of Abraham's sacrifice of Isaac (Genesis 22), to the threshing floor purchased by David (2 Samuel 24:18-25), to the building of the first temple (1 Kings 6), Jerusalem became the center of corporate worship. Virtually every corner of the city carries significance to the Jewish man or woman. Jerusalem is, to the Jew, the city that God has chosen for them and is symbolic of God's covenant.

Jerusalem is identified with the rule of God over His blessed nation Zion among the Old Testament prophets, especially in their lamentations that the city and nation would be destroyed. When Jeremiah writes of the decimation of the "daughter of Jerusalem" in Lamentations 2:10-15 and the "children of Zion," he speaks of both the people and the land. Over two centuries before Jeremiah, Isaiah had voiced the same theme when he wrote: "As yet he will remain at Nob that day; he will shake his fist at the mount of the daughter of Zion, the hill of Jerusalem" (Isaiah 10:32).

Jerusalem also is the center of messianic expectation. Upon His ascent to the throne of David in Jerusalem, Messiah will establish God's kingdom:

> "Behold, the days are coming," says the LORD, "that the city shall be built for the LORD from the Tower of Hananel to the Corner Gate. The surveyor's line shall again extend straight forward over the hill Gareb; then it shall turn toward Goath. And the whole valley of the dead bodies and of the ashes, and all the fields as far as the Brook Kidron, to the corner of the Horse Gate toward the east, shall be holy to the LORD. It shall not be plucked up or thrown down anymore forever." (Jeremiah 31:38-40)

Even the hymn of the national Zionist movement, which in 1948 became the national anthem for the nation of Israel, reflects the importance of Jerusalem to their collective conscience. The anthem, called *"ha-Tiqvah"* ("Hope"), details the "eye that looks toward Zion," and the eschatological hope of a return to the "land of Zion and Jerusalem."

Why is Jerusalem so important to Christians?

The importance of Jerusalem to the Christian is a little more difficult to discern, since the land itself has less central salvific importance. Certainly there is emotional connection to the places where Christ taught and was arrested, scourged, crucified, died, buried, rose from the grave, and ascended to the Father. Pilgrimages to Jerusalem became crucial during the medieval period as a way to do penance and earn forgiveness in the theology of works practiced by Rome. These journeys to locations and sights chosen by Constantine's mother following his edict in 313 became quite fruitful to Rome. Defense of the land became vital even before the Crusades to ease the journeys of pilgrims.

Historically, Protestants have not viewed the land as having mystical value in the way that Roman Catholic pilgrims view it. Protestant Christians view Jerusalem as a consecrated place, and certainly a trip helps the believer put context to the study of Scripture. Seeing the Bible lands can be a meaningful experience. There is no concept of a "pilgrimage" through which Christians earn merit with God. Some have sought to be baptized in the Jordan River, but this experience carries only symbolic meaning.

Jerusalem is more important to Christians in view of what most believe *will* occur there in the future. As Christ ascended into glory from the Mount of Olives, outside of Jerusalem, the angels who guarded the proceedings told the disciples: "Men of Galilee, why do you stand gazing up into heaven? This same Jesus, who was taken up from you into heaven, will so come in like manner as you saw Him go into heaven" (Acts 1:11). Most take this to mean that Jesus will descend to the same spot upon His return, called "the Second Coming" in Christian theology. This return will initiate His millennial reign, as described by the Old Testament prophets and in the New Testament.

The question remains: If Christ's return and ascension to the throne of David is His work alone, and nothing remains to be done to prepare Jerusalem to receive Him, why do evangelical Christians stand so fervently for the Jewish claims to Jerusalem? For most evangelical Christians, this has more to do with the importance of the Jews as God's special covenant recipients than with the place. The defense of Israel, including Jerusalem, is commanded in Scripture. God's people are to "pray for the peace of Jerusalem" (Psalm 122:6). God Himself issues the initial promise of the land to Abraham: "I will bless those who bless you, and I will curse him who curses you; and in you all families of the earth shall be blessed" (Genesis 12:3).

Israel's connection to the land is even central to the portion of Deuteronomy 6 called the *shema Yisrael*. This command with central significance for Jews and Christians is given in verses 4–5: "Hear, O Israel: The LORD our God, the LORD is one! You shall love the LORD your God with all your heart, with all your soul, and with all your might." This comes in the midst of a section on the land promises made to Israel found in Deuteronomy 6:1–19. We quote the entire section to show the significant role that the land plays in the promise:

> Now this is the commandment, and these are the statutes and judgments which the LORD your God has commanded to teach you, that you may observe them in the land *which you are crossing over to possess*, that you may fear the LORD your God, to keep all His statutes and His commandments which I command you, you and your son and your grandson, all the days of your life, and that your days may be prolonged.
>
> Therefore hear, O Israel, and be careful to observe it, that it may be well with you, and that you may multiply greatly as the LORD God of your fathers has promised you—"a land flowing with milk and honey."
>
> Hear, O Israel: The LORD our God, the LORD is one! You shall love the LORD your God with all your heart, with all your soul, and with all your might. And these words which I command you today shall be in your heart. You

shall teach them diligently to your children, and shall talk of them when you sit in your house, when you walk by the way, when you lie down, and when you rise up. You shall bind them as a sign on your hand, and they shall be as frontlets between your eyes. You shall write them on the doorposts of your house and on your gates.

So it shall be when *the Lord your God brings you into the land of which He swore to your fathers, to Abraham, Isaac, and Jacob,* to give you large and beautiful cities which you did not build, houses full of all good things, which you did not fill, hewn-out wells which you did not dig, vineyards and olive trees which you did not plant—when you have eaten and are full—then beware, lest you forget the LORD who brought you out of the land of Egypt, from the house of bondage.

You shall fear the LORD your God and serve Him, and shall take oaths in His name. You shall not go after other gods, the gods of the peoples who are all around you (for the LORD your God is a jealous God among you), lest the anger of the LORD your God be aroused against you and destroy you from the face of the earth. You shall not tempt the LORD your God as you tempted Him in Massah. You shall diligently keep the commandments of the LORD your God, His testimonies, and His statutes which He has commanded you. And you shall do what is right and good in the sight of the LORD, that it may be well with you, and that you may go in *and possess the good land of which the Lord swore to your fathers,* to cast out all your enemies from before you, as the LORD has spoken.[5]

Isn't the conflict in Jerusalem a perpetual one?

Jerusalem has been the perennial battleground of the ages. Based on our view of what the Bible teaches about the culmination of history, we believe that today's conflict has taken on new dimensions that are exponentially more dangerous. Two substantial changes have increased the regional tensions to a frightening level.

First, we again note the appearance of female jihadin (see previous question). While the Wahhabis do allow women in that role, the fact that women actually are carrying out suicide attacks is a new development. Historically, the war has been fought only with men. Civilian women, by and large, were off-limits. One reason might be that Israel has traditionally conscripted men and women for military service. The women bombers also might be reacting in part to the number of Palestinian women and children who have been casualties in Israeli attacks on terrorist centers. Civilian women have long been "collateral damage" casualties in the Middle East conflicts. Never before in recent memory, however, has fighting been carried out by women.

From a terrorist's perspective, the addition of women is debilitating to the enemy's morale. Now, everyone on the street must be suspect. A pregnant woman entering the market may actually be laden with high explosives and shrapnel.

Second, in modern times there has always been tacit agreement among the warring parties that some "sacred places" are off-limits. While churches, holy sites, and mosques have sustained damage due to war, they have rarely been actual targets. Not since 1948 have Jerusalem holy places been picked out as centers for fighting. This changed in 2002 when gunmen took over Bethlehem's Church of the Nativity and Jewish soldiers laid siege to it. Imagine the implications if holy sites are now "fair game" for warfare?

Hasn't Islam contributed much to intellectual history?

Muslims sometimes fall back on "red herring" arguments when confronted with the claims of Christ. One is that Westerners show their prejudice when they perceive that Muslims are a backward people in need of spiritual enlightenment. Actually, Islam is not a religion of dark ages and third-world conditions but is the source of some of the West's greatest ideas. Muslims often ask questions related to academic history, to see what the Christian understands about world cultural history.

It is at this point that the Christian can legitimately extend a point of connection to the Muslim and begin to build a bridge. We can appreciate and commend the outstanding cultural and scientific contributions of Islam. Christian and secular thought owe a large debt to medieval Muslims who studied the Greek philosophers and classical mathematicians and scientists. Before Muhammed, the Arabian Peninsula was a morass of warring tribes. Upon Muhammed's return from Medina, he began to unite the region under the aegis of Islam. He succeeded remarkably. Ancient enemies became compatriots.

Soon Islamic thinkers had the peaceful environment and academic freedom to explore the mental world. Theologians (ulema) began to search the writings of Aristotle, which had largely been lost on the Christian world. One reason Christians had not studied the classical thinkers was language. The Western world was united under Latin, while most of Aristotle's works had remained in Greek. One of the few real contributions of the Crusades was to introduce Muslim books to the West. Scholars learned Arabic to gain access to them, and Aristotle's works were reintroduced to the European continent as the first universities were beginning. Aristotelian rationalism and scholasticism transformed Christian thinking, contributing to the philosophical streams that led to the Reformation of the church.

To whom do we credit the preservation of Aristotle's realism? The point could be made that, were it not for the Muslim academic community, Aristotle's importance would have gone largely ignored, and the West would be a far more primitive society today.

Many historians credit the Islamic community with introducing the university system itself. Europe's first major universities began in the thirteenth century. Universities were established in Oxford, Paris, and Bologna in about 1200. Cambridge followed in about 1209 and Naples in about 1224. Some date Islamic schools of learning to over a century earlier. Some of these claims are disputed by historians, but there is certainly much evidence that the Muslim world set the stage for schools of higher learning in philosophy, science, medicine, and education.

The modern Western perception that Islamic lands are primitive until reached with the gospel lacks intellectual integrity and damages authentic gospel witness. Muslims still value education and tend to be highly educated when the opportunity is afforded them. The issue is that, regardless of status, learning, intellect, history, or wealth, all Western and Muslim thinking alike remains in darkness without Christ as the foundation for truth.

Hasn't Islam contributed much to philosophy?

While this question is largely covered in the previous answer, the question of contributions in philosophy does deserve special attention. Again, the answer is strongly in the affirmative. One does not have to look any earlier than the eleventh century to see the vast influence of Muslim philosophers on both secular and sacred thought.

A prime example of the Muslim influence in philosophy is the interplay of Christian and Islamic thought in the writings of Thomas Aquinas. Aquinas (1224-1275) is the most influential of the high medieval Christian theologians. He was a Dominican monk, a preacher, a professor at the University of Paris, and a student of world philosophies. His underlying thesis was simple: If Christianity is to be offered universally, and if it is in fact universal truth, then it must engage every culture, every philosophy, and every system. His system of evidential apologetics held that every person is created in the image of God *(imago Dei)*. Although fallen and depraved, humanity still is created for a relationship with the Creator. Therefore, since all truth is God's truth, then philosophy, intellect, and knowledge can draw people to recognize the existence of God, and human culpability before Him.

Aristotle provided most of the fundamental thought for Thomas's ideas, and he gained access to this stream of Aristotelian philosophy through Muslim writers. It was their considerations that stimulated his apologetic "proofs" for the existence of God. Muslim philosophers had both preserved the texts and interacted insightfully with them. One need only read Aquinas's *Summa Theologica* to see that he is in dialogue with great Christian philosophers such as Augustine of Hippo (354-430) and Cyprian (200-258), the great Jewish philosopher Moses ben Maimonides (1135-1204), and the profound Muslim philosophers Averroes (1126-1198) and Avicenna (980-1037).

Modern Western thought owes much to the Muslim world, a point that can serve to enter into dialogue with Muslim intellectuals.

Were the Crusades ordered by God?

The Crusades had a lot to do with the political and social situation of the medieval world and some theological errors. These events had absolutely nothing to do with the will of God in Christ or the teachings of Scripture. For the Christian, these wars remain the darkest chapter of our history. The slaughter of hundreds of thousands of Muslims and Jews did irreparable harm to the cause of Christ in the Middle East, causing our witness to be stunted, shunned, and mocked for hundreds of years. No thinking Christian tries to defend or explain away the Crusades as anything but misguided, horrifically sinful, and embarrassing. It has caused Muslims around the world to view Christians with a suspicion and bitterness as erroneous as the animosity shown toward all Muslims because of a small number of jihadin.

In November of 1095, the church in Rome faced several serious dilemmas, including persecution of Christian pilgrims by Muslims who controlled Palestine and Jerusalem. The Eastern Orthodox world was threatened by Islamic invasion as well, and the patriarch of Constantinople had called upon Rome for help. A relief force from Rome might help heal the schism that had divided Eastern and Western Christians in 1054. But how could Pope Urban II assemble such a force? The church's control over European society was tenuous. The region was divided into a patchwork of tiny governments and petty rulers who continually found reasons to go to war with each other to gain land and wider political dominion. European Christendom needed a unifying cause that would force rulers to set aside their differences.

Urban's answer was to break a thousand-year tradition of noninvolvement in wars by organizing a Christian army under the banner of the Cross. To those who would go to war, Urban would grant forgiveness of sins. In a simple paragraph within the anonymous

Gesta version of Urban's sermon at the Council of Clermont that fateful day, we see Urban's logic:

> And so Urban, Pope of the Roman see, with his archbishops, bishops, abbots, and priests, set out as quickly as possible beyond the mountains and began to deliver sermons and to preach eloquently, saying: "Whoever wishes to save his soul should not hesitate humbly to take up the way of the Lord, and if he lacks sufficient money, divine mercy will give him enough." Then the apostolic lord continued, "Brethren, we ought to endure much suffering for the name of Christ—misery, poverty, nakedness, persecution, want, illness, hunger, thirst, and other (ills) of this kind, just as the Lord saith to His disciples: 'Ye must suffer much in My name,' and 'Be not ashamed to confess Me before the faces of men; verily I will give you mouth and wisdom,' and finally, 'Great is your reward in Heaven.'" And when this speech had already begun to be noised abroad, little by little, through all the regions and countries of Gaul, the Franks, upon hearing such reports, forthwith caused crosses to be sewed on their right shoulders, saying that they followed with one accord the footsteps of Christ, by which they had been redeemed from the hand of hell.[6]

Thus, in one sermon, Pope Urban II launched the equivalent of a Christian jihad. Notice the promise of salvation to the warrior.[7] To further support Urban's emphasis, Baldric of Dol includes this frightening point in Urban's speech: "You should shudder, brethren, you should at raising a violent hand against Christians; it is less wicked to brandish your sword against Saracens (Muslims). *It is the only warfare that is righteous,* for it is charity to risk your life for your brothers."[8]

No, God did not order the Crusades, and many false teachers will be held accountable in eternity for their violent and blasphemous misrepresentation of Christ.

Were the Inquisitions ordered by God?

Second in horror to the Crusades were the periods in which Rome tried to stamp out dissent against its teachings through torture, imprisonment, and murder. All through the period of the Crusades, there were murderous pogroms against Jews in Europe and violence by church and state authorities against any attempts to reform or correct church practice. The Inquisitions developed as an institution in fifteenth-century Spain under a Spanish Dominican monk named Tomas de Torquemada (1388–1468). Organized programs of arrest, trial, torture, imprisonment, and execution in the name of pure theology had been standard operating procedure against heretics, reformers, and political enemies of the pope since the eleventh century. The name *inquisition* grew out of Spain, where it was used to terrorize Muslims and Jews, among others. It was imported into Europe to help deal with the early Protestants who could be arrested in Rome-controlled territories.

Torquemada perfected the methods of public trial and private torture to elicit recantations of wayward members of the Roman Catholic Church who had strayed from allegiance to Rome. For hundreds of years, Protestants were stretched, garroted, tortured, torn asunder, and murdered in other ways for their refusal to rescind their separation. In the logic of the time, Rome believed it was better to torture the body to save the soul, which would be eternally damned without the protection of the holy Church.

Again, it must be emphatically stated that the Middle Ages and Reformation persecutions, under whatever label, were not from God, who never called Christians to torture anyone in order that they "find faith." Such uses of the secular sword have always been an abomination to God and an affront to the very definitions of faith. Faith must be personal and voluntary, not forced.

Didn't the medieval church hate Muslims?

As can be seen from the answers above, the institutional church of the Middle Ages did hate, hunt down, and kill Muslims—and anyone else who did not follow the pope without question. For almost two hundred years, from 1096 to 1270, seven Crusades were launched to brutalize Muslims and break the Islamic hold on Jerusalem, Antioch, and Acre. The Crusaders were just as murderous toward Jews and other unbelievers within reach of their swords.

However, in the midst of all the venomous hatred that Rome spewed toward the Muslim, not all medieval Christian scholars saw the advent of Islam as an apocalyptic challenge. For one, Thomas Aquinas saw the rationalism and scholasticism of Islam as an opportunity to enrich apologetics and engage secular culture. Nor was he alone in denouncing the Crusades. Perhaps his words, spoken over eight centuries ago, should give us pause as well:

> Muslims and pagans do not agree with us in accepting the authority of any Scripture we might use in refuting them, in the way in which we can dispute against Jews by appeal to the Old Testament and against heretics by appeal to the New. These people accept neither. Hence we must have recourse to natural reason, to which all men are forced to assent.[9]

Did the Reformers encounter Muslims?

Certainly the Reformers did encounter Islam, although usually at a distance. There was not a great deal of discussion between the two peoples. It has been noted that, in God's timing, the Turks saved the Protestants from certain massacre by encroaching militarily on Europe at the very moment when the reform movement could not have adequately defended itself. The common threat also gave Protestants and Catholics at least one area in which they could speak as one out of mutual fear.

Since not many understand exactly what happened and when in the Protestant Reformation, it should be noted that when we speak of "Reformers" we are referring to five movements that followed Luther's emergence in 1517 in Germany. For the sake of clarity, they can be listed thusly:

1. *The German Reformation* began in debates between Martin Luther (1483-1546) and Roman representatives, culminat-

ing in three great treatises against the church in 1520. He was excommunicated in January 1521. The most significant event of this period was Luther's translation of the New Testament into German between 1522 and 1524. Philipp Melanchthon (1497-1560) was Luther's chief aide and successor. Melanchthon never gave up his dream of healing the breach with the Roman Church. He pulled Lutherans back to a theology close to that of Roman Catholicism.

2. *The German-Swiss Reformation* began in 1523 under Ulrich Zwingli (1484-1531). When Zwingli tried to negotiate theological union with Luther, they could agree on every point except for the meaning of the Lord's Supper. Zwingli believed the supper was a simple memorial, while Luther believed it had a more supernatural significance. After Zwingli was killed at the Battle of Kappel in 1531, the movement was taken by Heinrich Bullinger (1504-1575), who eventually tried to merge with the followers of John Calvin.

3. *The Swiss Brethren Reformation* began as a group that separated from Zwingli on January 21, 1525, over the meaning of baptism. They believed baptism to be solely a memorial act, an outward act that portrays an inward repentance and salvation so that baptism is only for believers. They rebaptized adults who had been baptized as infants and so were called "Anabaptists." After leader Balthasar Hubmaier (1480-1528) was burned at the stake, the biblical and orthodox Anabaptists organized under Menno Simons (1496-1559), among others. Anabaptists were persecuted by Protestant and Catholic alike.

4. *The French-Swiss Reformation* began in Geneva in 1534 under Guillaume Farel (1489-1565) but was quickly identified with the publication of the first edition of *Institutes of the Christian Religion* by Calvin in 1536. Calvin's theology was marked by his understanding of the majesty of God and His sovereignty over every sphere of life. Among other distinctives, this implied that Christians should actively promote God's priorities in government, so governments influenced by this movement developed a partnership between church and state

that could become theocratic in practice. After Calvin's death in 1564, the movement was further developed by Theodore Beza (1519–1605) and numerous other theologians in Scotland, England, and the Lowlands (Netherlands).

5. *The English Reformation* was launched over the marital problems of King Henry VIII (1491–1547) in 1534. Henry was a fervent believer in Roman theology, but he wanted a male heir and sought to replace his wife because she did not give birth to one. Rome did not allow divorce, especially on those grounds, and the pope had political reasons to oppose the English. Henry started his own state-run church. Depending on the current state of politics and the leanings of rulers, the resulting beliefs of churches of England and Scotland were pulled here and there. A number of leaders, some good but more bad, guided the churches—the only stability under the strong but mediating hand of Queen Elizabeth I (1533–1603). After her death, the rivalries and persecutions boiled until the English Civil War in the 1640s. The Anglican churches remained a halfway mix of Roman and Protestant ideas.

Islam received its first converts in 621, and Luther's expulsion from the Roman Church came in 1521. Islam, therefore, was a mature nine hundred years old when the Protestant movement began. Because Islam remained bent on world dominion, the first Protestants learned about Muslim theology in the context of terror that the Turks would massacre citizens of Vienna. Reformers, therefore, might be forgiven if their comments on Islam were not very insightful and sometimes shrill.[10]

Luther believed that Muslims wanted to "eradicate the Christians," and that Muhammed had the spirit of the Antichrist. He believed much the same about the pope in Rome.

Hubmaier was a little more reasoned. He wrote that "a Turk or a heretic cannot be overcome by our doing, neither by sword nor by fire, but alone with patience and supplication, whereby we patiently await divine judgment."[11]

Calvin wrote that Muhammed, "allowed men the brutal liberty

of chastising their wives and thus corrupted that conjugal love and fidelity which binds the husband to the wife. . . . [Muhammed] allowed full scope to various lusts—by permitting a man to have a number of wives. . . . [Muhammed] invented a new form of religion."[12] He added, "The sect of [Muhammed] was like a raging overflow, which in its violence tore away about half of the church,"[13] and "It is about a thousand years since those cursed hellhounds were made drunk with their follies."[14]

Did early American evangelicals encounter Islam?

While most of the contemporary furor between Bible-believing Christians and Muslims has centered on the more recent encounters, Christians of the past sometimes glanced at Islam. Usually they dismissed it as a works-centered religious movement, designed and birthed in direct contradiction to Christianity. As such, they have traditionally viewed Islam as the inverse of the grace of atonement and the lordship of Jesus Christ.

Jonathan Edwards (1703–1758) was a colonial preacher, yet his studies and writings were remarkably broad. He asserted that Satan had established two great anti-Christian kingdoms, Roman Catholicism and Islam, "which have been, and still are, two kingdoms of great extent and strength. Both together swallow . . . up the Ancient Roman Empire. . . . In the Book of Revelation . . . it is the destruction of these that the glorious victory of Christ at the introduction of the glorious times of the Church, will mainly consist."[15]

How have secular historians and philosophers viewed Islam?

Of late, effusive praise has poured out upon Islam by those pursuing political correctness. Indeed, modern culture seems intent on portraying Islam as a peaceful and palatable world religion that is beyond criticism, while evangelical Christians are the source of all evil. Such has not always been the case. As Ibn Warraq[16] aptly illustrates, the deafening chorus of praise has not always been the standard within academia.

Two past secular philosophers did not spare their barbs regarding the Muslim worldview. David Hume (1711–1776), who was no friend of Christianity either, described the Qur'an as a "wild and absurd performance. Let us attend to his (Muhammed's) narration; and we shall soon find that he bestows praise on such instances of treachery, inhumanity, cruelty, revenge, and bigotry as are utterly incompatible with civilized society. No steady rule of right seems there to be attended to; and every action is blamed or praised, so far only as it is beneficial or hurtful to the true believers."[17] Warraq notes that Hume refers to Muhammed as "the pretended prophet."[18]

Even before Hume, the skeptic Englishman Thomas Hobbes (1588–1679) mocked Muhammed for his attempt to, "set up his new religion, pretending to have conferences with the Holy Ghost in form of a dove."[19]

Among historians, the most scathing critiques came from Edward Gibbon (1737–1794). After reading the Qur'an in preparation for writing his monumental world history, Gibbon called the Qur'an an "endless incoherent rhapsody of fable, and precept, and declamation, which seldom excites a sentiment or an idea, which sometimes crawls in the dust, and is sometimes lost in the clouds." He did not spare Muhammed from his analysis either:

> The use of fraud and perfidy, of cruelty and injustice, were often subservient to the propagation of the faith; and Muhammed commanded or approved the assassination of the Jews and idolaters who had escaped from the field of battle. By the repetition of such acts the character of Muhammed must have been gradually stained. . . . Of his last years ambition was the ruling passion; and a politician will suspect that he secretly smiled (the victorious impostor!) at the enthusiasm of his youth, and the credulity of his proselytes . . . In his private conduct Muhammed indulged the appetites of a man, and abused the claims of a prophet. A special revelation dispensed him from the laws which he had imposed on his nation; the female sex, without reserve, was abandoned to his desires.[20]

Such criticisms often speak less to the condition of Islam than to the condition of the culture from which the critics come. The ethical and governmental problems within Islam have existed in perpetuity, but we have entered a period when critique of any sort of any worldview (except Christianity) is seen as the equivalent of a mortal sin. No Christian should be as biting in our criticism of Islam as were some of our forefathers, but it does not help discourse if any criticism is met with a cacophony of howls. The human errors within Christianity are certainly open to criticism, satire, and attack. We defend every person's right to do so. Yet in Islam, such criticism is regarded as heresy and blasphemy, and tantamount to treason, for which the offender can be put to death.

Wasn't Hitler a Christian?

Often Muslims cite historical figures known to have done horrifying evil deeds as "Christians" to balance horrors committed by terrorists or others who profess Islam. A favorite foil for this tactic has been Adolph Hitler, the dictator who led National Socialist Germany into the nightmare of the 1930s and 1940s. Was Hitler a Christian, perhaps one who acted upon some personal belief that Christ called him to destroy entire races?

Two worldviews came together in German National Socialism, neither of them remotely Christian. Adolph Hitler longed for a return to ancient teutonic pagan mythology. He was intrigued by occult mysticism, and some of his colleagues were passionate followers of occultism and black magic. The other belief system he followed was the nihilism of Friedrich Nietzsche (1844-1900). Hitler despised serious Christians as much as he hated the Jews and Slavic peoples.

Hitler believed that he could enable an evolved race of superhumans by cleansing the earth of races he deemed to be inferior. He used Germany's state church heritage for political purposes, so he sometimes twisted Christian language. At the outset of his rise to power from the "brownshirts," Hitler demanded that churches in Germany ally themselves with his geopolitical German nationalism. Tragically, many did. If that were the end of the story, a case could be made that German Christians acquiesced as silent partners to genocide.

A number of church leaders did give wholehearted approval to the evolutionary hypothesis of the "survival of the purest," and others were bullied into compliance. A large portion of German Christians, however, courageously resisted. In 1934, a group of their leaders formed the "Confessing" church. Their Barmen Declaration publicly repudiated any political misuse of Jesus Christ as blasphemy. Signers knew that their stand endangered themselves and their families. Confessing Church Christians were active in the underground resistance. Many Protestants and Roman Catholics died alongside the Jews in the death camps or were imprisoned and sometimes executed as traitors.

Hitler is a classic example of the unbeliever Christ referred to in Matthew 7:21–23 (NIV): "Not everyone who says to me, 'Lord, Lord,' will enter the kingdom of heaven, but only he who does the will of my Father who is in heaven. Many will say to me on that day, 'Lord, Lord, did we not prophesy in your name, and in your name drive out demons and perform many miracles?' Then I will tell them plainly, 'I never knew you. Away from me, you evildoers!'"

One of the most remembered Christians of the period was Dietrich Bonhoeffer (1906–1945). Bonhoeffer was a pastor, college professor, and published author who had already strongly condemned Christian worldliness. He was lecturing in the United States when Hitler's repression began in earnest, but he returned to his homeland to share its time of crisis. A pacifist by philosophy, Bonhoeffer came to believe that Nazism was so evil that violence was the only faith response. He joined the resistance and became involved in an attempt to assassinate Hitler. Arrested and condemned as a traitor, Bonhoeffer was hanged five days before Allied forces reached the prison where he was held. Bonhoeffer's testimony alone bespeaks the clear rejection of any claim by Hitler that he was acting on behalf of Christ.

Is it sinful for Christians to fight in war or defend themselves?

Bonhoeffer is an example of the struggles Christians have had in time of war. We speak often against killing in the name of Allah but insist that Christians are called to love the Muslim. So we are sometimes asked at public forums whether we take a theological position of pacifism. The question is a fair one, given our belief that Christ called us to, "love your enemies, bless those who curse you, do good to those who hate you, and pray for those who spitefully use you and persecute you" (Matthew 5:44). Does that mean that it is sinful for a Christian to participate in warfare? Does that mean that we would not defend ourselves?

We are not pacifists in the sense that Mennonites, for example, completely reject Christian participation in a country's military defense. We believe that Christians can use Scripture to discern the differences between fighting to defend one's country and killing capriciously. We draw a sharp distinction between just war, in which God's people can fight, and "holy war" causes that we should always condemn—whoever is defining what makes the excuse for violence "holy."

God calls us to be obedient to secular governing authorities:

> Let every soul be subject to the governing authorities. For there is no authority except from God, and the authorities that exist are appointed by God. Therefore whoever resists the authority resists the ordinance of God, and those who resist will bring judgment on themselves. For rulers are not a terror to good works, but to evil. Do you want to be unafraid of the authority? Do what is good, and you will have praise from the same. For he is God's minister to you for good. But if you do evil, be afraid; for he does not bear the sword in vain; for he is God's minister, an avenger to execute wrath on him who practices evil. Therefore, you must be subject, not only because of wrath but also for conscience' sake. (Romans 13:1–5)

There have always been Christians in national armies, and sometimes governments call Christians to wage war on soldiers who are brothers in Christ. This is profoundly different than organizing a "Christian army." Also, there have been times when Christians such as Bonhoeffer believed that their governing authority had crossed a line of evil that Christians could no longer tolerate.

It can be difficult for a Christian to balance the sanctity of life with demands by government. Historically, Christian ethics have emphasized the defense of the oppressed against injustice. Augustine (354–430) in *The City of God* suggests that war is both the product of sin, and the weapon to contain sin's injustice: "To carry on war and extend a kingdom over wholly subdued nations seems to bad men to be foolishness, to good men necessity. . . . But it is beyond doubt that it is greater (choice) to have a good neighbor at peace, than to conquer a bad one by making war."[21]

In short, war is sometimes needed to maintain peace. What criteria determine whether a war is "just"? D. J. Atkinson summarizes Augustine's just-war criteria:

1. The tradition does not offer a justification of all wars. There is a distinction to be made between a "just war" and the crusading militarism of a "holy war." The professed aim of a just war is peace through the vindication of justice.
2. There are circumstances in which the proper authority of the state may use force in defense of its people.
3. War may only be waged by legitimate civil authority, and there must be a formal declaration of war.
4. The purpose for which the war is fought must be just.
5. The recourse to war must be a last resort.
6. The motive of war must be just.
7. There must be reasonable hope of success.
8. The good consequence to be expected from going to war must outweigh the evils incurred.
9. The war must be waged in such a way that only the minimum force needed to achieve the aims of the war may be used.[22]

Can such aims be achieved? Can war actually be waged within these specific justifications? Certainly the defense of the oppressed for the purpose of their self-determinism is a proper goal, even if war must be waged to facilitate their freedom. Also, unless the criteria are obviously being violated, the Christian who is a citizen of a country at war can fight within the criteria of Romans 13. Under this justification, a soldier usually can fight with a clear conscience. In the ideal, the Christian experiences the horrors of warfare so that others may live in peace and liberty.

Notes

1. Some scholars believe that Jerusalem was actually the first site toward which Muslims were instructed to pray, instead of Mecca. The Arabic title is designated ʿula al-qiblatheyn ("the first of the two directions of prayer"). However, there is little proof of this.
2. Abdullah Yusuf ʿAli, *The Meaning of the Holy Qurʾan* (Brentwood, Md.: Amana, 1992), 671. All spelling, capitalization, and spacing is in the original text of ʿAli.
3. Ibid.
4. The Surah 53 vision includes the controversial allusions to three of the precleansing idols in the Kaʾaba. See 53:19–20.
5. Emphasis added by the authors.
6. Rosalind M. Hill, *Gesta francorum et aliorum Hierosolymitanorum: The Deeds of the Franks* (London: Penguin, 1962), 141.
7. Emphasis added by the authors.
8. A. C. Krey, *The First Crusade: The Accounts of Eye-Witnesses and Participants* (Princeton, N.J.: Princeton University Press, 1921), 33–36. Krey translated from *Recueil des historiens des croisades, Historiens occidentaux,* 5 vols. (Paris: Biblioteque, 1844–95), IV.Occ.IV. Emphasis added by the authors.
9. Cited in Anthony Kenny, *Aquinas* (New York: Hill & Wang, 1980), 6. See also Timothy Renick, *Aquinas for Armchair Theologians* (Louisville: Westminster John Knox, 2002), 12.
10. Taken from Dr. Peter Hammond, *The Challenge of Islam According to the Reformers,* frontline.org.za.
11. *On Heretics and Those Who Burn Them.*

12. *Commentary on the Book of the Prophet Daniel.*

13. *Commentary on Second Thessalonians.*

14. *Sermons on Timothy and Titus.*

15. Jonathan Edwards, "A History of the Work of Redemption," found at frontline.org.za.

16. Ibn Warraq, *Why I Am Not a Muslim* (Amherst, N.Y.: Prometheus, 1995), 10.

17. David Hume, *Of the Standard of Taste*, 3.450, as cited in Warraq, *Why I Am Not a Muslim*, 10.

18. Warraq, *Why I Am Not a Muslim*, 10.

19. Ibid.

20. Edward Gibbon, *Decline and Fall of the Roman Empire* (1776–88), 5:240ff, as cited in Warraq, *Why I Am Not a Muslim*, 10.

21. Augustine, *The City of God*, trans. Marcus Dods (New York: Christian Literature Company, 1887), 72–74.

22. D. J. Atkinson, "Just War Criteria," in R. K. Harrison, gen. ed., *Encyclopedia of Biblical and Christian Ethics* (Nashville: Thomas Nelson, 1992), 215–16.

12

QUESTIONS CONCERNING
CONTROVERSY AND JIHAD

THIS FINAL SECTION SAMPLES A variety of topics and issues with one common theme: All are somewhat controversial in nature. These questions are part of Christian-Muslim dialogue, but they do not readily fit into the other categories around which we have organized this book. All have been asked on multiple occasions, and all merit attention.

Doesn't *jihad* mean "personal struggle"?

The word *jihad* has become part of the current cultural dialect. It is used as a noun to refer to a party or movement that is actively engaged in a war—declared or undeclared officially—against those who have been perceived to pose a threat to Islam. A related term, *jihadin,* means "holy warriors," and military confrontations against these fighters have dramatically changed the way the West approaches military conflict. World military strategy has struggled to respond to this army's hit-and-run tactics. Unless a force can be isolated in a geographical region, as in Afghanistan, there is often no discernible battlefield. This army wears no uniforms, declares only peripheral or no allegiance to any single country, crosses racial and ethnic lines, and is united solely by a common hatred. Usually that hatred is directed toward a vague perception of infidel Christian hordes, whose identity can be shifted as need arises.

Jihadin use the rhetoric of a book held as sacred by more than one billion people, but they often number among their enemies any who hold this book dear yet do *not* take up arms with them. They prefer death to surrender, for they believe death grants them eternal bliss, a happiness that eludes them on this planet. They will not negotiate. Jihad as it is practiced in the early twenty-first century is not like the warfare of conquest practiced by Islam in the past.

Because the phenomenon is new, the term used for this struggle, *Jihad,* is a little tricky to pin down. As we have enumerated in our book *Unveiling Islam,* the Qur'an and Hadith are full of references to "holy war" (*jihad*) and its protocols that must be observed. In the main, these passages refer to military conflict. However, *jihad* is used in a personal inner context to mean "personal struggle." Ian Richard Netton has noted that "all Muslims are obliged to wage a spiritual jihad in the sense of striving against sin and sinful inclinations within themselves: this is the other major sense of *jihad.*"[1] Why do we emphasize this point? We encounter many anxious Christians who tremble in fear for their lives whenever they have come into contact with Muslims, be it at the grocery store, in the workplace, or at the retail shopping mall. These people have truly been terrorized by the continuing reports of suicide bombings and other terrorist attacks, with their constant invocation of Allah's cause. They see every Muslim as their potential murderer, which is unfair and blatantly untrue.

The average Muslim follows jihad only in the sense of personal struggle. Frankly, most are as terrified by the sectarian violence as are non-Muslims. Those living in the West are personally caught in the backlash by those angered by the work of extremists. Those living in Islamic societies are anxious because Muslim radicals from another sect or extreme fringe may choose to attack their countries.

Further, because they refuse to take up arms in the fatwa, the call to take up a violent jihad, they are mocked as backslidden and errant by the militant jihadin. They also are confused, because they have never before been exposed to this overtly violent form of jihad.

The extremists hold that those who refuse to pick up guns and bombs are indeed cowardly and without genuine fidelity to Islam.

The Christians they meet will either ease or heighten these feelings, depending on whether the Christians reflect Christ's love or their own prejudices. When followers of Christ express hatred, mistrust, or even discomfort, the gospel will not be heard and honestly evaluated. Muslims will not even be aware of it. God has not called His believers to hate the Muslim, however hateful and violent some Muslims may be. Christians give up the "right" to hatred and vengeance when God forgives their sins and grants eternal mercy to them in Christ. Forgiven people are to love and show mercy, as Christ has shown it to us.

There are important implications of that love. Christians can ease the plight of peaceful Muslims who have become accustomed to vilification and rage. Muslims are not accustomed to receiving unconditional love and acceptance that comes solely because Christ commanded it. Beyond the Muslim store owner down the street, Christians are called to actively pray for the salvation of those who actively hate and war against us. As long as Usamah Bin Ladin and the leaders of the Taliban are alive, they can be turned to truth for their eternal salvation in Jesus Christ.

Have Muslim groups rejected violent jihad?

Such Muslim groups as the Kharijites and the Ibadis believe in jihad so intensely that they consider it the sixth pillar of Islam. Others, however, have publicly and privately repudiated jihad as warfare. In particular, Sufi sects such as the Qadiriya and the Indian Chishtiya have banished the doctrine of warfare from their Islamic theology. The problem is that many Sunni and Shi'ite Muslims do not accept the Sufi as true Muslims. Sufi themselves are vulnerable targets of violent persecution. For that matter, any prominent Muslim who openly speaks of peace is in danger of being killed. Extremists perceive that such a blasphemer has been compromised by exposure to the West.

Most Muslims living in the West also have renounced jihad warfare. They or their parents may have fled poverty and violence.

They long to have good jobs and live in peace. Sadly, the fields of world conflict illustrate that the vast majority of Islamic leaders do not share their sentiments.

Don't some Christians now fight in jihad-type warfare?

Although not so frequently as during previous eras, violence still is perpetrated in the name of Christ Those who would practice some personal version of jihad are an embarrassment to genuine followers of Christ.

In a televised interview, we were asked by a prominent anchorman, "Are there not alleged Christians who have taken up arms for the cause of their religion, and killed in the name of their God?" The answer is that there are, but there are differences between Christians and Muslims, especially in light of the current conflict.

When some aberrant alleged Christian promotes or instigates violence in the "name of Jesus," a chorus of other Christians immediately condemn the actions and call for gunmen to lay down their arms. There is a unanimous public declaration that such actions are ungodly. It is unthinkable that other Christians would leave their homes, quit their jobs, and rush to the "warrior's" side to help him engage the enemy. The outpouring of condemnation never occurs in the Islamic community. Where are the Muslim voices calling on all Muslims to lay down arms and stop killing? How many Muslims decry the acts of the Taliban and testify that the suicide bombers in Jerusalem are not serving the will and pleasure of Allah? Sadly, while many Muslim apologists will not condone the acts of recent days, neither have they been willing to *condemn* those acts.

On December 11, 2002, the Associated Press reported that 461 Pakistani women had been slaughtered during the year in purported "honor killings." The story gives frightening details:

> Pakistan's main human rights body said . . . that at least 461 women have been killed by family members in so-called "honor killings" this year. . . . In such killings, women are murdered to protect the "family honor" for immoral be-

havior ranging from sex outside of marriage, dating, talking to men, being raped or even cooking poorly. . . . According to the commission's figures, out of the 161 slain women in Punjab state, 67 were killed by their brothers, 49 by their husbands . . . (and) in seven cases, seven sons killed their mothers.[2]

Where is the outcry from Muslims who find such acts deplorable? To kill a woman for being the victim of a rape is ghastly, yet oddly there has been no uproar from Western Muslims against such acts. Rather, Western Muslims tend to excuse them as cultural differences. In the United States, some once took such a stance regarding slavery, and in retrospect that view seems shameful. Yet tragically, no one is raising voices to halt unjustified murder of these defenseless women.

Who are the "People of the Book"?

In Arabic, the term *ahl al-kitab* is used with some frequency in the Qur'an. Translated "People of the Book," the phrase appears in such surahs as 2:101: "And when there came to them a Messenger from Allah, confirming what was with them, a Party of the People of the Book threw away the book of Allah behind their backs. As if (it had been something) they did not know!"[3] Do these "People of the Book" have the truth of God and are thus "secret" believers in Allah, somewhat like Karl Rahner's (1904–1984) "anonymous Christian" theory? No, they are the Jews and Christians who have abandoned the truth of Allah and distorted the truth contained within their own writings, according to Islam. ʿAli comments on the aforementioned verse with a very interesting point:

I think that by "the Book of Allah" here is meant, not the Qur'an, but the Book which the People of the Book had been given, viz., the previous Revelations. The argument is that Muhammed's message was similar to Revelations which they had already received, and if they had looked into their own books honestly and sincerely, they would have found proofs in them to show that the new Message was true and from Allah. But they ignored their own Books or twisted or distorted them according to their own fancies. Worse, they followed something that actually was false and mischievous and inspired by the evil one. Such was the belief in magic and sorcery.[4]

Netton in *The Popular Dictionary of Islam* expounds upon the concept of *ahl al-kitab:*

The name initially referred to the Jews and the Christians whose scriptures like the Torah and the Gospel were completed in Muslim belief by the Islamic revelation of the Qur'an. The term was later broadened to cover adherents of other religions like Zoroastrianism. Differences on the same subject between the Qur'an and, for example, the Gospels are accounted for by the doctrine of corruption (tahrif) according to which Christians are believed to have corrupted or distorted the original Gospel text. Qur'anic references to the "People of the Book" are a mixture of the friendly and the hostile. In early Islamic history of the "People of the Book" had a protected status, provided they pay a poll (protection) tax, (called) *jizya.*[5]

It is a reference to the Islamic belief that Jews and Christians had originally been given the truth of Allah but had ruined the message. As seen in surah 2:83: "And remember We (Allah) took a Covenant from the Children of Israel (to this effect): Worship none but Allah. . . . Then did ye turn back, except a few of you and ye backslide even now."

Does this "backsliding" mean that Islam teaches that Jews and Christians who adhere to their faith shall make it into heaven? Apparently not. The fifth and sixth levels of hell (*al-Hutama* and *Laza,* respectively) are specifically designated for Jews and Christians who do not turn to Allah.[6]

The term *People of the Book* carries only one special dispensation in the Islamic dialogue with Christians and Jews. It enables Muslims to say, "Well, of course we worship the same God," when in fact they mean that all religious "people of the Book" worship Allah. "In original form, you were called to worship Him, but you abandoned the truth of Allah. Unless you accept Allah, repent and do good works, you shall end in hell."

What role do Black Muslims play in world Islam?

In the United States the status of the Black Muslim movement within the larger scope of Islam has always been confusing. This is a national movement, largely focused in the United States, which originated in the "Five-Percenter" movement in the early twentieth century. As described in some detail in our book *Unveiling Islam,* the movement significantly changed as its leaders adopted Islam as their religion of choice. No one seems to have a reliable count of the number of adherents, but there are hundreds of thousands, if not millions, of Black Muslims.

How do Muslims worldwide view this movement? Azad and Amina, themselves Muslim authors, write:

> After World War II an Islamic movement arose among blacks in the United States; members called themselves the Nation of Islam, but they were popularly known as Black Muslims. Although they adopted some Islamic social practices, the group was in large part a black separatist and social protest movement. Their leader, Elijah Muhammed, who claimed to be an inspired prophet, interpreted the doctrine of Resurrection in an unorthodox sense as the revival of the oppressed ("dead") peoples. The popular leader and spokesman Malcolm X (el-Hajj Malik el-Shabazz) broke with Elijah Muhammed and adopted more orthodox Islamic views. He was assassinated. . . . In 1975, the group was renamed (the) World Community of Islam in the West and officially abandoned its separatist aims. The name was again changed in the late 1970s, to American Muslim Mission (AMM).[7]

The Nation of Islam still exists, although there have been changes in belief. Its leaders primarily reach public consciousness when they weigh in on social and political issues. The AMM has achieved some credibility within the Sunni branch of Islam and continues to grow rapidly.

Why does Nation of Islam thrive in urban centers of the United States?

In our estimation, the Nation of Islam (NOI) is largely successful in urban centers because the orthodox Christian church has written off the urban African-American culture. It was not always so. Black churches once saturated their communities with a biblical gospel message and spiritual care. But for a variety of reasons, much of this strong evangelical heritage has almost died out. To be sure, some notably successful churches reach such areas as Manhattan and Brooklyn in New York City. But the strong, active church ministries are too few to make more than a ripple in the pond of despair and desperation.

We have mentioned the life and martyrdom of theologian Dietrich Bonhoeffer (see p. 244). Bonhoeffer saw the ineffectiveness of Christians to disciple Germany. Christianity, Bonhoeffer railed, fails when it offers a "cheap grace" that demands no real discipleship. Christians fervently revel in the unmerited favor of God and the free offer of salvation. It seems one is preaching works righteousness to demand righteous living in the family and responsibility in the secular and religious community.

During the 1990s, one successful men's movement among evangelicals brought more honest discipleship into the church. This movement tackled the lack of spiritual leadership by men in the home and the sins of sexual impurity and racism. But the Promise Keepers revival was more of a rousing success among the suburban middle class than in areas of deep urban poverty. It warmed the hearts of many cold Christians but did not reach many unbelievers.

On the other hand, NOI has actively confronted the festering open wounds of inner-city life—drugs, violence, and the lack of moral male role models. Perhaps Christians are so fearful of offending the men who languish in this mire that we treat them like children who can never grow up. Cheap grace seems loving when it is merely paternalistic disrespect. Respect demands that new creatures *act* new (2 Corinthians 5:17). Real love doesn't turn a blind eye to lives that are destroying themselves and their families through drugs and crime.

This criticism may seem harsh to churches who are endeavoring a great work in the midst of the blight. They feel alone and overwhelmed by the responsibility of ministering to those who suffer in the darkness. They pour energy into helping battered spouses, malnourished children, and displaced families, often with little help. Then there are other institutions that once offered a helping hand in the name of God's truth, but along the way they lost their gospel foundation. They have become social agencies that help the symptoms but never suggest a cure.

Meanwhile, NOI marches firmly into these urban centers and tells the men engaged in sin that Allah is judging and destroying them. They will go to hell, unless they rise up, get jobs, act with dignity, return to their families, get off drugs and out of crime, and become responsible members of the community. Having the respect to challenge the sinner with condemnation offers self-respect. Men and women can be part of something greater than themselves. Since Islam is the ultimate works-centered religion, every deed, from finding gainful employment to taking responsibility for one's children, helps balance the scales. In the city and in prisons, NOI is largely succeeding because Christians have been silent. It is not that NOI offers more than does Christianity to those in poverty and distress. Rather they offer something.

The offer of salvation, as has been said, is free, but it is not cheap. It cost Jesus Christ His life, which is of infinite value. The lordship of Christ demands more than just a casual Sunday only faith.

Does the number *19* mean anything in Islamic theology?

At the Million-Man March in Washington D.C., a rally to promote male leadership in African-American society, black Islamic activist Louis Farrakan gave an elaborate speech about how numbers should provide significant meaning to the Black Muslim. What exactly did he mean by his constant refrain and repetition of the number *19* in that speech? While we cannot be certain of the meaning or motive, there is a small numerology based movement within the Islamic community. The Hurufis sect today is quite small, but it keeps alive a mysticism based on numerology. Hurufis are among the Ithna-ashariyya Shiʾites. According to Azad and Amina,

> Many Muslim tales, legends, and traditional sayings are built upon the mystical value of numbers, such as the threefold or sevenfold repetition of a certain rite. This is largely explained by examples from the life of a saintly or pious person, often the Prophet himself, who used to repeat . . . formula(s) . . . so many times. The number "40," found in the Qurʾan . . . as the length of a period of repentance, suffering, preparation and steadfastness, plays the same role in Islam where it is connected. . . . To each number, as well as to each day of the week, special qualities are attributed through the authority of both actual and alleged statements of the Prophet. . . . The importance given to the letters of the Arabic alphabet were assigned numerical values: the straight *alif* (numerical value one), the first letter of the alphabet, becomes a symbol of the uniqueness and unity of Allah; the *b* (numerical value two), the first letter of the Qurʾan, represents to many mystics the creative power by which everything came into existence.[8]

Interestingly, Azad and Amina believe that the purported reoccurrence of the number *19* in the Qurʾan is proof that Islam will conquer the world because:

1. There are 114 chapters in the Qurʾan, and 114 is the sixth multiple of 19.
2. The first verse of the Qurʾan, known as the "Bismillah," has nineteen Arabic letters.

3. The first word of the first verse, *bism,* occurs exactly nineteen times in the entire Qurʾan. Further, the second word in this verse, *Allah,* is found exactly 2698 times in the Qurʾan. This number is 142 multiples of 19.[9]

The authors continue to make such calculations throughout the Qurʾan, and conclude that *19* is the structure of the Qurʾan.[10] They believe such numerical precision proves the supernatural nature of the Qurʾan: "Now that we all know that the Holy Qurʾan came directly from Allah and is being guarded by Him, it is safe to say that everything in the Holy Qurʾan is true, and Islam will conquer all other religions and American power will diminish."[11]

Who are the female suicide bombers?

In *Unveiling Islam,*[12] we looked to the Hadith to find the protocols of jihad. One clear stipulation was that women are not to fight in jihad. Muhammed said, "a woman's hajj (pilgrimage to Mecca) is her jihad." Yet in the winter of 2001, female suicide bombers began to carry out their martyrdom in Jerusalem. Does this portend a shift in Muslim violence? What this means is that those attacks were carried out by members of the Wahhabi sect of Islam, which allows women to be jihadin. The Wahhabis were begun by a Sunni named ibn Taymiya (d. 1328). The Wahhabis spread from Arabia to India under the leadership of Sayd Ahmed. Some Pentagon and World Trade Center "martyrs" were from this group. The Wahhabi allow women to be martyrs, with a profound distinction. Male martyrs expect to recline on couches at the highest level of Paradise and be attended by seventy virgins. For a woman to be attended by seventy men, however, would seem more annoying than inviting. So the Wahhabi developed the doctrine of "compatriot paradise." When the woman dies in a suicide bombing, she may pick anyone she wishes to accompany her into Paradise. Usually the women name compatriots whose salvation they wish to sponsor before they carry out the act itself.

Female martyrdom, then, is an act of loving sacrificial atonement. The woman picks wayward sons, brothers, or loved ones whose level of righteousness does not seem likely to tip the scales in their favor. Then she dies to give them her righteousness. She dies for a few others. This is a remarkable act of self-sacrifice, yet it saddens those of us who recognize its futility. The role of sacrifice for the sins of others has been taken by Jesus Christ. His death alone is a sufficient atonement for whosoever will call upon the name of the Lord (Romans 10:13).

Aren't Turks hated by both Muslims and Christians?

The authors are of Turkish heritage (see p. 19). Our previous book, *Unveiling Islam,* shares our conversion experience as Turkish immigrants and Muslims who became believers in Jesus Christ. In many television, radio, and newspaper interviews, we have presented our testimonies, often with fascinating reactions from Muslims. On one occasion, Ergun returned to his college faculty office from a speaking engagement and listened to a long and rather graphic phone message. "You dirty Turks are not even real Muslims. You are an embarrassment to us and will fill hell," was the jist of it.

Were the accusations valid? Some Muslims hold bitter resentment against Turkish Muslims. Turkey enraged world Muslims after World War I when Mustafa Kemal Atatürk (1881–1938) abolished the caliphate. Muslims saw the once monolithic voice of Islam silenced by a man they considered a renegade. Many Muslims believe they have a valid grudge against Turkey.

This is not to say that Turkey has been a peaceful state. Our proud people must live with the shame that we slaughtered millions of Armenian Christians, Kurds, and Cossacks. However, we dispute the charge that the Turkish people somehow are inferior in their Islamic faith. Turkey has tens of millions of faithful Muslims, who attend the mosque devoutly. Until we accepted Christ as Savior, we were among them.

Was Aisha actually six years old when she married Muhammed?

As referred to above (p. 200), an international furor arose in the summer of 2002 when an eminent U.S. pastor, speaking at a Southern Baptist gathering, referred to Muhammed's marriage to Aisha, when he was over fifty years old, and she was only six years old. The speaker's judgment that Muhammed had acted in a way that would now be regarded as pedophilia drew a blast of media and public fury. We consider the speaker a dear friend and had actually made a similar comment when speaking in his church, which is one of the largest in the nation. He had checked the information that we first supplied when he unwittingly unleashed the ire of both Muslims and Christians.

For the record, his statement was factual. Sahih al-Bukhari Hadith 7.62.64 plainly records the marriage as narrated by Aisha herself: "Narrated Aisha: that the Prophet married her when she was six years old, and he consummated his marriage when she was nine years old, and then she remained with him for nine years (until Muhammed's death)." The following verse (65) repeats the testimony: "Narrated Aisha: that the Prophet married her when she was six years old and he consummated his marriage when she was nine years old. Hisham said: I have been informed that 'Aisha remained with the Prophet for nine years.'"

The facts of the matter have never been in debate. Following the debate, some scholars protested that this doesn't mean Muhammed was a pedophile, for the "Western mind can not understand the culture of Arabia in that period. This was the culture of the day."

Point granted. Perhaps it was a more acceptable action at the time in that cultural norm. However, that is vastly different than condemning the speaker as incorrect. He was simply citing the Hadith, a source that Muslims hold dear and indisputably true.

Don't most Islamic scholars believe that she was actually a teen?

Some modern Muslims disagree with the dates of Aishah's age at marriage and reinterpret the terms used. For example, what does it mean that the marriage was "consummated." In the interest of fairness, we include four arguments:

1. *Variants in Ahadith texts:* Three hadithic texts state three

different ages. One reports that she was six years old when she married Muhammed and nine years old at consummation. Sahil al-Muslim says she was seven when she was married and nine when the marriage was consummated. Neil-Al-awtar (6.120) puts Aishah in her teens, although this hadithic source has lower standing for reliability.

2. *The Qur'an's teaching:* Surah 4:6 states that a young girl cannot get married until puberty "until they reach the age for marriage." It is argued that Muhammed would not violate a key teaching of the Qur'an by marrying someone too young. In other matters, however, Muhammed believed Allah gave him a special dispensation. For example, he married thirteen women, which certainly exceeded the limit for the number of wives, which also was set in surah 4.

3. *Cultural maturity:* In some cultures, young women tend to mature more rapidly and reach puberty at a younger age. Again, this is a valid point, although few cultures sanction marriage of a six-year-old.

4. *Terminology:* One scholar argued that the terms used meant different things in Muhammed's day. To "marry" would simply mean to be promised in a parental contract. To "consummate" would refer to cohabitation but not necessarily sexual intercourse. Few, if any, Islamic scholars have held such a view previously.

Until 2002, Muslims in the West never were called upon to defend the personal morality of Muhammed. In other Muslim societies, the matter still is not an issue, and Muslims tend to dismiss the problem as a matter of Western ignorance. Parenthetically, in the same summer of 2002, Iran officially changed the legal age at which a young woman could marry without her parents' permission—from nine to thirteen.

Don't such discussions define *hate speech*?

The statement by our friend was not the only tempest stirred by Christian critiques of Islam in 2002. A number of Christian leaders were accused of "hate speech" and "Islamophobia." Christian criticism of Islam is hardly new. Christians perhaps are called upon to speak on the subject more frequently since Islamic terrorism became front page news in the United States and other Western countries. In the past, some Christians have been recorded as making truly reactionary statements with far less notice. We have seen statements from other times that called on governments to deport all Muslims, or worse.

When does negative comments and criticisms in the context of debate become uncivil and inappropriate "hate speech"? In a culture that prides itself on not being judgmental, any statement of absolutes has become a high crime. Evangelicals who take seriously and testify to the absolutes of Scripture can expect to be tarred and feathered in reaction as "hatemongers."

We believe there are things that Christians should never say as representatives of Christ. True "hate speech" has no respect for others or the truth. It seeks to diminish another's personal rights, based on personal animosity. We do not hate anyone. On the contrary, we believe that Jesus Christ is the only Lord, Redeemer, and King, and we love the Muslim enough to want them to find the peace with God that we found. Christians are called to engage culture and reach the Muslim with the gospel. Before anyone is ready to receive Jesus as Savior and God, they must first recognize that they need what Jesus offers. This means they must realize that the system upon which they are basing their lives is insufficient and untrue where it counts.

This is not "hate speech." People who speak from a heart of hate rejoice to see someone else defeated, killed, and sent to hell. Christians may speak harshly. Sometimes anyone who speaks in the public eye may say something that might be better restated or left unsaid. But what Christians rejoice to say is that "Christ is Lord. He died for you. Come unto Him and gain everlasting life."

Do good Muslims go to hell?

Easy question, and one of the most-oft asked. Though we have dealt with this question in detail in section 9, it is so essential, we include it here as well. The answer is, good *Baptists* go to hell. Neither your goodness, nor your denominational affiliation, nor your membership in a religious body merits salvation. Only by surrendering to Jesus Christ as Lord in repentance and faith is the individual saved. We are not attempting to win Muslims to faith in the Southern Baptist Convention; we are attempting to win them to Christ. Only He can save.

Has the United States overreacted to attacks, when this sort of thing has occurred before?

The West has persevered in the past through global problems that loomed as large as the conflict with Islam. Sadly, we have become a less patient nation. In our contemporary culture, we have become a nation of convenient solutions, to our great peril. We now want our food quickly, solutions quickly, and even our oil changes quickly. We stand before our microwaves, impatiently tapping our feet, while the microwave prepares food in two minutes. We can send mail around the world in microseconds by Internet. We can pay bills in mere moments. We want our wars to end as quickly as we solve our communication needs.

In September 2002, the media attempted to memorialize the World Trade Center tragedies. Television broadcasts, moments of silence, and newspaper eulogies were ubiquitous. The dilemma was— the war against terrorism is not over. Why did America not attempt to memorialize the Pearl Harbor tragedy in 1942, a year after the bombing? Because we were in the midst of a war effort. We were busy sacrificing and rationing and fighting to ensure our freedom. Our country had a long-range view of the conflict, which our present culture despises. Tragically, we want "quick fixes," and this will lessen our resolve and lessen our chances for victory.

Will the West survive this ordeal?

Since the United States felt a major terrorist attack firsthand, we have encountered fearful people in our speaking engagements who anxiously ask whether we are heading toward a great disaster. Usually at the end of a "question-and-answer" session, someone will tentatively rise and ask if the East-West difficulties can be overcome. Yes, we believe that the free world will survive, under one condition—we must return to our "tapestry" ideal.

We are immigrant U.S. citizens. Like millions before us, our family came to fit into the American landscape. One of the shining distinctives of the United States has been its melting pot tendency, a weaving of mingling colors and threads of varying tensile strength, brought together as a beautiful fabric. Historians argue that U.S. culture has always been somewhat ethnically fragmented, and the tapestry motif is more an ideal or myth than a reality. But the fact that most immigrant cultures have come with the idea of eventually melting into an "American dream" of freedom and prosperity has defined our society.

Of late, however, the United States has shown less of a tapestry mentality than the mind-set of a patchwork quilt, a loose menagerie of independent patches with connecting threads that stretch and break easily. No one quilt patch relates to the others. We now seemingly prefer to be a confederacy of subgroups, agendas, and special interests.

If the distinctive North American culture is to survive as a world influence, it must return to its tapestry ideal. We must desire to be amalgamated into this large swirling culture of freedom. To this end, we immigrants to the United States and Canada make a plea: Stop hyphenating us. We are immigrants and we are Americans. Many of our American neighbors came to these shores several generations ago. Other neighbors are relative newcomers like us, and we expect that our descendents will be part of Western culture for many generations to come.

So we are not Turkish-Americans, Middle Eastern-Americans, Christian-Americans, or immigrant-Americans. We are Americans. Period. No country will retain its historic freedoms if we accept a patchwork mentality. We pray that our readers will stop distinguishing themselves as African-Americans, Hispanic-Americans, or Asiatic-Americans. If you are woven into the fabric of the U.S. tapestry, complete with your racial and cultural heritage, then you are an American of U.S. citizenship. The same principles apply if you are Canadian or Irish or Australian or South African. If you are reading this in translation, the same principles apply if you are Mexican or German or Venezuelan. It is precisely the variations that bring beauty to a national identity. The only way we can withstand the onslaught of a bitter enemy is if we stand together, drawing on one another's strength and resolve in community.

How can I win my Muslim friend to Christ?

Muslims might be surprised to learn how deeply concerned their Christian friends are about them, and how fervently Christians want to reach out to them with our most important gift. The question of how to witness to a Muslim friend is asked more frequently than is any other.

The question both lifts our hearts, and saddens us, because there are no easy answers. Centuries of cultural difference, misinformation, and distrust lie between Christianity and Islam. It takes much longer to win the trust of a Muslim, let alone convince them of their need for Christ. It takes time and patience and open conversation to cut through the issues that this book has addressed. Christians must be ready to wait a long time, perhaps years, for a sincerely open heart. In the meantime, your Muslim friend is continually watching to see whether you are really interested in them and respect their feelings, or whether you would not give them a glance unless you had a hidden agenda

You will not see a Muslim turn to Christ after you hit them over the head with a fifty-pound family Bible that has a three-dimensional picture of Jesus looking like Ted Nugent on the cover. Muslims are intelligent and cautious. They will have questions.

Beyond being patient and not superficial, there are some definite dos and don'ts to sharing your faith with a Muslim:

1. As friends, Christians should carefully reflect gender distinctions. Unless the Muslims show that gender distinctions are not an issue, a man should avoid speaking directly to a Muslim woman, even as neighbors across the backyard fence. Women should be careful about offending male sensibilities

in the same way. When it comes to sharing Christ, men definitely should share only with men, and women only with women. Muslims tend to see cross-gender communication as offensive. Muslim men may misunderstand the intentions of a Christian women who approaches them. There are exceptions to this rule in the Muslim community, but Christians should never just automatically assume that they have the privilege of open conversation with a person of the opposite gender.

2. Be gentle in spirit. One should avoid being drawn into arguments regarding geopolitical matters. Be quick to listen to the Arab perspective and slow to begin a heated defense of U.S. or Israeli policies. Remember that you are not saved by national affiliation; you are saved because you are a Christian.

3. Be a genuine friend. To build bridges into the life of a Muslim, one must be willing to spend time together and take part in enjoyable activities in which religion is not a continual specter of potential conflict. Then when the right moment comes for religious discussion, it will come in the context of trust and honesty. That reflects the way Christ dealt with the people He encountered.

4. Purchase and read the Qur'an out of an open interest in a Muslim friend's world and perspective. Muslims aren't interested in dialogue with someone who has never taken the time to interact with the book they regard as the source of life and hope. This is the only way to legitimately suggest that they might read and discuss your foundational source.

5. Invite them to church initially to nonthreatening events. Many Muslims have never been in a Christian building where worship meets, let alone a church service. They may have some ideas about what goes on there that you would find strange. The Muslim family that enjoys music would enjoy being asked to come as a guest to a well-performed concert or cantata. Someone who enjoys drama will appreciate being asked to a well-done play. Churches sometimes sponsor art exhibitions or other special events that fit the interests of your Muslim friend, once you know what those interests are.

6. When the subject of Christ does come up, focus on the mercy and grace extended in the finished work of Christ. Do not be distracted by side issues. This, after all, is the center of Christianity for anyone who wants to know what we are about. Emphasize that good works are futile before a God who cares about holiness. Jesus has done everything necessary for our salvation, and any righteousness we contribute amounts to filthy rags. Remember that Jesus ascended to heaven to a throne, not because He was tired but because His saving work was complete.

Most Muslims do not have caring, concerned Christian people that they can call a "close friend." Like all people, they long for someone to care about them, and you may just be the person to break through. May God give you the opportunity to share the work of our Savior with a lost and dying world, which includes Muslims. Christ is more than a prophet. He is Prophet, Priest, and King.

Notes

1. Ian Richard Netton, *A Popular Dictionary of Islam* (Chicago: NTC, 1992), 136.
2. Associated Press, 11 December 2002.
3. Abdullah Yusuf ʿAli, *The Meaning of the Holy Qurʾan* (Brentwood, Md.: Amana, 1992). All citations in this section are taken from this approved Islamic translation.
4. Ibid., 102.
5. Netton, *The Meaning of the Holy Qurʾan*, 22–23.
6. See the Eschatology section for further information on the Islamic seven levels of hell.
7. Mohamed Azad and Bibi Amina, *Islam Will Conquer All Other Religions and American Power Will Diminish* (Brooklyn: Bell Six, 2001), 40.
8. Ibid., 87.
9. Ibid., 107
10. Ibid., 116.

11. Ibid., 125.

12. Ergun Mehmet Caner and Emir Fethi Caner, *Unveiling Islam* (Grand Rapids: Kregel, 2002).

ALSO FROM KREGEL PUBLICATIONS

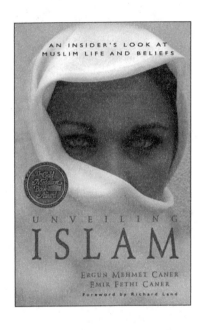

Unveiling Islam
An Insider's Look at Muslim Life and Beliefs
Ergun Mehmet Caner &
Emir Fethi Caner
0-8254-2400-3

Discover the reality of Islam—
written by two former Sunni
Muslims widely respected for
their ability to clearly explain
the Muslim mind. Also
available in Spanish.

> *"Must reading for all
> Christians."*—Zig Ziglar

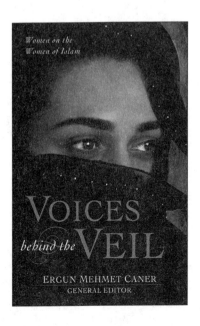

Voices Behind the Veil
Women on the Women of Islam
Ergun Mehmet Caner,
general editor
0-8254-2402-x

An unprecedented, sympa-
thetic, and wide-ranging
exploration of the mysterious
world of Islamic women—the
people behind the veils—by
female writers and Christian
workers.